The Institute of Chartered Accountants in England and Wales

PRINCIPLES OF TAXATION
Finance Acts 2015

For exams in 2016

Study Manual

www.icaew.com

Principles of Taxation
The Institute of Chartered Accountants in England and Wales

ISBN: 978-1-78363-207-7

Previous ISBN: 978-0-85760-987-8

First edition 2007

Tenth edition 2015

The content of this publication is intended to prepare students for the ICAEW
examinations, and should not be used as professional advice.

British Library Cataloguing-in-Publication Data
A catalogue record for this book is available from the British Library

Printed in Great Britain by Ashford Colour Press Ltd, Gosport, Hants

Welcome to ICAEW

I am delighted that you have chosen ICAEW to progress your journey towards joining the chartered accountancy profession. It is one of the best decisions I also made.

The role of the accountancy profession in the world's economies has never been more important. People making financial decisions need knowledge and guidance based on the highest technical and ethical standards. ICAEW Chartered Accountants provide this better than anyone. They challenge people and organisations to think and act differently, to provide clarity and rigour, and so help create and sustain prosperity all over the world.

As a world leader of the accountancy and finance profession, we are proud to promote, develop and support over 144,000 chartered accountants worldwide. Our members have the knowledge, skills and commitment to maintain the highest professional standards and integrity. They are part of something special, and now, so are you. It's with our support and dedication that our members and hopefully yourself, will realise career ambitions, maintain a professional edge and contribute to the profession.

You are now on your journey towards joining the accountancy profession, and a highly rewarding career with endless opportunities. So, if you are studying for our Certificate in Finance, Accounting and Business (ICAEW CFAB) or our world-leading chartered accountancy qualification, the ACA, you too have made the first of many great decisions in your career.

You are in good company, with a network of over 26,000 students around the world made up of like-minded people, you are all supported by ICAEW. We are here to support you as you progress through your studies and career; we will be with you every step of the way, visit page ix to review the key resources available as you study.

I wish you the best of luck with your studies and look forward to welcoming you to the profession in the future.

Michael Izza
Chief Executive
ICAEW

Contents

1 Introduction

ACA qualification

The ICAEW chartered accountancy qualification, the ACA, is a world-leading professional qualification in accountancy, finance and business.

The ACA has integrated components that give you an in-depth understanding across accountancy, finance and business. Combined, they help build the technical knowledge, professional skills and practical experience needed to become an ICAEW Chartered Accountant.

Each component is designed to complement each other, which means that you can put theory into practice and you can understand and apply what you learn to your day-to-day work. Progression through all the elements of the ACA simultaneously will enable you to be more successful in the workplace and exams.

The components are:

- Professional development
- Ethics and professional scepticism
- 3-5 years practical work experience
- 15 accountancy, finance and business modules

To find out more on the components of the ACA and what is involved in training, visit your dashboard at icaew.com/dashboard.

ICAEW Certificate in Finance, Accounting and Business

The ICAEW Certificate in Finance, Accounting and Business (ICAEW CFAB) teaches essential skills and knowledge in the three key areas of finance, accounting and business.

ICAEW CFAB consists of the same six modules as the first level of our world-leading qualification, the ACA. This means, it can serve as a stand-alone qualification or as a stepping stone on your journey towards chartered accountancy.

You can find out more about the ICAEW CFAB exams and syllabus at icaew.com/cfabstudents.

To learn more about the ACA qualification and chartered accountancy, visit icaew.com/careers.

2 Principles of Taxation

The full syllabus and technical knowledge grid can be found within the module study guide. Visit icaew.com/dashboard for this and more resources.

2.1 Module aim

To enable candidates to understand the general objectives of tax and to calculate income tax, national insurance contributions, capital gains tax, corporation tax and VAT in straightforward scenarios.

2.2 Method of assessment

The Principles of Taxation module is assessed by a 1.5 hour computer-based exam. 20% of the marks are allocated from two scenario-based questions. These will each cover a single syllabus area: income tax and NIC, and corporation tax. The remaining 80% of the marks are from 40 multiple choice, multi-part multiple choice, multiple response or numeric entry questions. These questions will cover the remaining areas of the syllabus in accordance with the weightings set out in the specification grid.

2.3 Specification grid

This grid shows the relative weightings of subjects within this module and should guide the relative study time spent on each. In each assessment, the marks available will equate to the weightings below.

		Weighting (%)
1	Objectives, types of tax and ethics	10
2	Administration of taxation	20
3	Income tax and national insurance contributions	26
4	Capital gains tax and chargeable gains for companies	10
5	Corporation tax	14
6	VAT	20

3 Key Resources

Student support team

Our student support team are here to help you, providing full support throughout your studies.

T +44 (0)1908 248 250
F +44 (0)1908 248 069
E studentsupport@icaew.com

Student website

The student area of our website provides the latest information, guidance and exclusive resources to help you as you progress through the ACA. Find everything you need (from sample papers to errata sheets) at icaew.com/dashboard.

If you are studying for the ICAEW CFAB qualification, you can access exam resources and support at icaew.com/cfab

Online student community

The online student community provides support and practical advice – wherever you are, whenever you need it. With regular blogs covering a range of work, life and study topics as well as a forum where you can post your questions and share your own tips. ACA and ICAEW CFAB students can join the conversation at icaew.com/studentcommunity.

Tuition

The ICAEW Partner in Learning scheme recognises tuition providers who comply with our core principles of quality course delivery. If you are receiving structured tuition with an ICAEW Partner in Learning, make sure you know how and when you can contact your tutors for extra help. If you are not receiving structured tuition and are interested in classroom, online or distance learning tuition, take a look at our recognised Partner in Learning tuition providers in your area, on our website icaew.com/dashboard

Faculties and Special Interest Groups

Faculties and special interest groups support and develop members and students in areas of work and industry sectors that are of particular interest.

Our seven faculties provide knowledge, events and essential technical resources. As an ACA or ICAEW CFAB student, you can register to receive a complimentary e-newsletter from one faculty of your choice each year throughout your studies.

Find out more about faculties and special interest groups at icaew.com/facultiesandsigs

Library & Information Service

The Library & Information Service is ICAEW's world-leading accountancy and business library. The library provides access to thousands of resources online and a document delivery service, you'll be sure to find a useful eBook, relevant article or industry guide to help you. Find out more at icaew.com/library.

CHAPTER 1

Ethics

Introduction
Examination context
Topic List
    1 Fundamental principles
    2 Threats and safeguards framework
    3 Ethical conflict resolution
    4 Conflicts of interest
    5 Tax avoidance and tax evasion
    6 Money laundering
Summary and Self-test
Technical reference
Answers to Interactive questions
Answers to Self-test

Introduction

Learning objectives

- Identify the five fundamental principles given in the IESBA Code of Ethics for Professional Accountants and ICAEW Code of Ethics, and the guidance in relation to a tax practice with regard to:

  - The threats and safeguards framework ☐

  - Ethical conflict resolution ☐

- Identify the following:

  - Conflicts of interest ☐

  - Money laundering ☐

  - Tax avoidance and tax evasion ☐

The specific syllabus references for this chapter are: 1f, g.

Syllabus links

The topics covered in this chapter are essential knowledge for the whole of your Taxation studies. They will ensure that advice and communication is appropriate and in keeping with the requirements of the ICAEW.

You will be using this knowledge again when you tackle the Tax Compliance paper and Business Planning: Taxation paper later on in the Professional Level.

Examination context

In the examination, in the objective test questions, candidates may be required to:

- Identify the five fundamental principles in straightforward scenarios and the safeguards to be put in place when these are threatened

- Demonstrate knowledge of the framework for ethical conflict resolution

- Determine which of the five fundamental principles conflicts of interest may threaten

- Differentiate between tax evasion and tax avoidance

- Identify the elements of money laundering in straightforward scenarios

For extra question practice on these topics go to the section of the Question Bank covering this chapter.

1 Fundamental principles

Section overview

- The International Ethics Standards Board for Accountants (IESBA) is an independent standard-setting body which aims to serve the public interest by setting robust, internationally appropriate ethics standards for professional accountants worldwide.

- The ICAEW Code of Ethics is derived in part from the IESBA 'Code of Ethics for Professional Accountants'. In particular, the five fundamental principles of professional ethics for accountants appear in both.

- The ICAEW Code of Ethics ('the Code') also contains additional requirements and discussion.

1.1 Fundamental principles

Definition

Professional accountant: a member of the ICAEW.

Professional accountants have a responsibility to act in the public interest as well as considering their client or employer. The Code requires professional accountants to comply with the following five fundamental principles:

- Integrity
- Objectivity
- Professional competence and due care
- Confidentiality
- Professional behaviour

1.2 Integrity

Definition

Integrity: to be straightforward and honest in all professional and business relationships.

Integrity also implies fair dealing and truthfulness.

A professional accountant shall not knowingly be associated with any information where the professional accountant believes that the information:

- Contains a materially false or misleading statement

- Contains statements or information furnished recklessly

- Omits or obscures information required to be included where such omission or obscurity would be misleading

1.3 Objectivity

Definition

Objectivity: to not allow bias, conflict of interest or the undue influence of others to override professional or business judgements.

A professional accountant shall not perform a professional service if a circumstance or relationship biases or unduly influences the accountant's professional judgment with respect to that service.

Conflicts of interest, which may threaten objectivity, are considered later in this chapter.

Worked example: Objectivity

Ayesha is a professional accountant working on the corporation tax return of Lever Ltd. The FD of the company has made it clear that she expects the company's tax payable to be less than £50,000 and that she doesn't care what Ayesha has to do to make this happen.

Requirement

Does Ayesha need to resign from this engagement?

Solution

Ayesha need only resign if she considers that the FD's request will unduly influence her professional judgement.

1.4 Professional competence and due care

Definition

Professional competence and due care: to maintain professional knowledge and skill at the level required to ensure that clients or employers receive competent professional service based on current developments in practice, legislation and techniques and act diligently in accordance with applicable technical and professional standards when providing professional services.

Competent professional service requires the exercise of sound judgement in applying professional knowledge and skill. Competence entails:

- Attainment of professional competence
- Maintenance of professional competence, requiring a continuing awareness and understanding of relevant issues

Continuing professional development enables a professional accountant to develop and maintain the capabilities to perform competently within the professional environment.

The professional accountant shall take steps to ensure that those working under the professional accountant have appropriate training and supervision.

Users of the accountant's professional services should be made aware of any limitations in those services.

1.5 Confidentiality

Definition

Confidentiality: to respect the confidentiality of information acquired as a result of professional and business relationships and, therefore, not disclose such information without proper and specific authority unless there is a legal or professional right or duty to disclose, nor use the information for their personal advantage or the advantage of third parties.

A professional accountant shall maintain confidentiality, including in a social environment, being alert to the possibility of inadvertent disclosure, particularly to a close business associate or a close or immediate family member.

A professional accountant shall consider the need to maintain confidentiality of information within the firm. All reasonable steps shall be taken to ensure that staff under the professional accountant's control and persons from whom advice and assistance is obtained respect the professional accountant's duty of confidentiality.

A professional accountant shall also maintain confidentiality of information disclosed by a prospective client or employer.

The need to comply with the principle of confidentiality continues even after the end of relationships between a professional accountant and a client or employer.

Worked example: Confidentiality

Greg is a professional accountant who has recently changed employer. He has gone out for the evening with his new colleagues who are asking him whether he has ever worked for anyone famous and whether he knows how much they earn. In his previous job, Greg helped prepare tax returns for a number of celebrities. He met with one particularly well-known entertainer who did not go on to engage the firm. He also got talking to a famous actor whom he happened to sit next to on the flight back from his last summer holiday.

Requirement

What information learned before he began his current job may George disclose to his colleagues?

Solution

Greg is bound by the fundamental principle of confidentiality. The social context and the change of employer do not alter this. Greg may not disclose any information regarding the clients or prospective clients of his old employer.

However, there is nothing to stop Greg discussing his meeting with the actor last summer, since this was not a business meeting.

1.6 Professional behaviour

Definition

Professional behaviour: to comply with relevant laws and regulations and avoid any action that discredits the profession.

This includes actions which a reasonable and informed third party, having knowledge of all relevant information, would conclude negatively affects the good reputation of the profession.

Professional accountants shall conduct themselves with courtesy and consideration towards all with whom they come into contact and shall not:

- Make exaggerated claims for the services they are able to offer, the qualifications they possess, or experience they have gained

- Make disparaging references or unsubstantiated comparisons to the work of others

2 Threats and safeguards framework

Section overview

- The circumstances in which professional accountants operate may give rise to specific threats to compliance with the five fundamental principles.

- The Code provides a framework to help identify, evaluate and respond to these threats.

- The professional accountant is then able to apply safeguards to eliminate the threats or reduce them to an acceptable level so that compliance with the five fundamental principles is not compromised.

2.1 Threats

When a relationship or circumstance creates a threat, such a threat could compromise, or could be perceived to compromise, a professional accountant's compliance with the fundamental principles.

Threats to compliance with the fundamental principles fall into one or more of the following categories:

- **Self-interest threats**, which may occur as a result of the financial or other interests of a professional accountant or of an immediate or close family member

- **Self-review threats**, which may occur when a previous judgment needs to be reevaluated by the professional accountant responsible for that judgment

- **Advocacy threats,** which may occur when a professional accountant promotes a position or opinion to the point that objectivity may be compromised

- **Familiarity threats,** which may occur when, because of a close relationship, a professional accountant becomes too sympathetic to the interests of others

- **Intimidation threats**, which may occur when a professional accountant may be deterred from acting objectively by actual or perceived pressures, including attempts to exercise undue influence over the professional accountant

2.2 Safeguards

Safeguards are measures that may eliminate threats or reduce them to an acceptable level. The nature of the safeguards to be applied will vary depending on the circumstances.

Safeguards include:

- Educational, training and experience requirements for entry into the profession

- Continuing professional development requirements

- Corporate governance regulations

- Professional standards

- Professional or regulatory monitoring and disciplinary procedures

- External review by a legally empowered third party of the reports, returns, communications or information produced by a professional accountant

Certain safeguards may increase the likelihood of identifying or deterring unethical behaviour, for example:

- Effective, well-publicised complaints systems operated by the employing organisation, the profession or a regulator, which enable colleagues, employers and members of the public to draw attention to unprofessional or unethical behaviour

- An explicitly stated duty to report breaches of ethical requirements

A professional accountant may encounter situations in which threats cannot be eliminated or reduced to an acceptable level. In such situations, the professional accountant shall decline or discontinue the specific professional service involved or, when necessary, resign from the engagement or employment.

3 Ethical conflict resolution

Section overview

- To ensure compliance with the fundamental principles a professional accountant may need to resolve a conflict in applying the principles.

- The Code lists factors for consideration and details the steps to be followed.

3.1 Conflict resolution process

When initiating an ethical conflict resolution process, a professional accountant should consider the following factors:

- Relevant facts
- Relevant parties
- Ethical issues involved
- Fundamental principles related to the matter in question
- Established internal procedures
- Alternative courses of action

Having considered these factors, the appropriate course of action may be determined, weighing the consequences of each alternative. If the matter remains unresolved, the professional accountant may wish to consult with other appropriate persons within the firm or employing organisation for help in obtaining resolution.

If a significant conflict cannot be resolved, a professional accountant may wish to obtain professional advice from the relevant professional body or legal advisors, and thereby obtain guidance on ethical and legal issues without breaching confidentiality. The ICAEW runs a confidential ethics helpline service.

It is advisable for the professional accountant to document the issue and details of any discussions held or decisions taken concerning that issue.

It is possible that, after exhausting all relevant possibilities, the ethical conflict remains unresolved. A professional accountant should, where possible, refuse to remain associated with the matter creating the conflict. The professional accountant may determine that, in the circumstances, it is appropriate to withdraw from the engagement team or specific assignment, or to resign altogether from the engagement or the firm.

Interactive question 1: Ethical conflict resolution   [Difficulty level: Exam standard]

James, a member of the ICAEW, is a tax manager working for a client which is a high-profile charitable organisation. Over the years he has become firm friends with the financial controller, Gordon.

Recently he has become concerned that refunds of tax under Gift Aid have been claimed from HMRC without the correct documentation to back these up. James has mentioned this to Gordon, who has told him not to worry about this. James does not wish to upset Gordon, but is not satisfied.

Requirement

Identify the main threat to the five fundamental principles here and the six factors to be considered by James when initiating the conflict resolution needed.

See **Answer** at the end of this chapter.

 Interactive question 2: Ethical conflict resolution   [Difficulty level: Exam standard]

The same facts as above.

After considering the six factors James decided to consult the Finance Director of the charity, Brenda.

James feels that Brenda has not taken sufficient steps to resolve the issue.

Requirement

Outline the options open to James.

See **Answer** at the end of this chapter.

4   Conflicts of interest

 Section overview

- The Code requires a professional accountant to take reasonable steps to avoid, identify and resolve conflicts of interest.

- Both actual and perceived conflicts must be considered.

4.1   Identifying a conflict of interest

A professional accountant shall take reasonable steps to identify circumstances that could pose a conflict of interest. These may give rise to threats to compliance with the fundamental principles.

A conflict may arise between the firm and the client or between two conflicting clients being managed by the same firm. For example, acting for both a husband and wife in a divorce settlement or acting for a company and an employee of the company being made redundant would most likely give rise to a conflict of interest.

A relevant test is whether a reasonable and informed observer would perceive that the objectivity of the professional accountant is likely to be impaired.

 Worked example: Conflict of interest

A professional accountancy firm initiates a joint venture with a major competitor of one of the firm's tax clients.

Requirement

Who is the conflict between here and which fundamental principle may be threatened by this conflict?

Solution

The conflict here is between the professional accountancy firm and its tax client. A threat to objectivity may arise.

4.2 The threat of a conflict of interest

Evaluation of threats from possible conflicts includes consideration as to whether the professional accountant has any business interests or relationships with the client or a third party that could give rise to threats. If threats are other than clearly insignificant, safeguards should be considered and applied as necessary.

Depending upon the circumstances giving rise to the conflict, safeguards should ordinarily include the professional accountant notifying all known relevant parties of the conflict.

A professional accountant may encounter situations in a conflict and the threats it poses to one or more of the fundamental principles cannot be eliminated or reduced to an acceptable level. In such situations, the professional accountant should conclude that it is not appropriate to accept a specific engagement or that resignation from one or more conflicting engagements is required.

5 Tax avoidance and tax evasion

Section overview

- Tax avoidance is legal while tax evasion is illegal.

- Tax evasion can lead to prosecution for the taxpayer and possibly their accountant.

5.1 Tax avoidance

Taxpayers may try to minimise their tax in various ways. These range from an individual opening a NISA account, which pays tax-free interest, to a multinational group of companies shifting profits to a country with a low rate of corporation tax.

There is no single definition of tax avoidance. The use of the term has varied over recent years, particularly in the media where it is used to describe a range of scenarios and is frequently confused with tax evasion, but all tax avoidance is legal.

The fact that avoidance is a legal method of reducing a taxpayer's liability does not mean that it will always be effective at saving tax. Anti-avoidance legislation is introduced to close legal 'loopholes' which taxpayers make use of. Certain tax avoidance schemes must be disclosed to HMRC. The courts strike down some planning schemes by ignoring elements of transactions which have no commercial purpose. A general anti-abuse rule (GAAR) has also been introduced to enable abusive tax avoidance arrangements to be challenged.

5.2 Tax evasion

Tax evasion is illegal. It consists of seeking to pay less tax than is due by deliberately misleading HMRC. This may be attempted by either:

- Suppressing information to which HMRC is entitled, for example by

    - Failing to notify HMRC of a liability to tax, or
    - Understating income or gains

  or

- Providing HMRC with false information, for example by

    - Deducting expenses that have not been incurred, or
    - Claiming capital allowances on plant that has not been purchased

Minor cases of tax evasion are generally settled out of court. Serious cases of tax evasion, particularly those involving fraud, continue to be the subject of criminal prosecutions which may lead to fines and/or imprisonment on conviction. There may also be money-laundering implications (see below).

5.3 Tax avoidance versus tax evasion

Tax avoidance is legal, whereas tax evasion is illegal. The distinction between tax evasion and avoidance is usually obvious since avoidance does not involve any intention to mislead HMRC.

As seen earlier in this section, the fact that a taxpayer is not acting illegally does not mean, though, that steps taken to minimise tax will necessarily be effective.

6 Money laundering

Section overview

- The ICAEW members' legal and regulatory guidance includes anti-money laundering guidance.

- This guidance has been prepared to assist professional accountants in complying with their obligations in relation to the prevention, recognition and reporting of money laundering.

6.1 Introduction

Accountants are required to comply with the Proceeds of Crime Act 2002 (POCA) as amended by the Serious Organised Crime and Police Act 2005 (SOCPA) and the Money Laundering Regulations 2007 (the Regulations).

The ICAEW Members' Regulations and guidance includes guidance issued by the Consultative Committee of Accountancy Bodies (CCAB) in December 2007.

6.2 Elements of money laundering

Definition

Money laundering: The term used for a number of offences involving the proceeds of crime or terrorist funds. It includes possessing, or in any way dealing with, or concealing, the proceeds of any crime.

Someone is engaged in money laundering under POCA where they:

- Conceal, disguise, convert, transfer or remove (from the United Kingdom) criminal property

- Enter into or become concerned in an arrangement which they know or suspect facilitates (by whatever means) the acquisition, retention, use or control of criminal property by or on behalf of another person

- Acquire, use or have possession of criminal property

Criminal property includes (but is by no means limited to)

- The proceeds of tax evasion, other tax-related offences (see below) or any other crime

- A benefit obtained through bribery and corruption (including both the receipt of a bribe and the income received from a contract obtained through bribery or the promise of a bribe)

- Benefits obtained, or income received, through the operation of a criminal cartel

- Benefits (in the form of saved costs) arising from a failure to comply with a regulatory requirement, where that failure is a criminal offence

Where a professional accountant suspects that a client is involved in money laundering there may be an obligation to report this.

6.3 Tax-related offences

Tax-related offences are not in a special category. The proceeds or monetary advantage arising from tax offences are treated no differently from the proceeds of theft, drug trafficking or other criminal conduct.

Tax evasion offences fall within the definition of money laundering and in certain cases individuals may be prosecuted under one of the money-laundering offences.

No offence is committed where the client reduces their tax liability using legal methods.

6.4 Anti-money laundering reports

Professional accountants are obliged by law to report suspicions of money laundering. Within an accountancy firm, an internal report would be made to the firm's Money Laundering Reporting Officer (MLRO). The MLRO, or the professional accountant if they are the MLRO for their firm, must then decide whether to submit a suspicious activity report (SAR) to the National Crime Agency (NCA).

6.5 Related offences

A professional accountant failing to submit a SAR when a report should be made is in itself an offence. Care should also be taken not to alert a money launderer when there is knowledge or suspicion that a SAR has been made. To do so would constitute tipping off, another offence under POCA.

6.6 Penalties

Money-laundering offences may be tried in a Magistrate's Court or in a Crown Court depending on severity. Cases tried in the Crown Court can attract unlimited fines and up to fourteen years' imprisonment for the main money-laundering offences. Failure to report and tipping off can attract unlimited fines and up to five years' imprisonment.

Interactive question 3: Money laundering   [Difficulty level: Exam standard]

Orla is a professional accountant working in sole practice handling Pay As You Earn (PAYE) compliance for various companies. Orla has acquired knowledge that one client has received money from the sale of a large number of stolen goods.

Requirement

Explain why a money-laundering report is needed, identify to whom any report should be made and outline any consequences if Orla lets the client know she is making a report.

See **Answer** at the end of this chapter.

Summary and Self-test

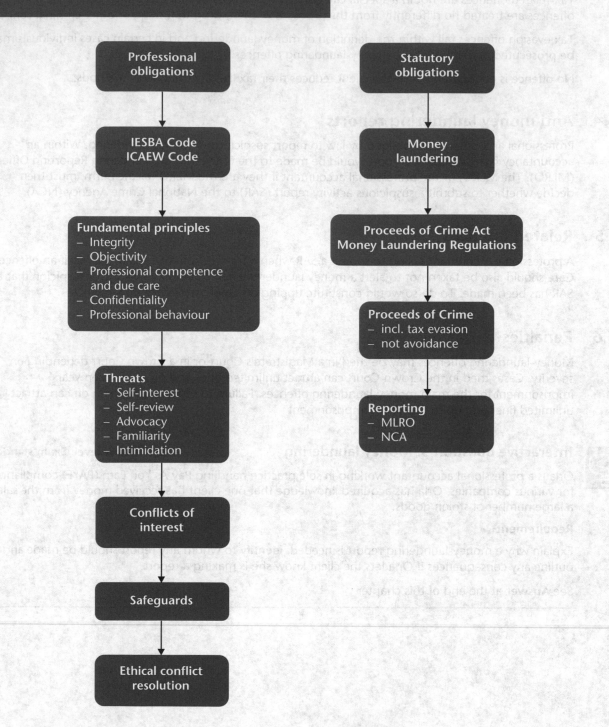

Professional obligations → **IESBA Code / ICAEW Code** → **Fundamental principles**
- Integrity
- Objectivity
- Professional competence and due care
- Confidentiality
- Professional behaviour

→ **Threats**
- Self-interest
- Self-review
- Advocacy
- Familiarity
- Intimidation

→ **Conflicts of interest**

→ **Safeguards**

→ **Ethical conflict resolution**

Statutory obligations → **Money laundering** → **Proceeds of Crime Act / Money Laundering Regulations**

→ **Proceeds of Crime**
- incl. tax evasion
- not avoidance

→ **Reporting**
- MLRO
- NCA

Self-test

Answer the following questions.

1   Which **TWO** of the following are **NOT** fundamental principles as stated in the ICAEW Code of Ethics?

   A   Integrity
   B   Professional intellect
   C   Objectivity
   D   Courtesy and consideration

2   A professional accountant is asked by her father, a partner in the firm employing her, to overstate the allowable expenses in a client's tax-adjusted accounts. He is offering to recommend she receive a bonus payment if she does this.

   Which **TWO** threats to objectivity is the professional accountant faced with in this situation?

   A   Self-interest
   B   Self-review
   C   Familiarity
   D   Intimidation

3   A professional accountant has been asked to act for a taxpayer who is negotiating a redundancy settlement with his employer. The employer concerned is a company which is one of the professional accountant's existing clients.

   Which of the following statements is true in this situation?

   A   The conflict here is between the accountant and the existing client.
   B   There is a perceived conflict of interest here but no actual conflict.
   C   The professional accountant must not inform the employer or the company of the situation.
   D   There is an actual conflict here between the company and the employee

4   Which of the following actions by a taxpayer would not constitute tax evasion?

   A   Obtaining tax-free interest by investing in a NISA
   B   Claiming capital allowances on a fictitious item of plant
   C   Choosing not to declare rental income received
   D   Failing to notify HMRC of a profitable trade commenced two years ago

5   What is the maximum prison sentence for the offence of tipping off?

   A   Two years
   B   Five years
   C   Seven years
   D   Fourteen years

Now go back to the Learning objectives in the Introduction. If you are satisfied you have achieved this objective please tick it off.

Technical reference

IESBA Code of Ethics for Professional Accountants

ICAEW Members' My guide to regulations: Code of Ethics

ICAEW Members' My guide to regulations: Anti-money laundering guidance for the accountancy sector

Proceeds of Crime Act 2002

Money Laundering Regulations 2007

ICAEW Ethics helpline service +44 (0)1908 248 250 http://www.icaew.com/members/advisory-helplines-and-services

> This technical reference section is designed to assist you. It should help you to know where to look for further information on the topics covered in this chapter. **You will not be examined on the contents of this section in your examination.**

Answers to Interactive questions

Answer to Interactive question 1

A familiarity threat arises from James's friendship with Gordon.

When initiating any conflict resolution process, James should consider the following:

- Relevant facts
- Relevant parties
- Ethical issues involved
- Fundamental principles related to the matter in question
- Established internal procedures
- Alternative courses of action

Answer to Interactive question 2

James may wish to seek professional advice from the ICAEW or legal advisors, and thereby obtain guidance on ethical issues without breaching confidentiality. James should consider seeking legal advice to determine whether there is a requirement to report.

If the ethical conflict remains unresolved, James should refuse to remain associated with the matter creating the conflict. He may determine that, in the circumstances, it is appropriate to resign altogether from the engagement.

Answer to Interactive question 3

Orla has acquired knowledge that her client is handling proceeds of crime (the stolen goods). This constitutes money laundering, therefore a report is required under anti-money laundering regulations.

Orla is in sole practice, so an internal report cannot be made. She must submit a Suspicious Activity Report to the NCA. If she fails to do this, this is a criminal offence carrying a maximum penalty of an unlimited fine plus up to five years in prison.

Answers to Self-test

1　B and D – Professional intellect and courtesy and consideration are required of a professional accountant but are not of themselves fundamental principles.

2　A and C – The family connection leads to a familiarity threat. The bonus offered constitutes a self-interest threat.

3　D – There is an actual conflict here between the company and the employee. This should be disclosed to both parties.

4　A – This is a legitimate way to reduce tax, whereas the others all constitute tax evasion and are illegal.

5　B

CHAPTER 2

Introduction to taxation

Introduction

Examination context

Topic List

    1 Objectives of taxation

    2 Liability to tax and tax administration

    3 Sources of tax law and practice

Summary and Self-test

Answers to Self-test

Learning objectives

Tick off

- Identify the objectives of tax in general terms of economic, social justice and environmental issues, the range of tax opportunities open to the government and the relative advantages of different types of tax in meeting the government's objectives ☐

- Recognise the impact of external influences, including EU tax policies, on UK tax objectives and policies ☐

- Classify entities as individuals, partnerships, or companies for tax purposes and state how they are taxed ☐

- Identify who is liable for the following taxes, how taxes apply to income, transactions and assets, identify the government bodies responsible for the taxes, and determine when an individual or entity comes within the scope of the taxes: ☐

  - Capital gains tax
  - Corporation tax
  - Income tax
  - National insurance
  - VAT

- Recognise the importance of the budget cycle, tax years and the following sources of UK tax law and practice: ☐

  - Legislation

  - Case law

  - HM Revenue & Customs manuals, statements of practice, extra-statutory concessions and press releases

Specific syllabus references for this chapter are: 1a, b, c, d, e.

Syllabus links

The topics covered in this chapter are essential background knowledge which will underpin the whole of your taxation studies.

Examination context

In the examination, in the objective test questions, candidates may be required to:

- Identify the social justice principles being applied for taxation purposes
- Recognise external influences on the UK taxation system
- Understand which taxes apply to different taxpayers eg partnerships, companies
- Identify the responsibilities of HM Revenue & Customs

For extra question practice on these topics go to the section of the Question Bank covering this chapter.

1 Objectives of taxation

Section overview

- The UK tax system has developed piecemeal and has been changed by successive governments in accordance with their political objectives.

- Governments use taxation to encourage or discourage certain types of economic activity.

- Taxation may be used to promote social justice but there is no political consensus on what is meant by this term.

- Environmental concerns have led to changes in taxation policy.

- External influences are increasingly important, in particular the European Union.

1.1 Introduction

The purpose of this chapter is to provide background information which will assist your understanding of the framework of the UK taxation system, why governments impose tax and the principles of taxation.

The UK taxation system has developed over centuries on a piecemeal basis. Successive governments have changed the taxation system in accordance with their political objectives. There has never been an all-party political consensus about how the UK taxation system should be changed and there probably never will be.

1.2 Management of the economy

The government has an effect on the level of economic activity in the UK by its withdrawal of money from the economy through taxation and the injection of money into the economy through public sector spending.

In the past, governments tended to make changes to taxation in the light of short-term changes in the economy such as inflation, unemployment and the balance of trade between imports and exports.

More recently, governments have believed that the impact of taxation takes a long time to have an effect. Government policies have therefore moved to longer-term planning. The government has also delegated the setting of interest rates to the Bank of England with specific targets for inflation, instead of trying to manage inflation by short-term interest rate changes.

Within the longer-term planning, the government aims to encourage or discourage certain types of economic activity.

The government encourages:

- Savings, for example by offering tax incentives such as tax relief on pension contributions

- Donations to charity, for example through the Gift Aid Scheme

- Investment into business, for example through Venture Capital Trust relief and the Enterprise Investment Scheme

- Entrepreneurs who build their own businesses, through reliefs from capital taxes

The government discourages:

- Smoking and alcoholic drinks, through substantial taxes on each type of product

- Motoring, through vehicle excise duty and fuel duties

Governments argue that these latter two taxes to some extent mirror the extra costs to the country of such behaviour, such as the burden placed on the National Health Service and maintenance of the road network.

However, the government also needs to raise money for other areas of public expenditure such as defence, law and order, overseas aid and the running of the government and parliament. There is no real link between any particular tax and this type of expenditure.

1.3 Social justice

Social justice lies at the heart of politics. What some think of as just is regarded by others as completely unjust. Attitudes to the redistribution of wealth are a clear example.

Some people believe in a free-market approach where individuals are allowed to generate income and capital and spend it as they choose, with relatively low levels of taxation. It is argued that since the economy overall increases in the free market, every individual will benefit in the long term.

The free-market approach could be criticised for resulting in the rich becoming richer and the poor poorer since economic power may become concentrated in relatively few hands.

Some people argue that taxation should be used to redistribute income and wealth away from the rich towards the poor. This is a key argument in favour of taxes on capital which, relative to the tax raised, cost a great deal to collect. The introduction of tax credits which benefit those on lower incomes, especially those with children, can also be seen as an attempt at wealth redistribution through taxation.

There are a number of principles which may be invoked today in the continued debate over social justice:

- The direct/indirect principle

    - Direct taxes (eg income tax, capital gains tax, corporation tax, national insurance contributions) are only paid by those who generate the funds to pay the tax

    - Indirect taxes (eg value added tax, excise duty) relate to consumption and it is up to individuals whether they spend money on such goods

- The progressive/regressive principle

    - Progressive taxes rise as a proportion of income as that income rises. For example, in the UK the lowest rate of income tax is currently 0% on the first few thousand pounds of certain taxable income, whereas the rate of income tax on income of over £42,385 is 40% and that on taxable income of over £150,000 is 45%

    - Regressive taxes rise as a proportion of income as income falls. The amount of duty paid on a packet of cigarettes is the same, regardless of the income of the purchaser. That amount will be a greater proportion of the income of a person with a low income than a person with a higher income. The argument that a regressive tax is just hinges on the benefit principle (below)

- The unit/value principle

    - A unit tax is calculated as a flat rate per item, regardless of value. Again, this hinges on the benefit principle (below)

    - A value tax is based on a percentage of the value of the item, such as value added tax. This argument partly hinges on the ability to pay principle (below)

- The income/capital/expenditure principle

    - Income tax is paid only by those who generate income

    - Capital taxes are just because people should not be able to live off the sale of capital assets without generating income

    - Taxes on expenditure are paid only by those who incur the expenditure

- The ability to pay/benefit principle

    - Taxes should be based on the ability of the taxpayer to pay them eg income tax, capital gains tax

    - Taxes should be based, at least partly, on the benefit that the taxpayer receives. For example, everyone should pay towards defence or law and order

- The neutrality principle

    - Tax should be neutral so as not to distort choice (but the examples given in 1.2 show that governments do not always want taxes to be neutral)

- The equity principle

  - Tax should be equitable or just. However, there are many different views as to what is equitable

- The efficiency principle

  - The cost of collecting the tax should be low in relation to the tax raised. Governments are generally only concerned with the cost to them of administration, not with costs incurred by the taxpayer. The Pay As You Earn scheme and value added tax, for example, impose a burden on the taxpayer to act as collector

1.4 Environmental concerns

The taxation system is slowly moving to accommodate environmental concerns such as sources of energy and global warming.

Many would agree that it is for the government to make sure that such concerns are dealt with through government policy, including taxation, instead of leaving it to individuals to modify their behaviour.

Examples of such taxes are:

- Climate change levy on businesses in proportion to their energy consumption

- Landfill tax to discourage the use of landfill sites for waste disposal and to encourage recycling

- Taxes on motor vehicles based on carbon emissions, such as cars provided to employees and vehicle excise duty, to encourage use of more environmentally friendly vehicles

1.5 External influences

In the past, the UK government tended to set its taxation policies based on domestic concerns with little external influence. However, over the last forty years, with the entry of the UK into the European Union (EU) and increased globalisation, the UK government has had to take much more account of external influences in setting its taxation policies.

We have already seen that the impact of environmental concerns has led to changes in UK taxation. This has been partly brought about by the influence of the international community and agreements entered into by the UK government such as the Kyoto Treaty on reduction of greenhouse gases, principally carbon dioxide.

However, the main external influence on UK taxation policy is the EU.

The overall aim of the EU is the creation of a single European market with no internal trade barriers and common policies relating to trade outside the EU.

There is no general requirement for member states to move to a common system of direct taxation and examples of specific European laws in relation to direct taxes have been very limited. However, states may provide for a common code of taxation within particular areas of their taxation system.

The most important example is indirect taxation such as value added tax (VAT), where the UK is obliged to pass its laws to conform to rules laid down by European law. There is a certain amount of flexibility between the member states, for example on rates of taxation.

Under the EU treaties, member states are also obliged to permit freedom of movement of workers and capital and freedom to establish business operations within the EU. These treaty provisions can be invoked by taxpayers. An example was a UK company which wished to make use of losses in a subsidiary based in another EU country. This was prohibited by UK tax law. The success of the UK company's case in the European Court has led to a change to UK tax law in this area.

Further examples of external influences affecting UK taxation policy are:

- The recent banking crisis: following this, the UK government and various other countries introduced the bank levy with a view to helping reduce the risks and impact of future such crises

- The Organisation for Economic Cooperation and Development (OECD): the OECD's model tax treaty forms the basis of many of the UK's international tax treaties

2 Liability to tax and tax administration

Section overview

- Individuals, partnerships and companies are liable to tax.
- Taxes in the UK are administered by HM Revenue & Customs (HMRC).

2.1 Individuals

An individual may be liable to the following taxes:

- Income tax (IT), for example on income from investments, income from employment and income from a business which he operates as a sole trader or as a member of a partnership

- Capital gains tax (CGT) on the disposal of capital assets owned by him as investments or used in his sole trade or partnership

- National insurance contributions (NICs) as an employee, as a sole trader or partner, and as an employer

- Value added tax (VAT) as the supplier of goods and services or as the final consumer of goods or services

An individual is taxed annually on his income and gains arising in a tax year.

Definition

Tax year: 6 April in one calendar year to 5 April in the next calendar year. The tax year running from 6 April 2015 to 5 April 2016 is called the 2015/16 tax year.

2.2 Partnerships

A partnership is a group of persons carrying on a business together with a view to making a profit.

Each partner is individually liable to tax on his share of income and gains of the partnership in a tax year, but not for tax on the shares of income and gains of the other partners.

The partners are jointly and severally liable for the following taxes:

- Income tax of employees deducted under the Pay As You Earn (PAYE) system

- National insurance contributions (NICs) as an employer (employer contributions and employee contributions are collected under the PAYE system)

- Value added tax (VAT) as the supplier of goods and services or as the final consumer of goods or services

'Joint and several' liability means that these taxes can be recovered from all or any of the partners.

2.3 Companies

A company is a legal person formed by incorporation under the Companies Acts. It is legally separate from its owners (shareholders) and its managers (directors).

A company is liable for the following taxes:

- Corporation tax (CT) on its income and gains

- Income tax of employees deducted under the Pay As You Earn (PAYE) system

- National insurance contributions (NICs) as an employer (employer contributions and employee contributions collected under the PAYE system)

- Value added tax (VAT) as the supplier of goods and services or as the final consumer of goods or services

The rate of corporation tax is determined by reference to the financial year.

Definition

Financial year: 1 April in one calendar year to 31 March in the next calendar year. The financial year running from 1 April 2015 to 31 March 2016 is called Financial Year (FY) 2015.

2.4 HM Revenue & Customs

All taxes in the UK are administered by HMRC.

The Commissioners of HMRC are a body of civil servants appointed by the Queen who exercise their duties on behalf of the Crown. They have a duty to implement the law relating to taxation and oversee the administration of taxation.

The Commissioners appoint 'Officers of Revenue & Customs' (known as Officers) to carry out the day-to-day work of HMRC. These officers mainly work in one of several hundred local district offices which are the front line point of contact between HMRC and the taxpayer.

Among the responsibilities of HMRC are:

- To collect and administer taxes including IT, CGT, NIC, CT and VAT

- To pay and administer universal credit, tax credits and child benefit

- To collect repayments of student loans

- To ensure all employers meet the minimum wage rules

- To protect UK society from tax fraud, alcohol and tobacco smuggling and illegal importation of drugs

3 Sources of tax law and practice

Section overview

- Tax law is set out in statute, supplemented by statutory instruments.

- A Finance Act is passed each year, following Budget proposals.

- Case law interpreting statute law must usually be followed in later cases.

- HMRC publishes its interpretation of tax law.

3.1 Legislation

3.1.1 Statutes and the Budget cycle

The basic rules of the UK taxation system are in a number of tax statutes (Acts of Parliament).

The tax law is amended each year by the **Finance Act**. This is based on proposals from the Chancellor of the Exchequer. Some of these are outlined in the Autumn Statement, a pre-budget report. Further proposals are then put forward in the Budget (Financial Statement) in March or April each year. A new Finance Bill is presented to Parliament each year to enact the proposals made by the Chancellor and bring them into law. This process is complete once the Finance Bill receives Royal Assent, becoming an Act.

There is usually one Finance Act for each tax year but when there is a change in government, there may be a number of Budgets and a number of Finance Acts in respect of a single tax year. However, the Finance Act generally relates to the tax year and financial year starting in April of that year, (although recent Finance Acts have also contained provisions in respect of future years). Therefore, the Finance Act 2015 relates mainly to the tax year 2015/16 and the Financial Year 2015.

Most of the statutory tax law is found in consolidated statutes which contain the law enacted by successive Finance Acts over the years. For example, VAT is dealt with in the Value Added Tax Act 1994 (*VATA 1994*).

The main direct tax law has also recently been rewritten in plainer English. An example is the Corporation Tax Act 2010 (*CTA 2010*).

3.1.2 Statutory instruments

Some tax statutes set out a general principal but provide for the detail to be changed, as required, in secondary or 'delegated' legislation. This is usually in the form of a statutory instrument (SI), introduced either by a parliamentary minister or a local authority.

The reason for this is that the procedure for making changes to a SI is less complicated than for a statute. A SI is simply laid before Parliament and usually automatically becomes law within a stated period, unless any objections are raised to it.

SIs most commonly take the form of Regulations, which deal with these detailed provisions. They are the biggest single source of tax law each year.

3.2 Case law

Over the years, many thousands of tax cases have been brought before the courts where the interpretation of statute law is unclear.

Decisions made by judges to resolve these cases form case law. Many judgements are precedent for future cases which means that they must be followed unless superseded by legislation or the decision of a higher court.

Knowledge of specific tax cases is not examinable at this level.

3.3 HMRC publications

HMRC must act according to tax law, but it has some discretion over how it applies the law. HMRC therefore publishes details of how the law is to be implemented in practice, for example on the gov.uk website – www.gov.uk/government/organisations/hm-revenue-customs.

These publications have no legal backing but do provide information on HMRC's interpretation of the law, which will be adhered to unless successfully challenged by a taxpayer in the courts.

HMRC publications include:

- Manuals, primarily for the guidance of its own staff but also mostly available to taxpayers and tax professionals on the HMRC website

- Statements of practice (SP) setting out HMRC's interpretation of tax legislation

- Extra-statutory concessions (ESC) which provide for a relaxation of the strict legal position to resolve anomalies and relieve hardship. An ESC may be given statutory effect by means of a Treasury Order. ESCs are gradually being either codified or withdrawn

- Press releases and explanatory notes dealing with changes in tax law, for example Budget proposals

- Leaflets which are mainly aimed at ordinary taxpayers and explain the tax system in non-technical language

Summary

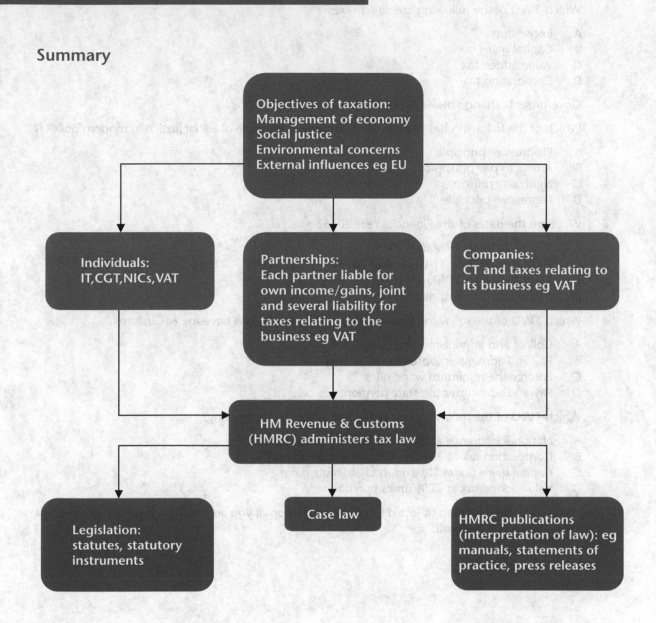

Objectives of taxation:
Management of economy
Social justice
Environmental concerns
External influences eg EU

Individuals:
IT,CGT,NICs,VAT

Partnerships:
Each partner liable for
own income/gains, joint
and several liability for
taxes relating to the
business eg VAT

Companies:
CT and taxes relating to
its business eg VAT

HM Revenue & Customs
(HMRC) administers tax law

Legislation:
statutes, statutory
instruments

Case law

HMRC publications
(interpretation of law): eg
manuals, statements of
practice, press releases

CHAPTER

2

Self-test

Answer the following questions.

1   Which **TWO** of the following are direct taxes?

    A   Excise duty
    B   Capital gains tax
    C   Value added tax
    D   Corporation tax

2   Governments change their tax policy to achieve 'social justice'.

Which of the following has **NOT** been an important principle of social justice in modern politics?

    A   Progressive principle
    B   Ability to pay principle
    C   Neutrality principle
    D   Regressive principle

3   What are the dates of the Financial Year 2015?

    A   1 April 2014 to 31 March 2015
    B   1 January 2015 to 31 December 2015
    C   1 April 2015 to 31 March 2016
    D   6 April 2015 to 5 April 2016

4   Which **TWO** of the following are functions carried out by HM Revenue & Customs?

    A   Collect and administer direct taxes
    B   Pay and administer jobseekers allowance
    C   Enforce the minimum wage rules
    D   Pay and administer the state pension

5   Which **TWO** of the following taxes may be payable by a company?

    A   National insurance at 2% on its taxable trading profits
    B   Corporation tax at 20% on its taxable trading profits
    C   Capital gains tax at 18% on its chargeable gains
    D   Value added tax at 20% on its purchases

Now, go back to the Learning objectives in the Introduction. If you are satisfied you have achieved these objectives, please tick them off.

Answers to Self-test

1   B and D – capital gains tax and corporation tax.

     The others are indirect taxes.

2   C – the neutrality principle (taxes should not distort choice).

     The encourage/discourage examples earlier in this chapter show that governments do not
     generally want taxes to be neutral.

3   C – Financial Year 2015 runs from 1 April 2015 to 31 March 2016.

4   A and C – collect and administer direct taxes and enforce the minimum wage rules.

5   B and D – corporation tax (payable by a company on its income and gains) and value added tax
     (as a supplier and a final consumer of goods and services). A company may pay national insurance
     on employees' earnings, but not on its own income and never at 2%.

CHAPTER 3

Introduction to income tax

Introduction

Examination context

Topic List

1 Chargeable and exempt income
2 Computation of taxable income
3 Computing tax payable
4 Personal allowances for taxpayers born before 6 April 1938
5 Allowances for married couples

Summary and Self-test

Technical reference

Answers to Interactive questions

Answers to Self-test

Introduction

Learning objectives

Tick off

- Recognise the main sources of taxable and non-taxable income ☐

- Calculate the personal allowance available to an individual according to personal circumstances including personal age allowances and married couples allowance ☐

- Calculate total taxable income and the income tax payable or repayable for employed and self-employed individuals ☐

The specific syllabus references for this chapter are: 3a, b, j.

Syllabus links

The topics covered in this chapter are fundamental to your understanding of income tax.

You will be using this knowledge again when you tackle the Tax Compliance paper and Business Planning: Taxation paper later on in the Professional Level.

Examination context

In the examination, in the scenario-based question for income tax, candidates may be required to:

- Differentiate between items which are taxable and exempt for income tax purposes

- Calculate taxable income where income has been received net of income tax or without deduction of tax at source

- Categorise taxable income as non savings, savings or dividend income

In the examination, in the objective test questions, candidates may be required to:

- Calculate the tax liability

- Identify how tax relief is given for Gift Aid

- Compute the personal allowances available for taxpayers with adjusted net income exceeding £100,000 and for taxpayers born before 6 April 1938

- Compute the allowances available for some married couples

For extra question practice on these topics go to the section of the Question Bank covering this chapter, and to the section of the Question Bank containing scenario-based questions for income tax. However, you will need to study Chapter 4 and Chapter 5 before attempting these scenario-based questions.

Candidates have historically prepared well for this area of the syllabus. Better prepared candidates are able to perform well in the more difficult areas of Gift Aid and allowances for taxpayers born before 6 April 1938.

1 Chargeable and exempt income

Section overview

- An individual's income may be chargeable to income tax or exempt from income tax.

- Chargeable income is employment income, trading income, property income, savings income, dividend income and miscellaneous income.

- Exempt income includes income from New Individual Savings Accounts and premium bond prizes.

1.1 Sources of income

Income can be broadly divided into two main types:

- Income which is chargeable to income tax – this may be called taxable income or chargeable income

- Income which is exempt from income tax – this may be called non-taxable income or exempt income

The first stage of an income tax computation is to prepare a computation of taxable income. To do this you will need to identify whether the income received by the taxpayer is chargeable or exempt.

1.2 Chargeable income

The main types of chargeable income are:

- Income from employment

- Income from trading

- Income from renting out property

- Income from investments such as interest on loans, bank and building society accounts

- Income from investments such as dividends

- Income from other sources (pensions income, some social security benefits, income from casual work)

1.3 Exempt income

Some income is specifically exempt from income tax including the following:

- Interest on National Savings Certificates

- Income (interest or dividends) from New Individual Savings Accounts (NISAs, previously ISAs) including Junior ISAs

- Betting, competition, lottery and premium bond winnings

- Some social security benefits such as housing benefit

- Scholarships

- Income tax repayment interest

2 Computation of taxable income

Section overview

- Some income is received with tax already deducted at source, such as most interest and employment income, and must be included gross in the income tax computation.

- Other income is received without tax being deducted at source, such as trading income and property income.

- Dividend income has a tax credit attached to it which must be included in the tax computation.

- There are three types of income in a total chargeable income computation: non-savings income; savings income; and dividend income.

- The total of all chargeable income is called 'net income'.

- Taxable income is net income less the personal allowance.

- The personal allowance is reduced for taxpayers with high income.

2.1 Income taxed at source

Some income is received by the taxpayer net of tax, which means that tax is already deducted at the source of the income. This simplifies the collection of tax for HMRC. You may be told in a question that the amount received is **net of income tax**. However, when working out the chargeable income you must include any tax deducted at source, and use the **gross** amount.

Most forms of interest are received net of 20% tax deducted at source. This includes most bank and building society interest and interest on loan stock issued by UK companies. Net interest must be **grossed up** by multiplying the net amount by 100/(100 – 20) (ie 100/80) to obtain the gross equivalent. For example, if you are given a figure for bank interest received of £160 in a question, you must multiply this figure by 100/80 to obtain the gross figure of £200 on which tax of £200 × 20% = £40 has been suffered. Alternatively, the question may give you the gross bank interest figure of £200.

Employment income is received net of income tax deducted under the Pay As You Earn (PAYE) system. The amounts of tax deducted under PAYE will vary according to the income and personal circumstances of the individual. The PAYE system is dealt with later in this text. For examination purposes, questions will normally quote employment income as the amount of income **before** any tax deducted, that is in **gross** terms. If required for the answer, the amount of income tax deducted at source via PAYE will be given separately.

Dividends from UK and overseas companies are received with a deemed tax credit. They are treated differently from other sources of income.

2.2 Income received without deduction of tax at source

The other sources of income are generally received without deduction of tax at source. This is called income received gross. You simply need to include the gross figure as given in the question as the chargeable income. The main types of income received gross are trading income and property income.

Some interest is received gross:

- Interest on National Savings and Investments (NS&I) Direct Saver and Investment Accounts

- Interest on government securities (gilt-edged securities or gilts) such as Exchequer Stock and Treasury Stock

- Interest received gross by an individual who has signed a declaration of non-taxpayer status and supplied a certificate to the bank or building society. This is called self-certification and is used mainly by children and pensioners

- Interest on non-commercial investments, such as a loan between friends

2.3 Dividend income

Dividends received from UK or overseas companies are dividend income. Dividend income is received with a deemed tax credit of 10% of the grossed up dividend. The amount received must be grossed up by 100/90 to obtain the gross equivalent. For example, if you are given a figure for a dividend received of £450 in a question, you must multiply the dividend by 100/90 to obtain the gross figure of £500 on which there is a tax credit of £500 × 10% = £50. Alternatively the question may give you the gross dividend income figure of £500.

2.4 Types of income

When you set out a taxable income computation, you need to use a standard format which divides the income into three types. This is because there are different rates of tax for each type of income.

The three types of income are:

- Non-savings income: Employment income, Trading profits, Property income, Miscellaneous income. Income that is not categorised as from a specific source is taxed as miscellaneous income.

- Savings income: Interest from investments

- Dividend income: Dividends from UK companies

Note that income received from a pension (pension income) and taxable social security benefits such as jobseeker's allowance (social security income) are taxed in the same way as employment income.

Definition

Net income: The total chargeable income before deducting the personal allowance (see later in this chapter).

Worked example: Net income

Andrew received the following income in 2015/16:

- Salary from his employment £10,000
- Building society interest £240
- Premium bond winnings £250
- Property income £2,000
- Dividends from UK companies £720

Requirement

What is Andrew's net income for 2015/16?

Solution

Net income

	Non-savings income £	Savings income £	Dividend income £	Total £
Employment income	10,000			
Property income	2,000			
Building society interest				
£240 × 100/80		300		
Dividends				
£720 × 100/90			800	
Net income	12,000	300	800	13,100

Premium bond winnings are exempt income and therefore not included in the above computation.

Interactive question 1: What type of income?   [Difficulty level: Easy]

Classify the following types of income as non-savings income, savings income or dividend income and show the taxable amount of each type of income that you would enter in the computation of taxable income.

Question	Fill in your answer
(a) Bank interest received from HSBC of £600	
(b) Property income of £1,000	
(c) Dividend received from overseas company of £495	
(d) Interest received on Treasury Stock of £525	
(e) Trading profits of £5,000	
(f) Interest received on NS&I investment account of £600	

See **Answer** at the end of this chapter.

2.5   Personal allowance

Definition

Taxable income: Net income after deduction of the personal allowance.

There is one further step that you need to undertake in order to arrive at the amount of taxable income. This is to deduct the personal allowance. Every individual taxpayer who is resident in the UK is entitled to a personal allowance from birth.

The basic personal allowance for taxpayers born after 5 April 1938 for 2015/16 is £10,600. There are enhanced personal allowances for taxpayers born before 6 April 1938 which are covered later in this chapter.

The personal allowance is deducted from the different types of income in the following order:

- Non-savings income
- Savings income
- Dividend income

ICAEW

Worked example: Taxable income

Charlotte receives the following income in 2015/16:

- Employment income £9,200
- Bank interest £500
- Dividends from UK companies £1,350

Requirement

What is Charlotte's taxable income for 2015/16?

Solution

Charlotte

Taxable income

	Non-savings income £	Savings income £	Dividend income £	Total £
Employment income	9,200			
Bank interest				
£500 × 100/80		625		
Dividends				
£1,350 × 100/90			1,500	
Net income	9,200	625	1,500	11,325
Less personal allowance	(9,200)	(625)	(775)	(10,600)
Taxable income	0	0	725	725

The full personal allowance of £10,600 is not available for individuals with an adjusted net income of more than £100,000. The personal allowance is reduced by £1 for every £2 that the individual's adjusted net income exceeds £100,000.

The personal allowance will be withdrawn completely where adjusted net income exceeds £121,200. Therefore any taxpayer subject to the additional rate of tax (see later in this chapter) will not be entitled to a personal allowance.

For the purposes of this exam, you may assume that net income is equal to adjusted net income.

Worked example: Reduction of the personal allowance

Julia, aged 30, had net income of £110,000 in 2015/16.

Requirement

What is Julia's personal allowance for 2015/16?

Solution

Julia

Personal allowance

	£	£	Total £
Personal allowance for 2015/16			10,600
(£110,000 – £100,000) = £10,000 × ½			(5,000)
Personal allowance for Julia			5,600

Interactive question 2: Computing taxable income [Difficulty level: Exam standard]

Max received the following income in 2015/16:

- Employment income £20,000
- Interest on New Individual Savings Account £600
- Interest on Barclays Bank account £280
- Dividends from UK companies £990

Requirement

Using the standard format below, compute Max's taxable income for 2015/16.

Max

Taxable income

	Non-savings income £	Savings income £	Dividend income £	Total £
Employment income				
Interest				
Dividends				
Net income				
Less personal allowance				
Taxable income				

See **Answer** at the end of this chapter.

3 Computing tax payable

Section overview

- Income tax is calculated first on non-savings income, then on savings income and lastly on dividend income.

- There are different rates of tax for each of the three types of income.

- Income tax may be payable by (or repayable to) a taxpayer after taking into account tax credits and tax deducted at source.

- Cash gifts to charity are given tax relief under Gift Aid, and affect the taxpayer's basic rate and higher rate band.

3.1 Computing tax liability

Definition

Tax liability: The total amount of income tax due from a taxpayer.

Once taxable income has been computed, you can calculate the income tax liability. Tax on the three types of income is calculated in the following order:

- Non-savings income
- Savings income
- Dividend income

For 2015/16, the rates of income tax for non-savings income are as follows:

• First £31,785 of taxable income	basic rate band	20%
• Taxable income between £31,785 and £150,000	higher rate band	40%
• Remainder over £150,000	additional rate band	45%

Worked example: Income tax liability on non-savings income

Krishan has trading profits of £55,000 in 2015/16. This is his only source of income in this tax year.

Requirement

What is Krishan's income tax liability for 2015/16?

Solution

Krishan

Income tax liability

	Non-savings income £
Trading profits/Net income	55,000
Less personal allowance	(10,600)
Taxable income	44,400
Tax	
	£
£31,785 × 20%	6,357
£12,615 × 40%	5,046
£44,400	
Income tax liability	11,403

Worked example: Income tax liability on non-savings income

Lois has employment income of £169,000 in 2015/16. This is her only source of income in this tax year.

Requirement

What is Lois's income tax liability for 2015/16?

Solution

Lois

	Non-savings income £
Employment income/Net income	169,000
Less personal allowance (note)	–
Taxable income	169,000
Tax	
£31,785 × 20%	6,357
£118,215 × 40%	47,286
£150,000	
£19,000 × 45%	8,550
£169,000	
Income tax liability	62,193

Note

As Lois' net income exceeds £121,200 her personal allowance is restricted to nil.

Interactive question 3: Computing tax on non-savings income

[Difficulty level: Exam standard]

Henry is an employee of Tilbury Ltd. His gross salary for 2015/16 is £45,465.

Requirement

Using the standard format below, compute Henry's income tax liability for 2015/16.

Henry

Income tax liability

	Non-savings income £
Employment income/Net income	
Less personal allowance	
Taxable income	
Tax	£
× 20%	
× 40%	
£	
Income tax liability	

See **Answer** at the end of this chapter.

A taxpayer is entitled to only one set of rate bands. The rate bands are used firstly by **non-savings income**. To the extent that any of the rate bands remain, they are used by savings income and then by dividend income. You will see how this works in the example below.

For 2015/16, the rates of income tax for savings income are as follows:

• First £5,000 of savings income	starting rate band	0%
• Next £26,785 of taxable income	basic rate band	20%
• Taxable income between £31,785 and £150,000	higher rate band	40%
• Remainder over £150,000	additional rate band	45%

The starting rate band of 0% for savings income applies **only** to taxpayers who have taxable non-savings income not exceeding £5,000. Where non-savings income, after deduction of the personal allowance (or personal age allowance) exceeds £5,000, the starting rate does not apply.

Worked example: Income tax liability on non-savings and savings income

Evie received the following income in 2015/16:

* Property income £10,689
* Building society interest £38,648

Requirement

What is Evie's income tax liability for 2015/16?

Solution

Evie

Income tax liability

	Non-savings income £	Savings income £	Total £
Property income	10,689		
Building society interest			
£38,648 × 100/80		48,310	
Net income	10,689	48,310	58,999
Less personal allowance	(10,600)		(10,600)
Taxable income	89	48,310	48,399

	£		£
Tax on non-savings income	89	× 20%	18
Tax on savings income:			
– in starting rate band	4,911	× 0%	0
	5,000		
– in basic rate band	26,785	× 20%	5,357
	31,785		
– in higher rate band	16,614	× 40%	6,646
	48,399		
Income tax liability			12,021

The £89 of non-savings taxable income is taxed first at 20%, the basic rate of tax for non-savings income.

Savings income is taxed next on a cumulative basis. Since the taxable non-savings income was less than £5,000 there is £4,911 of savings income in the starting rate band to tax at 0%.

On a cumulative basis a total of £5,000 of taxable income has been taxed so far. This leaves £26,785 (£31,785 – £5,000) of the basic rate band to tax the savings income at the basic rate of 20%.

Finally £16,614 of savings income falls in the higher rate band which is taxed at 40%.

For 2014/15, the rates of income tax for dividend income are as follows:

- First £31,785 of taxable income   basic rate band   10%
- Between £31,785 and £150,000   higher rate band   32.5%
- Remainder over £150,000   additional rate band   37.5%

Worked example: Income tax liability on all types of income

George receives the following income in 2015/16:

- Employment income £32,325
- Bank interest £4,040
- Dividends from UK companies £8,428

Requirement

What is George's income tax liability for 2015/16?

Solution

George

Income tax liability

	Non-savings income £	Savings income £	Dividend income £	Total £
Employment income	32,325			
Bank interest				
£4,040 × 100/80		5,050		
Dividends				
£8,428 × 100/90			9,364	
Net income	32,325	5,050	9,364	46,739
Less personal allowance	(10,600)			(10,600)
Taxable income	21,725	5,050	9,364	36,139

	£		£
Tax on non-savings income	21,725 × 20%		4,345
Tax on savings income:			
– in basic rate band	5,050 × 20%		1,010
	26,775		
Tax on dividend income:			
– in basic rate band	5,010 × 10%		501
	31,785		
– in higher rate band	4,354 × 32.5%		1,415
	36,139		
Income tax liability			7,271

Since the taxable non-savings income was more than £5,000 there is no starting rate band remaining to tax any savings income at 0%. All of the savings income therefore falls in the basic rate band and is taxed at 20%.

On a cumulative basis a total of £26,775 of taxable income has been taxed so far. This leaves £5,010 (£31,785 – £26,775) of the basic rate band to tax the dividend income at the basic rate of 10%.

Finally £4,354 of dividend income falls in the higher rate band which is taxed at 32.5%.

Worked example: Income tax liability on all types of income

Elise receives the following income in 2015/16:

- Employment income £95,875
- Property income £31,700
- Bank interest £21,140
- Dividends from UK companies £15,300

Requirement

What is Elise's income tax liability for 2015/16?

ICAEW

Solution

Elise

	Non-savings income £	Savings income £	Dividend income £	Total £
Employment income	95,875			
Property income	31,700			
Bank interest				
£21,140 × 100/80		26,425		
Dividends				
£15,300 × 100/90			17,000	
Net income	127,575	26,425	17,000	171,000
Personal allowance	–			
Taxable income	127,575	26,425	17,000	171,000

	£		£
Tax on non-savings income	31,785	× 20%	6,357
	95,790	× 40%	38,316
	127,575		
Tax on savings income			
– in higher rate band	22,425	× 40%	8,970
	150,000		
– in additional rate band	4,000	× 45%	1,800
Tax on dividend income			
– in additional rate band	17,000	× 37.5%	6,375
	171,000		
Income tax liability			61,818

3.2 Computing tax payable or repayable

Definition

Tax payable or repayable: The amount of income tax payable by a taxpayer (or repayable by HMRC) under self assessment after taking into account tax deducted at source.

The final stage that you may be asked to undertake is to compute the tax payable or repayable to the taxpayer under the self assessment system. Details of this system are covered later in this text.

The tax actually payable by the taxpayer must take into account:

- Tax credits received with dividends
- Tax deducted at source

Tax credits on dividends are set against the tax liability first (restricted to the tax credits on the taxable dividend). This is because dividend tax credits can only be used to reduce a taxpayer's tax liability. Any excess tax credits cannot be repaid.

Tax deducted at source on employment income and interest is used to reduce a taxpayer's tax liability and any excess tax deducted at source can be repaid to the taxpayer.

Worked example: Tax payable or repayable

Joe received the following income in 2015/16:

Property income	£5,475
Bank interest	£8,800
Dividends from UK companies	£549

Requirement

What is the tax payable by or repayable to Joe for 2015/16?

Solution

Joe

Tax payable/repayable

	Non-savings income £	Savings income £	Dividend income £	Total £
Property income	5,475			
Bank interest				
£8,800 × 100/80		11,000		
Dividends				
£549 × 100/90			610	
Net income	5,475	11,000	610	17,085
Less personal allowance	(5,475)	(5,125)		(10,600)
Taxable income	0	5,875	610	6,485

	£		£
Tax on savings income:			
– in starting rate band	5,000	× 0%	0
– in basic rate band	875	× 20%	175
	5,875		
Tax on dividend income:			
– in basic rate band	610	× 10%	61
	6,485		
Income tax liability			236
Less tax deducted at source:			
Dividend tax credit	£610	× 10%	(61)
Tax on bank interest	£11,000	× 20%	(2,200)
Income tax repayable			(2,025)

Since the taxable non-savings income was nil, there is £5,000 of savings income in the starting rate band to tax at 0%.

The dividend tax credit is used first to reduce the liability as it is not repayable.

3.3 Gift Aid

The Gift Aid Scheme gives tax relief for cash donations to charities.

In order to qualify for Gift Aid, a number of conditions must be satisfied, in addition:

- The donor must give the charity a Gift Aid declaration (in writing, by telephone or via the internet)

- The donor must pay an amount of income tax or capital gains tax which is at least equal to the amount of Gift Aid the charity will reclaim in the tax year in respect of the donor's donation

Basic rate tax relief is given by deeming the Gift Aid donation to be made net of basic rate tax. The charity will be able to recover this tax from HMRC. For example, if a taxpayer makes a Gift Aid donation of £160, the gross donation will be £160 × 100/80 = £200.

The charity will receive the actual tax credit of £200 × 20% = £40. There is no further tax consequence for the taxpayer if he pays tax at the basic rate. Gift Aid donations can therefore be ignored in computing the tax liability of a basic rate taxpayer.

If the taxpayer is liable to income tax at the higher rate or additional rate, further tax relief is given to the individual. This is done by extending the basic rate band and increasing the higher rate limit by the amount of the grossed up Gift Aid donation. For a higher rate tax payer, this will give a maximum additional (40% − 20%) 20% relief by reducing the amount of income taxable at the higher rate. For an additional rate taxpayer, this will give a maximum additional (45% − 20%) 25% relief by reducing the amount of income taxable at the additional rate.

Worked example: Gift Aid

In 2015/16, Roz has taxable income (all non-savings income) of £40,395 and makes a cash donation of £1,000 to charity under the Gift Aid Scheme.

Requirement

What is Roz's income tax liability for 2015/16?

Solution

Roz

Taxable income (all non-savings)	£40,395

Tax

	£
£31,785 × 20%	6,357
£1,250 (£1,000 × 100/80) × 20% (extended band)	250
£7,360 × 40%	2,944
£40,395	
Income tax liability	9,551

A taxpayer who makes a Gift Aid donation in 2015/16 can elect to treat the payment as if it had been made in 2014/15. This might be beneficial if the taxpayer was liable to higher rate tax in the previous year but not in the current year. The election must be made to HMRC no later than the date when the taxpayer files his tax return for the year for which the relief is claimed. If the taxpayer elects to treat the payment as if it had been made in 2014/15 then the election must be made by no later than 31 January 2016. This election does not affect the position of the charity.

4 Personal allowance for taxpayers born before 6 April 1938

Section overview

- Taxpayers born before 6 April 1938 are entitled to a personal age allowance (PAA).

- PAA is reduced once a taxpayer's adjusted net income reaches a certain level, but cannot be less than the basic PA unless adjusted net income exceeds £100,000.

There is a higher personal allowance available to older taxpayers, instead of the basic personal allowance.

The amount of the allowance is dependent on the level of net income.

A taxpayer who is was born before 6 April 1938 is entitled to a personal age allowance of £10,660.

Where the taxpayer's net income exceeds £27,700 in 2015/16, the personal age allowance is reduced by £1 for every £2 that the net income exceeds £27,700 until the amount of the basic personal allowance is reached. The PAA cannot fall below £10,600 unless adjusted net income exceeds £100,000, in which case it can be reduced to £0 – see 2.5 above.

You should assume a taxpayer is born after 5 April 1938 unless told otherwise.

Worked example: Personal age allowance

Robert was born on 23 August 1937. His net income for 2015/16 is £27,720.

Requirement

What is Robert's personal age allowance?

Solution

Robert is born before 6 April 1938.

	£
Personal age allowance	10,660
Less (£27,720 – £27,700) = £20 × ½	(10)
Reduced personal age allowance	10,650

Interactive question 4: Personal age allowance   [Difficulty level: Exam standard]

Pratish was born on 30 September 1935. His net income for 2015/16 is £28,360.

Using the standard format below, compute Pratish's personal age allowance.

Pratish is born before ....

	£
Personal age allowance	
Less (£.................... – ....) = £.................... × ½	(........)
Reduced personal age allowance	

See **Answer** at the end of this chapter.

5   Allowances for married couples

Section overview

- Married couples allowance (MCA) is available to married couples and civil partners where either one of the parties is aged 81 or over at 5 April 2016 (ie at least one spouse or civil partner must have been born before 6 April 1935).

- MCA is a tax reducer at the rate of 10%.

- Part of the personal allowance can be transferred between spouses/civil partners in limited circumstances. This is referred to as the marriage allowance and it is not age-specific.

- The marriage allowance gives a tax reduction to the recipient spouse at the basic rate.

5.1   Married couple's allowance (MCA)

There is an additional allowance available for older married couples and registered civil partners. The married couple's allowance (MCA) is not deducted from net income to arrive at taxable income like the personal allowance. Instead the MCA reduces an individual's income tax liability and is called a **tax reducer**. A tax reducer can reduce the tax liability to nil but no further. It is given before deducting any tax credits to arrive at tax payable or repayable. The MCA tax reducer is calculated at a fixed rate of 10% of the relevant MCA amount.

For civil partners and couples who married on or after 5 December 2005, the MCA is claimed by the spouse or civil partner who has the higher net income. The amount of the MCA depends on the net income of that spouse or civil partner. The exam will not test marriages before 5 December 2005.

The taxpayer is entitled to make a claim for the MCA if either spouse or civil partner was born before 6 April 1935 (in other words aged 81 by 5 April 2016).

The amount of the MCA is £8,355.

You should assume a taxpayer is single unless told otherwise. You should also assume that if a couple qualifies for the married couple's allowance, a claim is made for this and not the marriage allowance (see later in this Chapter).

Worked example: Married couple's allowance

Angus was married to Edna in January 2006. Angus was born on 16 September 1934 and Edna was born on 10 November 1941. Angus has net income of £15,590 in 2015/16 (all non-savings income). Edna has no taxable income.

Requirement

What is Angus' income tax liability for 2015/16?

Solution

Angus

Income tax liability

	Non-savings income £
Net income	15,590
Less PAA	(10,660)
Taxable income	4,930

	£
Tax	
£4,930 × 20%	986
Less: MCA tax reducer	
£8,355 × 10%	(836)
Income tax liability	150

In the year of marriage/civil partnership, the MCA is reduced by 1/12 for each complete tax month (running from the 6th of one month to the 5th of the following month) which has passed before the marriage/registration of the civil partnership.

Worked example: Year of marriage/civil partnership

Lucinda was born on 22 August 1937. Her net income for 2015/16 is £18,100. She entered into a civil partnership with Helen, who was born on 19 July 1933, on 10 December 2015. Helen has net income for 2015/16 of £12,380.

Requirement

What is the married couple's allowance for Lucinda in 2015/16?

Solution

The MCA is available because Helen was born before 6 April 1935. However, Lucinda is the taxpayer entitled to claim the MCA since she has the higher net income in 2015/16.

There are eight complete tax months between 6 April 2015 and 5 December 2015.

The MCA is therefore £8,355 × 4/12   £2,785

Note: The MCA tax reducer is £2,785 × 10% = £279.

When the relevant taxpayer's net income exceeds £27,700 and the Personal Age Allowance has been reduced to £10,600, any excess income reduces the MCA in the same way as for the PAA. However, the MCA cannot be reduced below the minimum amount of £3,220.

Worked example: Married Couple's Age Allowance

Simon was born on 19 July 1937. His net income for 2015/16 is £32,770. He married Jean, who was born on 22 August 1932, in January 2007. Jean has net income for 2015/16 of £12,380.

Requirement

Compute Simon's Personal Age Allowance and Married Couple's Allowance.

Solution

Simon is aged 78 and Jean aged 83 on 5 April 2016. The MCA is therefore based on Jean's age. However, Simon is the taxpayer entitled to claim the MCA since he has the higher net income in 2015/16 and the couple were married on or after 5 December 2005.

	£
Personal Age Allowance	10,660
Less: (£32,770 – £27,700) = £5,070 × ½ = £2,535 restricted to	(60)
Reduced Personal Age Allowance	10,600

	£
Married Couple's Allowance	8,355
Less: remainder of excess (£2,535 – £60)	(2,475)
Reduced Married Couple's Allowance	5,880

5.2 Marriage allowance

This section is new.

In 2015/16, in limited cases a spouse or civil partner may elect to transfer £1,060 (ie 10%) of their personal allowance to their spouse/civil partner. The transferor spouse must either have no tax liability or be only a basic rate taxpayer after such a reduction in their personal allowance. The recipient spouse must be a basic rate taxpayer.

The transferred allowance is given effect by a reduction in the recipient spouse's income tax liability at the basic rate.

If a claim is made for the married couple's allowance (see earlier in this Chapter) then this claim cannot also be made.

You should assume a taxpayer is single unless told otherwise.

Worked example: Marriage allowance

Sally and her civil partner, Josie, are both aged 40. In 2015/16, Sally has a part-time job earning £5,000 and no other income. Sally made a marriage allowance election. In 2015/16, Josie has employment income of £20,000.

Requirement

What is Josie's income tax liability for 2015/16?

Solution

Josie

Income tax liability

	Non-savings income £
Net income	20,000
Less PA	(10,600)
Taxable income	9,400
Tax	£
£9,400 × 20%	1,880
Less: marriage allowance reduction	
£1,060 × 20%	(212)
Income tax liability	1,668

Summary and Self-test

Summary

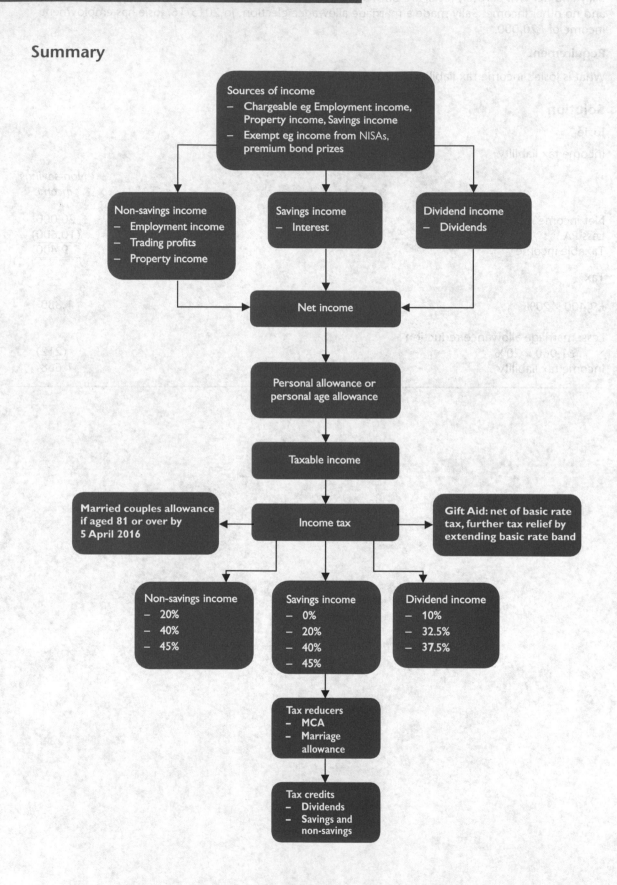

Self-test

Answer the following questions.

1   Which of the following is chargeable to income tax?

    A   Interest from a NS&I investment account
    B   Dividends received from a New Individual Savings Account
    C   £10 Lottery winnings
    D   Scholarship awarded by a university

2   Which **TWO** of the following sources of income are non-savings income?

    A   Interest from a building society
    B   Property income
    C   Dividend from a UK company
    D   Trading profits

3   At what rates is tax charged on savings income?

    A   10%, 32.5%, 37.5%
    B   0%, 20%, 40%, 45%
    C   0%, 20%, 32.5%
    D   20%, 32.5%, 40%, 45%

4   How is higher rate tax relief given for a Gift Aid donation?

    A   Deducted from net income
    B   Treated as paid net of higher rate tax
    C   Basic rate band extended by grossed up donation
    D   No higher rate tax relief given

5   A taxpayer born in May 1932 has net income of £27,800 in 2015/16.

    What personal age allowance is he entitled to?

    A   £10,660
    B   £10,610
    C   £10,600
    D   £10,560

6   A taxpayer born in June 1978 has employment income of £176,000 in 2015/16. This is her only source of income in this tax year.

    What is the income tax liability for 2015/16?

    A   £59,803
    B   £64,043
    C   £60,573
    D   £65,343

7   In addition to his salary of £24,000, Aaron received the following income in 2015/16:

	£
Interest received from a NISA	200
Interest received on National Savings & Investments Direct Saver Account	64
Income tax repayment interest	25

    His net income for the year is

    A   £24,025
    B   £24,289
    C   £24,064
    D   £24,200

8   In addition to his salary of £9,000, Nuru received the following income in 2015/16:

	£
Tips from customers	250
Interest received on a NISA investment	44
Income tax repayment interest	60

His net income for the year is

A   £9,000
B   £9,250
C   £9,310
D   £9,354

9   Perry received income from various sources during 2015/16.

Which **TWO** of the following are exempt from income tax?

A   £100 of National Savings & Investments Direct Saver Account interest
B   £80 of National Savings Certificate interest
C   £40 of interest received on a loan to his friend George
D   £56 of dividends received from a shareholding in X plc
E   £40 of dividends received on Y plc shares held in a stocks and shares NISA

10 During 2015/16 Leonard had earnings of £29,951 from his employer. His only other sources of income were a dividend received of £540 and bank interest received of £368. He also paid £352 as a Gift Aid donation to a registered charity.

What is Leonard's taxable income for 2015/16?

A   £31,011
B   £20,259
C   £20,411
D   £19,971

11 Gabriella is self-employed and has trading profits assessable in 2015/16 of £37,745. During 2015/16 she also received the following income:

Building society interest	£480
Premium bond winnings	£250
Dividend income	£720

What is Gabriella's taxable income for 2015/16?

12 Chloe is self-employed and has trading profits assessable in 2015/16 of £22,600. During 2015/16 she also received the following income.

Interest from a NISA	£205
Interest from a NS&I investment account	£190
Dividend income	£360

What is Chloe's net income for 2015/16?

13 Which **TWO** of the following items are treated as 'non-taxable income' for income tax purposes?

A   Income tax repayment interest
B   Interest paid on a loan between two friends
C   National Lottery winnings
D   Pension income
E   Tips given to staff by customers

14 Frederick works as an employee of Wood Ltd. Frederick's gross salary for 2015/16 was £25,815.

What is Fredericks's taxable income for 2015/16?

15 Josephine, aged 50, is self employed and has trading profits assessable in 2015/16 of £125,000. During 2015/16 she received dividends of £32,400.

What is Josephine's taxable income for 2015/16?

16 In addition to his wages, Massimo has received income from various sources during 2015/16.

   Which **TWO** of the following are exempt from income tax?

   A   Pension income
   B   Interest received on a loan to his son
   C   Dividends from shares held in a NISA
   D   Gratuities and tips received from customers
   E   Premium bond winnings

17 Identify the effect of the following items on the relevant tax liabilities.

   Mark has employment income in 2015/16 of £160,000, and no other sources of income. On
   1 February 2016 Mark paid £2,100 to a charity under the Gift Aid provisions.

   In 2015/16 the Gift Aid payment will

   A   increase Mark's income tax liability
   B   decrease Mark's income tax liability
   C   have no impact on Mark's income tax liability

18 In 2015/16 Margaret's only sources of income were £1,908 of bank interest received and £35,050
   of dividend income received.

   What is Margaret's income tax repayable for 2015/16?

19 April received the following interest in 2015/16:

	£
Interest received on National Savings Certificates	54
Interest received on National Savings & Investment Direct Saver account	72
Interest received on a building society account	36

   What is April's gross taxable interest for 2015/16?

   A   £162
   B   £108
   C   £135
   D   £117

20 In addition to his wages, Axel has received income from various sources during 2015/16.

   Which **TWO** of the following are exempt from income tax?

   A   £180 of tips received from customers
   B   £100 of dividends received from a NISA investment
   C   £56 of dividends received from a shareholding in X plc
   D   £50 received from an investment in premium bonds
   E   £75 of interest received on a loan to his cousin

21 In addition to his salary of £40,000, Pat received the following income in 2015/16:

	£
Betting winnings	200
Interest received on National Savings & Investments Direct Saver Account	76
Interest received on National Savings Certificates	52
Interest received on a building society account	24

   What is Pat's total net income for 2015/16?

Now go back to the Learning objectives in the Introduction. If you are satisfied you have achieved these
objectives, please tick them off.

Technical reference

Legislation

Income Tax (Earnings and Pensions) Act 2003 *(ITEPA 2003)*
Income Tax (Trading and Other Income) Act 2005 *(ITTOIA 2005)*
Income Tax Act 2007 *(ITA 2007)*

Employment income – definitions	ITEPA 2003 ss. 3 – 13
Trading income – definitions	ITTOIA 2005 ss. 3 – 8
Property income – definitions	ITTOIA 2005 ss. 263 – 265
Savings income – definitions	ITTOIA ss. 365 – 368
Miscellaneous income – definitions	ITTOIA ss. 574 – 577
Types of income and rates of tax	ITA 2007 ss. 3 –10, 12, 13, 16 – 20
Gift Aid	ITA 2007 ss.414 – 415,426
Personal allowances	ITA 2007 ss. 35 – 37
Married couples allowance	ITA 2007 s.46
Transferable tax allowance for married couples and civil partners (marriage allowance)	ITA 2007 ss.55A – 55E

This technical reference section is designed to assist you. It should help you to know where to look for further information on the topics covered in this chapter. **You will not be examined on the contents of this section in your examination.**

Answers to Interactive questions

Answer to Interactive question 1

(a) Bank interest received from HSBC of £600

Savings income, taxable amount £600 × 100/80 = £750

(b) Property income of £1,000

Non-savings income, taxable amount £1,000

(c) Dividend received from overseas company of £495

Dividend income, taxable amount £495 × 100/90 = £550

(d) Interest received on Treasury Stock of £525

Savings income, taxable amount £525

(e) Trading profits of £5,000

Non-savings income, taxable amount £5,000

(f) Interest received on NS&I investment account of £600

Savings income, taxable amount £600

Answer to Interactive question 2

Max

Taxable income

	Non-savings income £	Savings income £	Dividend income £	Total £
Employment income	20,000			
Bank interest				
£280 × 100/80		350		
Dividends				
£990 × 100/90			1,100	
Net income	20,000	350	1,100	21,450
Less personal allowance	(10,600)			(10,600)
Taxable income	9,400	350	1,100	10,850

Interest arising on a New Individual Savings Account is exempt income and therefore not included in the above computation.

Answer to Interactive question 3

Henry

Income tax liability

	Non-savings income £
Net income	45,465
Less personal allowance	(10,600)
Taxable income	34,865

Tax

	Non-savings income £
£31,785 × 20%	6,357
£3,080 × 40%	1,232
£34,865	
Income tax liability	7,589

Answer to Interactive question 4

Pratish

Pratish was born before 5 April 1938.

	£
Personal age allowance	10,660
Less (£28,360 – £27,700) = £660 × ½ = £330, restricted to	(60)
Reduced personal age allowance	10,600

The PAA cannot fall below £10,600 unless adjusted net income exceeds £100,000.

Answers to Self-test

1   A – interest from a NS&I investment account – chargeable. All the rest are exempt from income tax.

2   B and D – property income and trading profits are non-savings income.

    Interest from a building society is savings income.

    Dividend from a UK company is dividend income.

3   B – the rates at which tax is charged on savings income are 0% (starting rate band), 20% (basic rate band), 40% (higher rate band) and 45% (additional rate band).

4   C – higher rate tax relief is given by extending the basic rate band by the grossed up donation.

5   B – £10,610

	£
Personal age allowance	10,660
Less (£27,800 – £27,700) = £100 × 1/2	(50)
Reduced personal age allowance	10,610

6   D – £65,343

	Non-savings income £
Employment income/Net income	176,000
Less personal allowance	–
Taxable income	176,000
Tax	
£31,785 × 20%	6,357
£118,215 × 40%	47,286
£150,000	
£26,000 × 45%	11,700
£176,000	
Income tax liability	65,343

7   C   £24,064

    £24,064 only includes Direct Saver Account interest. NISA interest and income tax repayment interest are exempt from income tax.

8   B   £9,250

    Only include tips from customers

9   B   £80 of National Savings Certificate interest

    E   £40 of dividends received on Y plc shares held in a stocks and shares NISA

10 C   £20,411

	Non-savings income £	Savings income £	Dividend Income £	Total £
Employment earnings	29,951			
Dividends £(540 × 100/90)			600	
Bank interest £(368 × 100/80)		460		
Net income	29,951	460	600	31,011
Less personal allowance	(10,600)			(10,600)
Taxable income	19,351	460	600	20,411

Gift Aid does not affect the calculation of taxable income.

11   Gabriella's taxable income for 2015/16 is:

	Non-savings income £	Savings income £	Dividend income £	Total £
Trading profits	37,145			
Building society interest £480 × $^{100}/_{80}$		600		
Dividends £720 × $^{100}/_{90}$			800	
Net income	37,745	600	800	39,145
Less personal allowance	(10,600)			(10,600)
Taxable income	27,145	600	800	28,545

Premium bond winnings are exempt.

12   Chloe's net income for 2015/16 is:

	Non-savings income £	Savings income £	Dividend income £	Total £
Trading profits	22,600			
NS&I Investment interest (gross)		190		
Dividend income (£360 × $^{100}/_{90}$)			400	
Net income	22,600	190	400	23,190

NS&I interest is received gross

Interest on NISAs is exempt

13   A   Income tax repayment interest

      C   National Lottery winnings

14   Fredericks's taxable income for 2015/16 is:

	£
Salary	25,815
Less: Personal allowance	(10,600)
Taxable income	15,215

15   Josephine's taxable income for 2015/16 is:

	£
Trading income	125,000
Dividends (£32,400 × 100/90)	36,000
	161,000
Personal allowance	(0)
Taxable income	161,000

16   The correct answer is C and E

Pension income is taxable. Loans made on a non-commercial basis are still taxable. Tips and gratuities should be declared as income and are subject to tax.

17   The correct answer is B

Mark is an additional rate taxpayer so the basic rate band and the higher rate limit are both extended by the grossed up Gift Aid payment to reduce his tax liability (more taxable at 20% rather than 45%).

18 Income tax repayable for 2015/16 is:

	Savings income £	Dividend income £	Total £
Bank interest (£1,908 × 100/80)	2,385		
Dividend income (£35,050 × 100/90)		38,944	
Net income	2,385	38,944	41,329
Less personal allowance	(2,385)	(8,215)	(10,600)
Taxable income	0	30,729	30,729

	£
Tax on dividend income	
£30,729 × 10%	3,073
Income tax liability	3,073
Less tax-deducted at source	
Dividend tax credit	
(£30,729 × 10%) – restricted to taxable dividend	(3,073)
Bank interest (£2,385 × 20%)	(477)
Income tax repayable	(477)

19 The correct answer is D

	£
NSC interest – exempt	–
Direct Saver account interest received gross	72
Building society interest received net (£36 × 100/80)	45
	117

20 The correct answer is B and D

£100 of dividends received from a NISA investment
£50 received from an investment in premium bonds

21 The correct answer is £40,106

	Non-savings £	Savings £	Total £
Salary	40,000		
NS+I Direct Saver Interest – rec'd gross		76	
Building society interest (£24 × 100/80)		30	
Net income	40,000	106	40,106

Income from National Savings Certificates is exempt

CHAPTER 4

Employment income

Introduction
Examination context
Topic List
1 Calculation of assessable employment income
2 Taxable and exempt benefits
3 Pay As You Earn (PAYE) system
Summary and Self-test
Technical reference
Answers to Interactive questions
Answers to Self-test

Learning objectives

- Calculate assessable employment income for an employee or director, including taxable and exempt benefits ☐

- Identify the key features of the PAYE system and calculate PAYE tax codes for employees ☐

- Determine, in straightforward cases, due dates for employers' PAYE and national insurance payments ☐

Specific syllabus references for this chapter are: 2b, d, 3c.

Syllabus links

You will meet taxation of employees again in the Tax Compliance paper, so you need to be very familiar with the topics in parts 1 and 2 of this chapter to prepare you for the progression to the next level of your studies.

However, it is unlikely that the PAYE system (described in part 3 of this chapter) would be examined in the Tax Compliance paper. You should therefore expect it to be tested in detail in the Principles of Taxation paper.

Examination context

In the examination, in the scenario-based question for income tax, candidates may be required to:

- Determine how benefits are taxable on P11D employees
- Determine how benefits are taxable on P9D employees
- Identify which benefits are exempt

In the examination, in the objective test questions, candidates may be required to:

- Calculate an employee's coding
- Understand the operation of the PAYE system.

For extra question practice on these topics go to the section of the Question Bank covering this chapter and to the section of the Question Bank containing scenario-based questions for income tax. However, you will need to study Chapter 5 before attempting these scenario-based questions.

Candidates need to take great care when calculating the value of a benefit, as often one important piece of information is missed when working this out.

1 Calculation of assessable employment income

1.1 What is employment income?

Employment income includes income arising from an employment and the income of an office holder such as a director. We will use the term 'employee' to cover anyone who receives employment income.

There are two types of employment income:

- General earnings
- Specific employment income (not in your syllabus)

Definition

General earnings: Any salary, wages or fee, any gratuity or other profit or incidental benefit of any kind obtained by an employee consisting of money or money's worth, and anything else constituting an emolument of the employment, together with anything treated under any statutory provision as earnings (eg benefits).

General earnings therefore include bonuses, commissions, reimbursed expenses, expense allowances, inducements, tips and gratuities (even if received unsolicited from third parties).

1.2 Basis of assessment

The basis of assessment of general earnings is the **receipts basis**. This means that the actual amounts received between 6 April 2015 and 5 April 2016 are taxable in 2015/16.

General earnings consisting of money are treated as received on the earlier of:

- The time when payment is made
- The time when a person becomes entitled to payment

Worked example: Receipt of general earnings

Thomas is employed as a car salesman at a monthly salary of £2,100. In addition to his basic salary, he receives a bonus which is paid in May each year and relates to the sales made by Thomas in the year to the previous 31 October.

His recent bonuses are as follows:

y/e 31 October 2014	Paid 1 May 2015	£2,250
y/e 31 October 2015	Paid 1 May 2016	£4,850

Requirement

What are the general earnings from Thomas's employment for 2015/16?

Solution

	£
Salary (£2,100 × 12)	25,200
Bonus (received May 2015)	2,250
Taxable earnings 2015/16	27,450

General earnings not in the form of money (ie benefits) are taxable when they are received by the employee.

2 Taxable and exempt benefits

Section overview

- The benefits code deals with taxable benefits and applies in full to most employees.

- Certain parts of the benefits code do not apply to employees in 'excluded employment'.

- All employees are taxable on the receipt of vouchers and the provision of living accommodation.

- Employees not in excluded employment are also taxable on other benefits such as cars, fuel, vans and use of assets.

- There are a number of benefits which are exempt from the charge to income tax.

2.1 The benefits code

Taxable benefits are set down in legislation called the benefits code.

The benefits code generally applies to all employees. However, only certain parts of it apply to employees in 'excluded employment'.

Definition

Excluded employment:

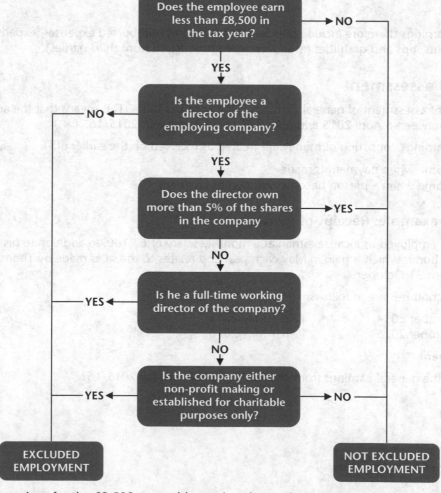

In calculating earnings for the £8,500 test, add together the total earnings and benefits that would be assessable if the employee were paid over £8,500. Do not deduct any expenses. (Allowable expenses are covered in the Tax Compliance paper.)

2.2 Employees in excluded employment

Employees in excluded employment are only taxable on benefits as follows:

- Benefits convertible into cash on the amount of cash that the benefit could be converted into: this is sometimes called the **second hand value**

- Vouchers

- Living accommodation (but not any associated expenses)

Employees in excluded employment are sometimes called 'P9D' employees. This is because their employers are required to submit form P9D to HMRC under the PAYE system giving details of their taxable benefits.

2.3 Employees not in excluded employment

Most employees are not in excluded employment. Such employees are sometimes called 'P11D' employees. This is because their employers are required to submit a form P11D to HMRC under the PAYE system giving details of their taxable benefits.

Employees not in excluded employment are subject to tax on all benefits in the benefits code, including:

- Vouchers
- Living accommodation
- Expenses connected with the provision of living accommodation
- Cars and fuel provided for private use
- Vans provided for private use
- Assets made available for private use
- Any other non-monetary benefit provided by reason of the employment

2.4 Vouchers

All employees, including those in excluded employments, are taxable on the provision of:

- Cash vouchers (vouchers exchangeable for cash) – the taxable amount is the sum of money for which the voucher is capable of being exchanged

- Credit tokens (eg a credit card) used to obtain money, goods or services – the taxable amount is the cost to the employer of providing the benefit, less any amount paid by the employee

- Vouchers exchangeable for goods and services (eg book tokens) taxable amount is the cost to the employer of providing the benefit, less any amount paid by the employee

2.5 Living accommodation

All employees, including those in excluded employment, are taxable on the provision of living accommodation unless it is 'job related accommodation'.

Definition

Job related accommodation: Accommodation is job related if:

(a) The accommodation is necessary for the proper performance of the employee's duties (eg caretaker); or

(b) The accommodation is provided for the better performance of the employee's duties and the employment is of a kind in which it is customary for accommodation to be provided (eg police officers); or

(c) The accommodation is provided as part of arrangements in force because of a special threat to the employee's security (eg members of the government).

A director can only claim one of the first two exemptions if he owns 5% or less of the shares in the employer company and either he is a full-time working director or the company is non-profit making or is a charity.

There are two potential benefits on the provision of living accommodation which does not qualify as job related:

Basic rental benefit

If the living accommodation is owned by the employer, the amount of the benefit is the rent that would have been paid if it had been let at its annual value (taken to be the rateable value).

If the living accommodation is rented by the employer, the amount of the benefit is the higher of the annual value and the rent actually paid by the employer.

The annual value will be given to you in the question.

Additional yearly rental benefit

This only applies to **expensive accommodation**. Expensive accommodation is purchased accommodation which cost the employer more than £75,000 to provide. The amount of the additional benefit is calculated as:

(Cost of providing the living accommodation less £75,000) × the official rate of interest at the start of the tax year

The cost of providing the living accommodation is the total of the original cost of the accommodation plus any capital improvements made before the start of the tax year in which the benefit is charged.

If the employee makes a payment to the employer for his occupation of the property, this reduces the taxable benefit. Any excess not set against the basic benefit will be used to reduce the additional benefit.

Worked example: Living accommodation

Kyle's employer provides him on 1 February 2015 with living accommodation consisting of a house owned by the employer. The annual value of the house is £7,500. The house originally cost the employer £150,000 and a conservatory was added at a cost of £15,000 in March 2015.

Kyle pays rent of £700 a month to his employer for use of the accommodation and occupies the house throughout 2015/16. The official rate of interest on 6 April 2015 is 3%.

Requirement

What are Kyle's taxable benefits in respect of the living accommodation in 2015/16?

Solution

Basic rental benefit

	£
Annual value	7,500
Less rent paid by Kyle	(7,500)
Taxable benefit	0

Additional yearly rental benefit

	£
Cost of provision (£150,000 + £15,000)	165,000
Less lower limit	(75,000)
	90,000
£90,000 × 3%	2,700
Less rent paid by Kyle	
(£700 × 12) = £8,400 – £7,500	(900)
Taxable benefit	1,800

If the accommodation is only available for part of the tax year, the benefit is time apportioned (for exam purposes, on a monthly basis).

If the property was acquired by the employer more than six years before it is first provided to the employee, use the market value of the property when it was first provided plus the cost of subsequent improvements to calculate the additional charge, instead of the original cost plus improvements.

However, unless the original cost plus improvements exceeds £75,000, the additional charge cannot be imposed, however high the market value.

Interactive question 1: Living accommodation [Difficulty level: Exam standard]

Susan is provided with living accommodation by her employer on 6 October 2015. The annual value of the accommodation is £2,500.

The original cost of the accommodation to the employer in 2002 was £80,000. The market value of the accommodation on 6 October 2015 is £190,000. The official rate of interest on 6 April 2015 is 3%.

Susan does not make any payment to her employer for the use of the accommodation.

Requirement

Using the standard format below, show the taxable benefit for Susan in respect of the provision of living accommodation for 2015/16.

Basic rental benefit

£

Additional yearly rental benefit

£

Cost of provision
Less lower limit

( )

Apply official rate of interest

....

Time apportionment

....

Taxable benefit is £

....

See **Answer** at the end of this chapter.

2.6 Expenses connected with the provision of living accommodation

In addition to the living accommodation benefits described above, P11D employees are also taxed on related expenses paid by the employer such as:

- Heat and lighting
- Council tax and water
- Cleaning, repairs, maintenance and decoration

The taxable benefit in each case is the cost to employer less any employee contribution.

Where an employee is provided with furnished living accommodation, the employee will also have a taxable benefit for the private use of the furniture provided by his employer (see later in this chapter).

2.7 Cars and fuel for private use

There is a taxable benefit for P11D employees on the provision of a car which is available for private use by the employee. Private use includes ordinary home-to-work travel.

There is no taxable benefit for incidental private use of a 'pool' car which is available for use by any employee and which is not normally kept overnight at or near an employee's residence.

The basis of the charge is the list price of the car plus any optional accessories originally provided with the car and any further accessories costing £100 or more which are provided at a later date.

Having worked out the list price of the car, the benefit is then calculated by applying a percentage to that price. The percentage depends on the carbon dioxide (CO_2) emissions of the car expressed in grams per kilometre (g/km). The CO_2 emissions figure will be given to you in the question.

The emissions thresholds are as follows:

- For cars with CO_2 emissions between 0g/km and 50g/km inclusive, the percentage is 5%.

- For cars with CO_2 emissions between 51g/km and 75g/km inclusive, the percentage is 9%.

- For cars with CO_2 emissions between 76g/km and 94g/km inclusive, the percentage is 13%.

- For cars with CO_2 emissions of 95g/km, the relevant threshold for the year, the percentage is 14%

- For every 5g/km over the 95g/km threshold (rounded down to the nearest 5g/km), an additional 1% is added, up to a maximum of 37%.

Where the car uses diesel instead of petrol, the percentage is increased by 3%, subject to the overall maximum of 37%.

If a car is not available for private use for the whole of a tax year, the benefit is time apportioned (for exam purposes on a monthly basis).

If the employee makes a contribution to the employer for the private use of the car, this contribution reduces the taxable benefit.

Worked example: Car benefit

Darren is employed on a salary of £25,000 per annum. He is provided with a car available for private use during the whole of 2015/16. The car has a petrol engine and CO_2 emissions of 121g/km. The car has a list price of £13,395, but the employer only paid £10,395 for it after discounts.

Darren contributes £50 per month for its private use.

Requirement

What is Darren's taxable benefit in respect of the car?

Solution

CO_2 emissions are 121g/km, round down to 120g/km

Appropriate percentage:

(120 – 95) = 25g/km in excess of threshold

25 ÷ 5 = 5%

14% + 5% = 19%

	£
List price £13,395 × 19%	2,545
Less contribution for use £50 × 12	(600)
Taxable benefit	1,945

The price actually paid by the employer is irrelevant.

Interactive question 2: Car benefit [Difficulty level: Exam standard]

Pedro is employed on a salary of £40,000 per annum. He is provided with a car for private use from 6 January 2016. The car has a list price of £17,820 and CO_2 emissions of 156g/km. It runs on diesel. Pedro makes no contributions towards the running costs of the car.

Requirement

Using the standard format below, calculate Pedro's taxable benefit in respect of the car.

CO_2 emissions are .... g/km, round down to .... g/km

Appropriate percentage:
(............. – 95) = ... g/km in excess of threshold

.... ÷ 5 = ... %

14% +....... % +....... % (diesel) = ... %

List price is £
£ .... × .... % = £ ....
Time apportionment

....

Taxable benefit

....

See **Answer** at the end of this chapter.

The car benefit charge is designed to cover the cost of running the car such as repairs, vehicle excise duty and insurance.

However, there is a separate charge for the provision by the employer of fuel for private use for a car provided by the employer with private use.

The benefit uses the same percentage calculated for the car benefit. This is then applied to a fixed amount which is £22,100 in 2015/16.

If the car for which the fuel is provided is not available for part of the tax year, the fuel benefit is time apportioned on the same basis as the car benefit.

There is no reduction in the benefit if the employee makes a partial contribution to the cost of private fuel. There is a full fuel benefit unless the employee reimburses the employer for all private fuel provided.

Worked example: Fuel benefit

Dilip is a P11D employee who is provided by his employer with a car for private use. The CO_2 emissions of the car are 202g/km and the car uses diesel. Dilip is required to pay a nominal amount of £30 per month towards the cost of private fuel.

Requirement

What is Dilip's fuel benefit?

Solution

CO_2 emissions are 202g/km, round down to 200g/km
Appropriate percentage:
(200 – 95) = 105g/km in excess of threshold
105 ÷ 5 = 21%
14% + 21% + 3% (diesel) = 37% (maximum)
£22,100 × 37% =   **£8,177**
No reduction for partial contribution for private fuel.

2.8 Vans for private use

P11D employees have a taxable benefit on the provision of a van available for private use. In this case, private use does not include travel from home to work, as long as the employee is not allowed any other private use that is more than insignificant.

The benefit is an annual amount of £3,150. The taxable benefit on the provision of a van for private use where the van has zero CO_2 emissions is £630 for 2015/16.

The benefit is time apportioned if the van is not available for the whole of the tax year (on a monthly basis for exam purposes). The benefit is reduced by any amount paid by the employee for the private use of the van.

There is a separate charge for the provision by the employer of fuel for private use of the van. The benefit is an annual amount of £594. If the van for which the fuel is provided is not available for part of the tax year, the fuel benefit is time apportioned on the same basis as the van benefit.

There is no reduction in the van fuel benefit if the employee makes a partial contribution to the cost of private fuel.

2.9 Assets available for private use

A taxable benefit arises to a P11D employee who is provided by the employer with an asset available for private use, including use by the taxpayer's family.

The amount of the taxable benefit is the higher of the annual value of the asset or any rent or hire charge payable by the employer. In both cases, any expenses relating to the provision of the asset are also added to the taxable benefit.

The annual value is 20% of the market value of the asset when first provided for private use to any employee.

If the asset is only provided for part of the year, the benefit is time apportioned (on a monthly basis for exam purposes).

The taxable benefit is reduced by any contribution made by the employee for private use.

There is no taxable benefit if private use of the asset is insignificant. For example, if an employee who works at home is provided with a laptop computer on which to work during the daytime, any private use of the computer during the evenings will be considered insignificant as the employer needs to provide the computer for the employee to do their job.

Worked example: Private use assets

Maria is provided with the following assets by her employer which are available for private use:

Television (provided on 6 October 2015) costing   £1,100
Computer (provided on 6 April 2015) costing   £2,700

Maria makes a contribution of £10 a month for private use of the television. Maria needs the computer for her work when visiting clients' sites and uses it to help her children research their homework on the internet.

Requirement

What are the benefits taxable on Maria for 2015/16 for private use of these assets?

Solution

Television
Annual value
20% × £1,100   £220

Available for six months in tax year

	£
£220 × 6/12	110
Less employee contribution £10 × 6	(60)
Taxable benefit	50

Computer
Insignificant private use therefore no taxable benefit   £0

2.10 Other benefits

If a P11D employee (or member of the employee's family or household) receives any other non-monetary benefit by reason of employment and there is no specific provision covering this type of benefit in the benefits code, the taxable benefit is the cost to the employer of providing the benefit less any amount paid by the employee for the benefit. Where benefits are provided in-house, the cost of the benefit is the marginal cost.

Worked example: Marginal cost

Leonard is a teacher at a public school. He pays a reduced fee of £2,000 in 2015/16 for his son to attend the school.

In 2015/16 the following figures relate to students attending the school.

	£
Normal fee payable per student	3,500
Average cost per student, including a proportion of fixed overheads	2,800
Additional cost of an extra student, including extra writing books, food etc	1,500

Leonard's son is taking up a place that would otherwise not be filled.

Requirement

What is the taxable benefit for Leonard for 2015/16 in respect of the school place?

Solution

First determine which fee cost is relevant.

The marginal cost of providing the place is the equivalent to the additional cost, ie £1,500.

Then deduct the contribution paid by Leonard ie £2,000

This cannot give rise to a negative benefit, so the benefit is nil.

2.11 Exempt benefits

There are a number of benefits which are specifically exempt from the charge on employment income. Exempt benefits include:

- Contributions by an employer to a registered pension scheme

- Pension advice available to all employees up to £150 per tax year (above which the full amount is taxable)

- Childcare facilities run by or on behalf of an employer

CHAPTER

4

- Childcare payments of up to £55 per week under a contract entered into before 6 April 2011 between the employer and an approved child carer or by childcare vouchers, provided that childcare payments are available to all employees, with some exclusions for those earning close to the national minimum wage.

  For those joining an approved childcare scheme from 6 April 2011 the amount that is exempt per week depends on the employee's basic earnings assessment.

  The basic earnings assessment is the individual's expected earnings for the current tax year. It is calculated by adding together the employee's basic earnings and taxable benefits and then deducting excluded income which includes occupational pension contributions, allowable expense payments and the personal allowance.

  The exemption is as follows:

  - Basic rate taxpayer in terms of basic earnings – £55 per week

  - Higher rate taxpayer in terms of basic earnings – £28 per week

  - Additional rate taxpayer in terms of basic earnings – £25 per week from 6 April 2013 (£22 between 6 April 2011 and 5 April 2013).

  For anyone already in a scheme at 6 April 2011, the £55 per week exemption continues to apply irrespective of their level of earnings.

- One mobile telephone (including smartphones) available for private use by an employee, including all calls

- Free or subsidised meals in a canteen where such meals are available to all staff

- Social events paid for by the employer up to £150 per head per tax year

- Entertainment provided by a third party (eg seats at sporting/cultural events)

- Non-cash gifts from third parties up to £250 per tax year from the same donor

- Provision of a parking space at or near the employee's place of work

- Awards of up to £5,000 made under a staff suggestion scheme

- Work-related training courses

- Sports and recreation facilities available to employees generally but not to the general public

- Payments towards the additional costs of an employee working from home (up to £4 per week without supporting evidence, payments in excess of £4 per week require documentary evidence that the payment is wholly in respect of such additional costs)

- Personal incidental expenses (eg cost of telephone calls home) whilst the employee is required to stay away overnight on business up to £5 per night in the UK, £10 per night abroad. If reimbursement by the employer exceeds these daily limits the total amount reimbursed is taxable.

- Works buses and subsidies for employees to use public bus services

- Travel expenses when public transport disrupted, late night journeys and where car sharing arrangements break down

- Use of bicycles or cyclists safety equipment if made available to all employees

- Reasonable removal expenses (maximum £8,000) paid for by an employer for a new employment position or on relocation

- Non-cash long service awards in respect of at least 20 years service, not exceeding £50 per year of service

- Eye tests required under health and safety legislation and specially prescribed glasses provided for employees who use VDU equipment

- Health-screening assessment or medical check up provided for an employee, by the employer (maximum of one of each per tax year)

- Up to £500 pa for recommended medical treatment to assist with a return to work

3 Pay As You Earn (PAYE) system

Section overview

- The PAYE system ensures that tax and NICs are paid on employment income.

- Amounts deducted under PAYE must usually be paid to HMRC by the 19th of each calendar month. The amount of tax deducted under PAYE depends on the employee's tax code.

- HMRC can require security payments from employers who are at risk of deliberately not paying PAYE.

- PAYE reporting uses the Real Time Information (RTI) system.

3.1 What is the PAYE system?

The aim of the PAYE system is to ensure that the correct amounts of income tax and national insurance contributions are paid on cash payments to employees. The system also ensures that taxable non-cash benefits are reported by the employer to HMRC.

The PAYE system applies to all cash payments made to employees (eg salaries, bonuses) and also to certain assets which can be readily converted into cash (eg gold bars, wine).

Income tax and national insurance contributions deducted under the PAYE system must usually be paid to HMRC 14 days after the end of the 'tax month' to which they relate. The tax month runs from the 6th day of one month to the following 5th day of the next month. Therefore, payment is required by the 19th of each calendar month.

Large employers (more than 250 employees) must pay electronically. Any other employer can pay electronically by choice. If payment is made electronically the payment deadline is extended to the 22nd of each calendar month.

Payments can be made quarterly instead of monthly where the average monthly total of the PAYE income tax and national insurance contributions does not exceed £1,500.

3.2 Security for payment of PAYE

HMRC can require employers to provide a security where amounts due under PAYE or NIC obligations are seriously at risk.

HMRC will require a security from employers who try to defraud the government by deliberately choosing not to pay PAYE and NIC, building up large PAYE or NIC debts (including penalties), or who do not respond to HMRC's attempts to contact them.

HMRC calculates the amount of the security on a case by case basis, depending on the amount of tax at risk and the previous behaviour of the employer. The form of the security is usually either a cash deposit from the business or director, held solely by HMRC or in a joint account with the taxpayer, or a bond from an approved financial institution.

The employer can appeal against either the notice requiring the security or the amount.

It is a criminal offence if a person required to give a security fails to do so. If that person is found guilty of the offence a fine of up to £5,000 may be imposed.

3.3 PAYE codes

The calculation of the PAYE income tax deduction is based on 'tax codes'.

For each tax year, the employee receives a PAYE coding notice (Form P2) setting out the allowances and deductions available to the employee in that year and the resultant tax code. The employer is informed of the PAYE code (Form P9(T)), but not the details of how it is calculated.

The tax code computation is as follows:

Allowances	£	Deductions	£
Personal allowance	X	Taxable benefits	X
Allowable expenses	X	Adjustment for underpaid tax	X
Adjustment for overpaid tax	X		
	X		X

If total allowances less total deductions gives a positive figure, the tax code is created by removing the last digit in the computation and adding a letter at the end. This is usually the letter L showing that the employee is entitled to the basic personal allowance.

If the employee is entitled to a full age personal allowance the letter to add is Y.

If a marriage allowance election is made (see earlier in this Text), and there is a deemed transfer of part of the personal allowance (£1,060) from one spouse to the other, the personal allowances effectively become £9,540 and £11,660 respectively, and the letter for the tax code will be N or M respectively. You should assume that a taxpayer is single unless you are told otherwise in any question on PAYE codes.

Worked example: PAYE code

Katie earns £24,000 a year. She is entitled to a basic personal allowance. She also receives taxable benefits of £4,795.

Requirement

What is Katie's PAYE code for 2015/16?

Solution

	£
Allowance: Personal allowance	10,600
Less deduction (taxable benefits)	(4,795)
Net allowances	5,805

The final digit is removed. Katie's tax code is therefore 580L.

If total allowances less total deductions give a negative figure, the tax code will have a letter K at the beginning. The application of a K code will mean that the taxable pay of the employee will be increased rather than decreased. A K code is calculated in the same way as other codes except that the code is decreased by 1.

Worked example: K code

Zack earns £18,000 a year. He is entitled to a basic personal allowance. He also receives taxable benefits of £11,807.

Requirement

What is Zack's PAYE code for 2015/16?

Solution

	£
Allowances: Personal allowance	10,600
Less deduction (taxable benefits)	(11,807)
Net allowances	(1,207)

Remove the last digit (gives 120) and deduct 1. Zack's tax code is therefore K119.

The code number can also reflect unpaid tax on income from earlier years. In this case, gross up the unpaid tax using the taxpayer's estimated marginal rate of income tax and deduct the grossed up unpaid tax from total allowances. There is a limit to the amount of tax which can be 'coded out' in this way (see later in this Text).

Worked example: Unpaid tax

Brandon earns £11,000 a year and has no other sources of income. He is entitled to a basic personal allowance. He has unpaid tax of £300 from 2014/15 which is to be paid through the PAYE system.

Requirement

What is Brandon's PAYE code for 2015/16?

Solution

Brandon is a basic rate taxpayer

	£
Allowances: Personal allowance	10,600
Less: Deduction (unpaid tax) £300 × 100/20	(1,500)
Net allowances	9,100

Brandon's tax code is therefore 910L.

3.4 Operation of PAYE system – Real Time Information

Most payroll systems now operate electronically. Software packages calculate income tax and NICs due at each pay day, given an employee's income and PAYE code. The software calculations spread an employee's allowances (as determined by their PAYE code) evenly over the tax year.

Under Real Time Information (RTI), employers are required to inform HMRC about tax, NICs and other deductions every time a payment is made to an employee, rather than after the end of each tax year. The introduction of RTI reporting removed the need for many of the paper forms previously required.

This information is sent online, integrated with employer payroll software, and enables HMRC to ensure the employee pays the correct amount of tax and NIC during the year.

Summary

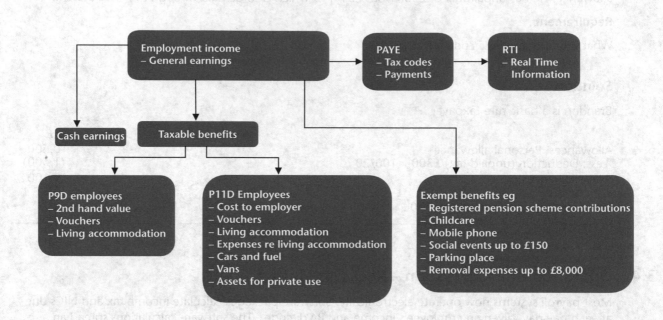

Employment income
– General earnings

PAYE
– Tax codes
– Payments

RTI
– Real Time Information

Cash earnings

Taxable benefits

P9D employees
– 2nd hand value
– Vouchers
– Living accommodation

P11D Employees
– Cost to employer
– Vouchers
– Living accommodation
– Expenses re living accommodation
– Cars and fuel
– Vans
– Assets for private use

Exempt benefits eg
– Registered pension scheme contributions
– Childcare
– Mobile phone
– Social events up to £150
– Parking place
– Removal expenses up to £8,000

Self-test

Answer the following questions.

1   Sandra works for Julian (a sole trader) as a part-time salesperson at a salary of £6,000 a year. On 31 December 2015, she received a bonus of £2,000 in respect of Julian's trading results for the year ended 30 September 2015. She expects to receive a bonus of £2,500 in December 2016 in respect of the year ended 30 September 2016.

     What are Sandra's assessable earnings for 2015/16?

     A   £6,000
     B   £7,250
     C   £8,000
     D   £8,250

2   Peter and Jane both work for Apple Ltd (a trading company).

     Peter is a director of Apple Ltd. He has no shares in Apple Ltd and works one day a week for a salary of £8,400.

     Jane is an employee and earns £8,600 working two days a week for Apple Ltd.

     Which of them is in an 'excluded employment'?

     A   Both of them
     B   Neither of them
     C   Peter
     D   Jane

3   Oliver is employed by Munton plc and earns £20,000 a year. He also receives the following benefits during 2015/16:

     Meal vouchers of £2 per day (240 working days in year)

     Pension advice costing £100

     Ticket to sporting event from a customer of Munton plc worth £50

     What are Oliver's taxable benefits for 2015/16?

     A   £0
     B   £480
     C   £580
     D   £530

4   Gerald is employed by Zoom plc at a salary of £30,000 a year. He is provided with a car available for private use from 1 November 2015. The car has CO$_2$ emissions of 122g/km and a list price of £18,000. The car has a diesel engine.

     What is the taxable car benefit in 2015/16?

     A   £3,960
     B   £3,420
     C   £1,650
     D   £1,425

5   Tricia (aged 30) is employed by Wilton Ltd at a salary of £11,000 per year. She is also entitled to taxable benefits of £2,960. She has no tax overpaid or underpaid from previous tax years.

     What is Tricia's tax code for 2015/16?

     A   1060L
     B   765L
     C   764L
     D   763L

6   David earns £60,000 a year. He is entitled to a basic personal allowance. He has unpaid tax of £920 from 2014/15 which is to be paid through the PAYE system.

     David's tax code for 2015/16 is ....

7   Harry is an employee of Table Ltd earning a salary of £30,000 per annum. Harry has been provided with a company car for a number of years. The car had a list price of £25,000 and CO_2 emissions of 172g/km. Table Ltd paid for all running expenses of the car including diesel fuel for private use.

The taxable benefits assessable on Harry in 2015/16 are ....

8   Newburgh Ltd has agreed to provide each of its employees, all of whom earn more than £8,500 per annum and are basic rate taxpayers, with a mobile telephone for the whole of 2015/16. The company will pay £420 per year to hire the telephone inclusive of all calls made by the employees. Newburgh Ltd will also provide its employees with vouchers worth £70 per week for 48 weeks per year for use with an approved child carer.

The additional employment income for each of the company's employees in 2015/16 as a result of the provision of the two benefits is ...

9   In 2015/16 Jacob was provided with various benefits by his employer Bony Ltd, a manufacturer of televisions, in addition to his salary of £50,000 per annum.

Identify the amount chargeable as employment income for each benefit.

Private health insurance, costing Bony Ltd £800. The same insurance would have cost Jacob £1,100.

A   £800
B   £1,100

A television out of stock which cost £200 to manufacture but would cost Bony Ltd £800 to buy in from another supplier.

C   £200
D   £800

A car parking space at a car park near to the office which cost Bony Ltd £500 in 2015/16.

E   £0
F   £500

10 John works for Ernley Ltd earning a salary of £18,000 per annum. On 1 May 2015 Ernley Ltd provided John with a new company van which had a list price of £6,700 and CO_2 emissions of 106g/km. John uses the vehicle for both business and private purposes (50/50 business/private). John pays for all of his private fuel.

What is John's taxable benefit for the van in 2015/16?

A   £983
B   £1,072
C   £2,888
D   £3,150

11 James who earns £6,000 per annum is given a bonus in the form of a washing machine by his employer. It cost his employer £700, although it normally retails at £900. James decided that he did not want the washing machine and sold it for £250 to a second hand shop.

How much additional employment income will James have relating to the washing machine?

A   £0
B   £250
C   £700
D   £900

12   Kyl Ltd has agreed to provide each of its employees with a bicycle costing £850 for use at home and for travelling to work. The bicycles will remain the property of Kyl Ltd. The company will also provide its employees with vouchers worth £25 per week for 44 weeks per year for use with an approved child carer. All of Kyl Ltd's employees earn more than £8,500 per annum and are basic rate or higher rate taxpayers.

How much additional employment income will each of the company's employees have in a full year as a result of the provision of the two benefits?

A   £0
B   £170
C   £1,100
D   £1,270

13   Blanche Ltd purchased a flat in Leeds in 2011 for £310,000. The company's finance director moved into the flat on 1 April 2015 and lived there throughout 2015/16. The market value of the flat on 1 April 2015 was £375,000. The company installed a new kitchen in May 2012 at a cost of £17,000 and double glazing in June 2015 at a cost of £16,000.

The 'cost' of the flat for the purpose of computing the additional yearly rental benefit for 2015/16 is...

14   Amy began working for Samuel Ltd on 6 July 2015. On that day she received a company car with a list price of £20,000 and CO_2 emissions of 162g/km. Samuel Ltd paid for all running expenses of the car including petrol, for Amy's private use.

The taxable benefit assessable on Amy in 2015/16 is...

15   Ping has worked for Brakes Ltd for many years. From 1 July 2015 he had use of a company car with a list price of £15,000 and CO_2 emissions of 177g/km. Brakes Ltd paid for all running expenses of the car except diesel fuel.

The car benefit assessable on Ping in 2015/16 is

A   £3,375
B   £3,713
C   £4,500
D   £4,950

16   Pirro was first provided with a computer by his employer in October 2011 when it was purchased for £2,800. He still has use of the computer for both private and essential business purposes during 2015/16, although his employers have retained ownership.

The benefit assessable on Pirro in respect of the computer is ...

17   Identify whether the following statements are correct or incorrect.

Pippin is provided with a van with CO_2 emissions of 190g/km by his employer Joker Ltd. Joker Ltd pays for all petrol for the van.

Pippin has an assessable fuel benefit based on the CO_2 emissions.

A   Correct
B   Incorrect

Piers makes a nominal contribution towards the fuel cost on his company car of £10 per month. This accounts for about 95% of his private use.

Piers is able to reduce his fuel benefit by £120 pa.

C   Correct
D   Incorrect

18   Monet Ltd purchased a flat in London in 1998 for £280,000. On 1 March 2009, when the flat had a market value of £565,000, Mustafa joined the company and began to live in the flat. The annual gross rateable value of the flat is £8,675.

The taxable benefit of the flat in 2015/16 is...

Use an official rate of interest of 3%.

19 Gerrard works for Frame Ltd. He has use of a staff canteen which is available to all employees. The meals in the canteen cost him £1.50 per day although the cost of providing the meals equates to £2.50 per day. He uses the canteen 200 days each year. He was also reimbursed overnight expenses totalling £30 when he worked away from home in Edinburgh for four nights.

How much additional employment income will Gerrard have as a result of the provision of the two benefits?

A £230
B £210
C £30
D £10

20 Jacob receives a monthly salary of £3,000 and an annual bonus payable on 30 April each year, although the bonus actually relates to the previous year ended 31 March. His recent bonuses have been as follows:

Relating to	Date paid	Amount
Year ended 31 March 2015	30 April 2015	£16,500
Year ended 31 March 2016	30 April 2016	£13,400

What is Jacob's employment income assessment for 2015/16?

A £52,500
B £49,400
C £16,500
D £13,400

21 Select whether the following statement is true or false.

Employees in excluded employment are taxed on benefits which can be converted into cash. The assessable amount is the marginal cost to the employer.

A True
B False

Select whether the following statement is true or false.

Employees in excluded employment are sometimes called 'P9D' employees.

C True
D False

22 Emily is provided with a company flat as a benefit of her job in addition to her annual salary of £66,000. Emily's employer rents the flat at an annual cost of £15,000. The annual rateable value of the flat is £8,900. Emily makes a contribution to the rent of £7,000 per annum.

What is the taxable benefit of the flat?

A £15,000
B £8,900
C £8,000
D £1,900

23 Your manager has made the following statements about what qualifies as job related living accommodation.

1   The accommodation is provided for the better performance of an employee's duties and it is customary to be so provided.

2   The accommodation is provided for security reasons.

3   The accommodation enables the employee to work longer hours by reducing time spent commuting.

4   Accommodation provided to directors owning more than 5% of the company is never job related.

Select which of the following options identifies which of these statements is/are true.

A   All of them
B   1 and 2 only
C   1, 2 and 3 only
D   1, 2 and 4 only

24 Sally is provided with accommodation which originally cost her employer £45,000 in 1982. In 2007 £15,000 was spent on capital improvements. Sally first occupied the property on 6 April 2015 when its market value was £425,000. The annual rateable value of the property is £18,000. Sally has an annual salary of £49,000.

What is the taxable benefit of the living accommodation for 2015/16?

A   £18,000
B   £10,500
C   £28,500
D   £60,000

Assume an official rate of interest of 3%.

25 Sumira moved into a house provided by her employer on 6 August 2015. The house cost £465,000 in January 2011. The annual rateable value of the property is £21,000. Sumira's annual salary is £26,000.

What is the taxable benefit for the living accommodation in 2015/16?

A   £11,700
B   £21,000
C   £21,800
D   £32,700

Assume an official rate of interest of 3%.

26 Lesley first occupied accommodation provided by her employer on 6 January 2016. The property was originally purchased by her employer in 2012 for £325,000. Capital improvements were made to the property in 2013 at a total cost of £45,000. Lesley pays her employer £12,000 per annum in rent. The annual rateable value of the property is £19,000. Lesley's annual salary is £94,000.

What is the value of the taxable benefit for the living accommodation in 2015/16?

A   £3,963
B   £15,850
C   £3,625
D   £8,850

Assume an official rate of interest of 3%.

27 Gertrude has been provided with a petrol company car by her employer since 6 April 2015 in addition to her annual salary of £14,500. The car has CO_2 emissions of 100g/km and a list price of £10,000. Gertrude is also provided with petrol for business and private use. She repays 5p per mile for the private fuel although current petrol prices equate to 15p per mile. Gertrude estimates her private mileage at 5,000 miles for 2015/16.

What is the taxable benefit for the car and fuel for 2015/16?

A   £4,815
B   £4,565
C   £2,000
D   £1,500

28 Wilma has been provided with a diesel company car for a number of years with CO_2 emissions of 90g/km. It had an original list price of £33,000 although the company bought it second hand for £24,000. Wilma pays her employer £50 per month towards the private use of her car. Wilma has an annual salary of £48,650.

What is the taxable benefit for the car for 2015/16?

A   £5,280
B   £4,680
C   £3,690
D   £3,240

29 Fred is provided with a two-year-old van by his employer. In addition to home to work journeys, Fred uses the van extensively at weekends. The van has a list price of £8,950 and CO_2 emissions of 101g/km. Fred's employer pays for all his private petrol. Fred's annual salary is £12,455.

What is the taxable benefit for 2015/16?

A   £4,658
B   £3,744
C   £3,150
D   £1,343

30 Jasper has an annual salary of £4,000 and has received the following benefits during 2015/16:

•   Use of a three-year-old company van. Jasper uses the van most of the time as he does not own a car; and

•   Gift of video equipment with a market value of £50 which cost £400 six weeks ago.

Select which of the following correctly identifies Jasper's taxable benefits for 2015/16.

A   £3,550
B   £3,200
C   £400
D   £50

31 Robert has an annual salary of £56,000 and has received the following benefits during 2015/16:

•   Childcare vouchers of £45 per week (£2,340 per year); and
•   Meal vouchers of £5 per day for 240 days of the year.

Robert has been receiving these benefits since 2009.

Select which of the following correctly identifies Robert's taxable benefits for 2015/16.

A   £2,084
B   £3,540
C   £1,200
D   £884

32 Alexandra works for an airline. She has an annual salary of £66,000 and has received the following benefits during 2015/16:

- Gifts of jewellery from a customer worth £200; and

- Provision of free flights when there are spare seats available on the plane. The market value of the flights taken during the year is £4,550.

Select which of the following correctly identifies Alexandra's taxable benefits for 2015/16.

A £4,750
B £4,550
C £200
D £0

33 Hettie has worked for the same employer (a manufacturing company) for 30 years. She has an annual salary of £12,000 and has received the following benefits during 2015/16.

- Long service award of an original oil painting worth £1,400; and

- Free bus pass worth £455 to enable Hettie to travel from home to work on a public bus service which the employer subsidises.

Select which of the following correctly identifies Hettie's taxable benefits for 2015/16.

A £1,855
B £1,400
C £455
D £0

34 Sunil is employed as a hairdresser by Hairy Monsters. He is paid £30,000 per annum and provided with a number of benefits.

Select whether the following benefits are taxable or exempt from income tax.

Employer contributions to occupational pension scheme

A Taxable
B Exempt

Childcare vouchers for use with an approved provider worth £40 per week

C Taxable
D Exempt

Living accommodation

E Taxable
F Exempt

35 Charlie commenced work as an employee of House Medical Corporation on 1 July 2015. Charlie earns £35,000 per annum. On 1 July 2015 Charlie was also provided with a company car which runs on diesel with a list price of £18,000 and CO_2 emissions of 150g/km. Charlie pays for all his private fuel.

In calculating Charlie's total employment income for 2015/16, the amount which will be included for the car benefit is …

36 Freddie's employer provides him with a diesel company car with a list price of £16,000 on 6 April 2015. The car has CO_2 emissions of 45g/km.

What is Freddie's car benefit for 2015/16?

A £1,440
B £800
C £1,280
D £1,920

37 Diana and Camilla are employees of Dark Ltd. Diana receives a company car which she uses for both business and private purposes. Camilla receives living accommodation at Dark Ltd's expense which does not qualify as job related.

Identify the extent to which the benefits provided by Dark Ltd are taxable.

Company car provided to Diana

A   Exempt benefit
B   Taxable benefit if employment earnings are at least £8,500 pa
C   Taxable benefit irrespective of level of earnings

Living accommodation provided to Camilla

D   Exempt benefit
E   Taxable benefit if employment earnings are at least £8,500 pa
F   Taxable benefit irrespective of level of earnings

38 On 1 October 2015 Mariano started his employment with Punch Ltd and was immediately provided with a car. The car has CO_2 emissions of 127g/km and a list price of £14,000. Mariano pays for all of his own petrol relating to the car.

What is Mariano's car benefit for 2015/16?

39 Since 1 January 2014 Amy has been provided with an apartment by her employer. The annual value of the accommodation is £1,500. The original cost of the apartment to her employer in 2000 was £81,000. The market value of the apartment on 1 January 2014 was £165,000, and on 6 April 2015 was £180,000. The official rate of interest at 6 April 2015 is 3%.

What is Amy's accommodation benefit for 2015/16?

A   £1,500
B   £1,680
C   £4,200
D   £4,650

40 Duncombe Ltd purchased a flat in London in 2000 for £280,000. On 6 February 2016 the company recruited a new sales director and allowed him to live in the flat for the remainder of 2015/16. The market value of the flat in February 2016 was £375,000. The company installed double glazing in March 2006 at a cost of £14,000 and air-conditioning in March 2016 at a cost of £29,000.

What is the 'cost' of the flat for the purpose of computing the additional yearly rental benefit for 2015/16?

A   £404,000
B   £375,000
C   £323,000
D   £389,000

41 Pryor, Feinstein and Hill are employees of Boxer Ltd each earning £40,000 per annum. Boxer Ltd is to provide Pryor with a company van, Feinstein with a company car and Hill with a company bicycle. Pryor and Feinstein will use their vehicles for business and for commuting to work only. Hill will use his bicycle for commuting only. All employees had the option of a company bicycle.

Identify whether each of the employees has a taxable or exempt benefit in relation to their mode of transport.

Pryor's company van is

A   Taxable
B   Exempt

Feinstein's company car is

C   Taxable
D   Exempt

Hill's company bicycle is

E   Taxable
F   Exempt

42 Schoolteachers working at Eastminster School Ltd (a private fee paying school) are provided with places for their children to attend the school at £2,000 pa. The normal fee levels are £10,000 pa. The average total cost to the school of providing a place is £7,500 pa but the additional cost per child of providing a place is £3,000 pa.

The employment income assessable on a teacher sending his only child to the school is...

43 Amanda is employed and has a salary as follows.

Employer's year ended

31 December 2015   £36,000 pa
31 December 2016   £37,500 pa

Amanda is paid on the last working day of every month. During 2015/16 she also received dividend income of £360.

What is Amanda's total taxable income for 2015/16?

A   £36,735
B   £36,775
C   £26,135
D   £26,175

44 Matilda works part-time with an annual salary of £4,000 and taxable benefits of £4,000 per year.

The taxable benefits consist of a company car and fuel for private use.

Which of the following statements is true?

A   Matilda is in excluded employment
B   Matilda is not in excluded employment

Which of the following statements is true?

C   Matilda will pay income tax on employment income of £8,000 per year
D   Matilda will pay income tax on employment income of £4,000 per year

45 Esmerelda has been provided with a diesel company car by her employer for a number of years in addition to an annual salary of £44,000. The diesel car has CO_2 emissions of 120g/km and an original list price of £19,000. Esmerelda left the employment on 5 February 2016.

What is the taxable benefit for the car for 2015/16?

A   £4,180
B   £3,610
C   £3,483
D   £3,008

C
H
A
P
T
E
R

4

46 Quasimodo has been provided with a petrol company car by his employer since 6 October 2015. The petrol car has CO_2 emissions of 105g/km and a list price of £22,000. Quasimodo chose optional accessories worth £4,500 and three months after acquisition he had 'go faster' stripes added at a cost of £95. Quasimodo has an annual salary of £46,000.

What is the taxable benefit for the car for 2015/16?

A   £2,120
B   £2,128
C   £4,240
D   £4,255

47 Frollo's employer provides him with a petrol company car on 6 July 2015. The petrol car has CO_2 emissions of 90g/km. Frollo's employer provides all fuel, for which Frollo pays £5 per month to the employer. The full cost of private fuel is at least £50 per month.

What is Frollo's fuel benefit for 2015/16?

A   £2,873
B   £2,813
C   £2,155
D   £2,110

48 Joshua is given the use of some music equipment by his employer on 6 September 2015 for private purposes. At the time it was first made available to Joshua it had a market value of £8,460 although it originally cost £10,000 two years ago when purchased for company use. Joshua's annual salary is £23,000.

What is the taxable benefit for the music equipment for 2015/16?

A   £987
B   £1,167
C   £1,692
D   £2,000

49 Dewi and Dilys are both 70 and are married. Dewi is a basic rate taxpayer and Dilys pays no tax. Dilys has elected to transfer £1,060 of her personal allowance to Dewi.

Which letter will complete Dewi's tax code?

A   L
B   M
C   N
Y   Y

Now go back to the Learning objectives in the Introduction. If you are satisfied you have achieved these objectives, please tick them off.

ICAEW

Technical reference

Legislation

References relate to Income Tax (Earnings and Pensions) Act 2003 (*ITEPA 2003*) unless otherwise stated

Tax on employment income	ss.6-8
When general earnings are received	ss.18-19
The benefits code (general)	s.63
Excluded employment	ss.216-220
Vouchers	ss.73-96A
Living accommodation	ss.97-113
Expenses connected with provision of living accommodation	ss.313-315
Cars and fuel for private use	ss.114-153, 167
Vans for private use	ss.154-164
Assets available for private use/transfer	ss.204-210
Other benefits	ss.201-203
Exempt benefits	ss.227-326
PAYE codes	Income tax (Pay As You Earn) Regulations 2003 paras 13-17
PAYE payment of tax	Income tax (Pay As You Earn) Regulations 2003 paras 68-70

HMRC manuals

Employment Income Manual (Found at http://www.hmrc.gov.uk/manuals/eimanual/index.htm)

Employment income: introduction	EIM00510
Employment income: basis of assessment for general earnings	EIM42200
Employment income: general earnings: amounts treated as earnings	EIM00513

This gives an overview of the benefits code and provides links to further guidance on individual types of benefit.

Employment income: alphabetical list of particular items	EIM01005

This gives links to more unusual types of benefit from employment, including those which are not taxable.

PAYE Manual can be found at http://www.hmrc.gov.uk/manuals/pommanual/index.htm

---

This technical reference section is designed to assist you. It should help you to know where to look for further information on the topics covered in this chapter. **You will not be examined on the contents of this section in your examination.**

C
H
A
P
T
E
R

4

Answer to Interactive question 1

	£
Basic rental benefit	
Annual value	2,500
Additional yearly rental benefit	
Cost of provision (MV at provision)	190,000
Less lower limit	(75,000)
	115,000
Apply official rate of interest	
£115,000 × 3%	3,450
Time-apportionment	
(£2,500 + £3,450) = £5,950 × 6/12	
Taxable benefit is	2,975

Answer to Interactive question 2

CO_2 emissions are 156g/km, round down to 155g/km

Appropriate percentage:

(155 – 95) = 60g/km in excess of threshold

60 ÷ 5 = 12%

14% + 12% + 3% (diesel) = 29%

List price is £17,820

£17,820 × 29% = £5,168

Time-apportionment

£5,168 × 3/12

Taxable benefit is £1,292

Answers to Self-test

1 C – £8,000

Sandra's basic salary is £6,000. She is also taxed on the bonus of £2,000 received in the tax year 2015/16. Note that in terms of any benefits, Sandra is a P9D, or excluded, employee.

2 B – Neither of them

Peter earns less than £8,500, but he is a director who does not work full-time and the company is not non-profit making nor charitable. Therefore Peter is not in excluded employment.

Jane earns over £8,500 a year and so is not in excluded employment.

3 B – £480

Meal vouchers = £2.00 × 240 = £480

Pension advice up to £150 is exempt (assume available to all employees)

Entertainment provided by third party is exempt

4 C – £1,650

CO_2 emissions are 122g/km, round down to 120g/km

Appropriate percentage:

(120 – 95) = 25g/km in excess of threshold

25 ÷ 5 = 5%

14% + 5% + 3% (diesel) = 22%

List price is £18,000

£18,000 × 22% = £3,960

Available for 5 months in tax year

£3,960 × 5/12 = £1,650

5 C – 764L

	£
Allowance: Personal allowance	10,600
Less deduction (taxable benefits)	(2,960)
Net allowances	7,640

Tricia's tax code is therefore 764L.

6 830L

	£
Allowance: Personal allowance	10,600
Less deduction (unpaid tax) £920 × 100/40 – higher rate tax payer	(2,300)
Net allowances	8,300

David's tax code is therefore 830L.

7 The taxable benefits assessable on Harry in 2015/16 are £15,072

$$\frac{170-95}{5} = 15$$

Percentage = 14 + 15 + 3 (diesel) = 32%

Car benefit = 32% × 25,000 = £8,000

Fuel benefit = 32% × 22,100 = £7,072

8　The additional employment income for each of the company's employees in 2015/16 as a result of the provision of the two benefits is £720

Telephone = £0

Childcare = £(70 − 55) × 48 weeks = £720

9　Private health insurance, costing Bony Ltd £800. The same insurance would have cost Jacob £1,100.

　　A　£800

　　　　PHI = £800 as cost to employer

　　A television out of stock which cost £200 to manufacture but would cost Bony Ltd £800 to buy in from another supplier.

　　C　£200

　　　　Television = £200 as marginal cost to employer

　　A car parking space at a car park near to the office which cost Bony Ltd £500 in 2015/16.

　　E　£0

　　　　Car parking space = Nil as exempt

10　C　£2,888

　　　　£3,150 × 11/12 = £2,888 = Pro rated van benefit

　　　　There is no fuel benefit as no private fuel is paid for by the employer.

11　B　£250

　　　　For non P11D employees (ie employees earning less than £8,500 per the emoluments test), benefits in the form of assets are taxable at the amount for which they can be exchanged into cash (second hand value).

12　A　£0

　　　　No benefit for cycle equipment made available to all employees.

　　　　No benefit for childcare vouchers of less than or equal to £55 per week for those in the scheme prior to 6 April 2011.　For those joining the scheme on or after 6 April 2011 there is no benefit for childcare vouchers of less than or equal to £55 per week for a basic rate taxpayer or £28 per week for a higher rate taxpayer.　In all cases they must be for use with approved childcare providers.

13　The 'cost' of the flat for the purpose of computing the additional yearly rental benefit for 2015/16 is £327,000

£327,000 = original cost plus enhancement pre 2015/16

　　　　　= £(310,000 + 17,000)

Market value is only relevant if owned for six years prior to first use. The double glazing is not included because it was not installed before the start of this tax year, however it will be used to calculate the benefit in 2016/17.

14　The taxable benefit assessable on Amy in 2015/16 is £8,525

$$\frac{160 - 95}{5} = 13$$

Percentage = 14 + 13 = 27%

Car benefit = 27% × 20,000 × 9/12 = £4,050

Fuel benefit = 27% × 22,100 × 9/12 = £4,475

15 B £3,713

$$\frac{175-95}{5} = 16$$

Percentage = 14 + 16 + 3 (diesel) = 33%

Car benefit = 33% × 15,000 = £4,950 × 9/12 = £3,713

16 The benefit assessable on Pirro in respect of the computer is zero

As the private use of the computer is insignificant (computer required for essential business use), there will be no assessable benefit.

17 Pippin is provided with a van with CO_2 emissions of 190 g/km, by his employer Joker Ltd. Joker Ltd pay for all petrol for the van. Pippin has an assessable fuel benefit based on the CO_2 emissions.

B Incorrect – the fuel benefit on a company van is £594 per annum irrespective of emissions.

Piers makes a nominal contribution towards the fuel cost on his company car of £10 per month. This accounts for about 95% of his private use. He is able to reduce his fuel benefit by £120 pa.

D Incorrect – a contribution towards private fuel only reduces the benefit if it is a 100% contribution (reducing the benefit to nil)

18 The taxable benefit of the flat in 2015/16 is £23,375

	£
Annual value	8,675
Additional yearly rental benefit £(565,000 – 75,000) × 3%	14,700
Taxable benefit	23,375

19 C £30

No benefit for the canteen as it is made available to all employees.

As the overnight expenses exceed £5 per night the whole amount becomes chargeable.

20 A £52,500

Jacob's employment income for the year is the amount actually received in the tax year, ie his salary of £36,000 plus the bonus of £16,500 received on 30 April 2015.

21 B Employees in excluded employment are taxed on benefits which can be converted into cash. The assessable amount is the marginal cost to the employer. False.

Employees in excluded employment are taxed on benefits which can be sold. However, the assessable amount is based on their second hand value. Employees not in excluded employment are assessed on the marginal cost of providing an asset where no specific rule exists as to how the value of that asset should be quantified.

C Employees in excluded employment are sometimes called 'P9D' employees. True.

Employees in excluded employment are often referred to as P9D employees. Employees not in excluded employment are often referred to as P11D employees.

22 C £8,000

The taxable benefit is the higher of the annual rateable value and the rent paid by the employer (if any) less any contribution by the employee:

	£
Higher of rent/rateable value	15,000
Less employee contribution	(7,000)
Taxable benefit	8,000

23 B 1 and 2 only

Accommodation is not job related simply because it enables the employee to work longer hours by reducing time spent commuting. Accommodation provided to directors owning more than 5% of the company is only job related if it is provided for reasons of security.

24 A £18,000

The taxable benefit of expensive living accommodation is calculated in two parts. Where accommodation is provided more than six years after its acquisition and its original cost plus improvements as at first occupation exceeds £75,000 market value is used instead of original cost. In this case Sally first occupies the property more than six years after its acquisition. However its original cost plus improvements is only £60,000. Thus the property does not qualify as expensive accommodation (despite its current market value) and Sally is only taxable on the annual rateable value.

25 C £21,800

The taxable benefit for expensive accommodation is the annual rateable value plus: ((original cost less £75,000) × official rate of interest). The taxable benefit then needs to be prorated for the actual period of use in the tax year, ie 6 August 2015 – 5 April 2016 for 2015/16:

[£21,000 + ((£465,000 – £75,000) × 3%)] × 8/12 = £21,800

26 A £3,963

The benefit is calculated as follows.

	£
Annual rateable value	19,000
Less: contribution by employee	(12,000)
	7,000
Additional yearly rent	
(£325,000 + £45,000 – £75,000) × 3%	8,850
Total benefit	15,850
Pro rate for actual occupation in the year × 3/12	3,963

Note that the additional yearly rent is based on the original cost plus capital improvements made before the start of the tax year in which the benefit is charged, ie prior to 6 April 2015 in this case.

27 A £4,815

The taxable benefit for the petrol company car is:

$$\frac{100-95}{5} = 1$$

Percentage = 14 + 1 = 15%

Car benefit = 15% × £10,000 = £1,500

Fuel benefit = 15% × £22,100 = £3,315

Where private fuel is only partly repaid by the employer no reduction is given to the taxable benefit. Either the private fuel benefit is fully reimbursed by the employee or the full £22,100 at the appropriate percentage is taxable on the employee.

28 B £4,680

The taxable benefit for the diesel company car, which has CO_2 emissions exceeding 75g/km but less than 95g/km, is:

13% + 3% (diesel) = 16%

16% × £33,000 (car list price) - £600 (employee contribution) = £4,680

The original list price is used to compute the taxable benefit.

29 B £3,744

The taxable benefit for a company van with private use is £3,150. The van fuel benefit is £594. Private use of vans does not include home to work.

30 D £50

As Jasper is in excluded employment (earnings + benefits as if were not in excluded employment <£8,500) there is no benefit in respect of the van.

Any assets which can be converted into cash, ie sold, are assessed based on their second hand value. The benefit of the gift of video equipment is therefore just £50.

31 C £1,200

Childcare vouchers of up to £55 per week are exempt as Robert was in the scheme prior to 6 April 2011 (otherwise only £28 per week would be exempt as he is a higher rate taxpayer). Meal vouchers are taxable in full.

32 D £0

Non-cash gifts from a third party of up to £250 per tax year from the same donor are exempt.

Where an employee not in excluded employment receives a benefit for which there is no specific rule under the benefits code, the benefit should be assessed based on the marginal cost to the employer. Given that the plane would operate with or without Alexandra on board and there were always spare seats available, the marginal cost to her employer of Alexandra's travel is nil. Her total taxable benefit is therefore £0.

33 D £0

Long service awards are exempt where minimum service is 20 years and are not in cash and equate to less than £50 per year of service.

Subsidies to public bus services with free travel for employees in return, are exempt.

Hettie's taxable benefits are therefore £0.

34 B Employer contributions – Exempt

D Childcare vouchers – Exempt

E Living accommodation – Taxable

35 In calculating Charlie's total employment income for 2015/16, the amount which will be included for the car benefit is £3,780

150 – 95 = 55g/km

55 ÷ 5 = 11%

Taxable percentage 28% (14% + 11% + 3% diesel)

£18,000 × 9/12 × 28% = £3,780

The benefit is time apportioned as the car was available from 1 July 2015

36 C The car has emissions not exceeding 50g/km so the percentage used is 5%.

As it is a diesel car this must then be increased by 3% to 8%.

£16,000 × 8% = £1,280

37 The correct answer is B, F

A company car is only taxable on employees with employment earnings of at least £8,500 pa. Living accommodation is taxable on all employees regardless of earnings.

38 The correct answer is £ [1,400]

127g/km = 14 + (125 – 95) ÷ 5 = 20%

Mariano only has the car for six months of the year.

Car benefit = 20% × £14,000 × 6/12 = £1,400

39   The correct answer is C

	£
Annual value	1,500
plus	
(Cost – 75,000) × 3%, but cost is replaced with MV when first made available if more than 6 years after purchase £(165,000 – 75,000) × 3%	2,700
	4,200

40   The correct answer is B

£375,000

More than six years since acquisition so use market value at first use. Market value at Feb 2016 will already include increase for March 2006 enhancement. March 2016 enhancement not included until 2016/17.

41   The correct answer is B, C, F

Pryor's company van.

Exempt – as the only private mileage is commuting

Feinstein's company car.

Taxable – as some private mileage

Hill's company bicycle.

Exempt – as available to all employees

42   The correct answer is £1,000

	£
Marginal cost of providing the place	3,000
Less employee contribution	(2,000)
	1,000

43   The correct answer is D

	Non- savings income £	Dividend income £	Total £
Salary			
9/12 × £36,000	27,000		
3/12 × £37,500	9,375		
Dividend (£360 × 100/90)		400	
Net income	36,375	400	36,775
Less personal allowance	(10,600)		(10,600)
Taxable income	25,775	400	26,175

44   The correct answer is A, D.

Matilda is in excluded employment

Matilda will pay income tax on employment income of £4,000 per year

Excluded employment is defined as earnings of less than £8,500 per annum including the value of any taxable benefits assessed as if the employee were not in excluded employment.

As Matilda is in excluded employment the only benefits which are taxable are those convertible into cash, vouchers and living accommodation. She is therefore only taxable on employment income of £4,000, ie her salary.

45   The correct answer is C

The taxable benefit for the diesel company car is:

120g/km – 95g/km ÷ 5 = 5% + 14% + 3% diesel supplement = 22%

22% × £19,000 × 10/12 pro rated for time of Esmerelda's employment = £3,483

46   The correct answer is A

The taxable benefit for the petrol company car is:

$(105 - 95) \div 5 = 2\% + 14\% = 16\%$

$16\% \times (£22,000 + £4,500) \times 6/12$ pro rated for actual use = £2,120

Optional accessories added after the time of purchase which cost less than £100 are excluded from the calculation.

47   The correct answer is C

With emissions exceeding 75g/km but less than 95g/km, the percentage is 13%.

$£22,100 \times 13\% = £2,873$

Available for 9 months: $9/12 \times £2,873 = £2,155$

No deduction is allowed for an employee's contribution to payment for private fuel unless the employer is reimbursed in full.

48   The correct answer is A

Use of an employer asset is taxable based on the market value when first used by an employee × 20%:

$£8,460 \times 20\% \times 7/12$ (pro rated for actual use in tax year) = £987

49   The correct answer is B

M in Dewi's code indicates he is the recipient of the marriage allowance.

CHAPTER 5

Trading profits

Introduction

Examination context

Topic List

    1   Badges of trade

    2   Adjustment to profits

    3   Allowable and disallowable expenditure

    4   Other adjustments

Summary and Self-test

Technical reference

Answer to Interactive question

Answers to Self-test

Introduction

Learning objectives

- Recognise the badges of trade

- Allocate given items of business expenditure as allowable or disallowable for tax purposes and calculate adjusted trading profits of a sole trader or partnership using the accruals basis

Specific syllabus references for this chapter are: 3d, e.

Syllabus links

The material in this chapter forms the basis of the charge to tax on business profits.

You will be expected to know the main adjustments to profit in the Tax Compliance paper later on in the Professional Level and also as technical background for the Business Planning: Taxation paper.

Examination context

In the examination, in the objective test questions, candidates may be required to:

- Identify and use the badges of trade in a given scenario

In the examination, in scenario-based questions, candidates may be required to:

- Determine whether expenditure incurred is allowable or disallowable in calculating trading profits
- Correctly deal with other adjustments required to calculate adjusted trading profits

For extra question practice on these topics go to the section of the Question Bank covering this chapter and to the section of the Question Bank containing scenario-based questions for income tax.

1 Badges of trade

Section overview

- Taxable trading profits arise from a trade.

- It is not always clear whether activities constitute a trade.

- The badges of trade are key factors which indicate whether a trade is being carried on.

- All the circumstances need to be taken into account to decide whether a taxpayer is carrying on a trade.

1.1 Is a trade being carried on?

Before considering the details of how to compute taxable trading profits, you need to ask whether a trade is being carried on. This is important in deciding how the profits or losses on a transaction are taxed. For example, the disposal of an asset might result in a trading profit or a capital gain; income received might be trading income or investment income.

A trade is defined in tax legislation as 'every trade, manufacture, adventure or concern in the nature of trade'. In practice, it is not always clear whether the activities of a taxpayer constitute a trading activity.

It has been left to the courts to interpret this definition and there are a number of decided cases identifying a number of key factors in deciding whether an activity constitutes a trade. These are known as the **badges of trade**. You will be expected to know the badges of trade and the facts of the cases described below. The case names are not examinable.

It is important to understand that no one factor is decisive. The badges of trade merely provide guidance to be used in conjunction with all the facts surrounding the transaction and with common sense.

1.2 Profit seeking motive

Trading requires a profit motive to exist when the asset is acquired. If it can be established that an asset was bought with the intention of reselling it at a profit, this would normally be regarded as an indicator that there is a trading activity.

An example was the purchase and resale of £20,000 of silver bullion as protection against the devaluation of sterling. The transaction was treated as a trading activity (*Wisdom v Chamberlain 1969*).

1.3 The number of transactions

A transaction which, by itself, might be regarded as of a capital nature, may be treated as a trading activity if a number of similar transactions are entered into.

An example was the purchase of a mill-owning company and the subsequent stripping of its assets (*Pickford v Quirke 1927*). Since this was the fourth such transaction, it was decided that a trade was being carried on.

1.4 Nature of the asset

The subject matter of the transaction may indicate whether a trade is being carried on.

There are three reasons for purchasing an asset:

- For personal use

- As an investment for its aesthetic value or to yield an income and/or a longer-term gain on the sale of the investment (examples include shares, land, works of art)

- For resale at a profit (which constitutes trading)

Examples of subject matter held to be for resale at a profit are 34,000,000 yards of aircraft linen (*Martin v Lowry 1927*) and 1,000,000 rolls of toilet paper (*Rutledge v Commissioners of Inland Revenue 1929*).

1.5 Existence of similar trading transactions or interests

The other activities of the taxpayer should be considered to see whether any similarities exist. For example, if an accountant sold a car it is unlikely that the accountant would be deemed to be trading. If however a car mechanic in business as a sole trader sold a car, there is a direct link between repairing and selling cars. HMRC may seek to tax the profit on the car sale as trading income.

1.6 Changes to the asset

If an asset is purchased and then subjected to a process before resale to enhance its marketability, the sale is more likely to be regarded as a trading activity.

An example was the purchase of a quantity of brandy which was blended and recasked before sale. The sale was treated as a trading activity (*Cape Brandy Syndicate 1921*).

Active marketing and advertising are also likely to lead to the conclusion that there is a trading activity.

1.7 The way the sale was carried out

Where a sale is carried out in a way that is typical of a trading organisation (eg through an agent), it is more likely to be considered as trading. For example a woodcutter who bought a consignment of whisky in bond and sold it through an agent was held to be trading.

1.8 Source of finance

If money was borrowed short-term to buy or improve the asset, this indicates a trading activity, especially if the loan could only be repaid by selling the asset.

1.9 Interval of time between purchase and sale

If an asset is bought and then resold shortly afterwards, this may indicate a trading activity.

1.10 Method of acquisition

An asset that is acquired by inheritance, or as a gift, is less likely to be the subject of trade.

2 Adjustment to profits

Section overview

- Trading profits cover income from a trade, profession or vocation.

- Profit and loss accounts must be drawn up under recognised accounting principles.

- The net accounting profit or loss may need to be adjusted for tax purposes.

2.1 Introduction

Having established that a taxpayer is carrying on a trade, it is necessary to work out what the taxpayer's **taxable trading profits** are. The same rules apply to income from professions (eg accountants) so we will simply refer to trading profits in this text. A taxpayer may carry on a trade as a sole trader or as a partner in a partnership.

2.2 Profit and loss account

UK tax law requires the use of accounts drawn up under recognised accounting principles. This will usually be in accordance with UK accepted accounting practice (UK GAAP). In some cases, company accounts may be prepared in accordance with International Accounting Standards (IAS) and International Financial Reporting Standards (IFRS).

However, unincorporated businesses such as sole traders are not bound to follow the same standards as companies when drawing up accounts.

2.3 Computing taxable trading profits

Whichever accounting method is used, the profit and loss account will show a figure for the net accounting profit or loss for a period of account. However, this figure needs to be adjusted to accord with tax law. This process is called the **adjustment to profits** and we will deal with the main adjustments in the rest of this chapter. The adjustments are those which apply to sole traders and partnerships. Broadly similar adjustments are required to compute tax adjusted trading profits for companies and we deal with the differences when we look at tax on companies later in this text.

Once the tax-adjusted profit or loss has been computed, capital allowances need to be taken into account to find taxable trading profits or trading losses. We deal with capital allowances in the next chapter.

The computation to determine tax-adjusted profits therefore takes the following form for a particular accounting period:

	£
Net profit per financial accounts	X
Add disallowable expenditure/income not shown in accounts	X
Less non-trade income in accounts/expenditure not in accounts	(X)
Tax adjusted profits before capital allowances	X
Less capital allowances	(X)
Tax-adjusted profit/(loss) after capital allowances	X

3 Allowable and disallowable expenditure

Section overview

- Expenditure is generally allowable if it is incurred wholly and exclusively for the purposes of the trade.

- Capital expenditure, appropriations of profit, general provisions, non-trade debts, most entertaining and gifts, and fines and penalties are disallowable.

- Some expenditure is specifically allowable such as legal costs on the renewal of a short lease. Some is specifically disallowed or restricted, for example leasing costs on cars with high emissions.

3.1 General principles

Definition

Allowable expenditure: Expenditure incurred wholly and exclusively for the purposes of the trade, not specifically disallowed by legislation.

In theory, if there is a dual purpose for expenditure (eg expenditure for both business and private use), the whole of the expenditure should be disallowed. In practice, however, HMRC will generally accept a reasonable apportionment between business (allowable) and private (disallowable) use.

Some expenditure is allowable for accounting purposes, but not for tax purposes. Such expenditure is **disallowable** and must be **added back** to the accounting profit or loss. Expenditure will be disallowable if it is too remote from the purposes of the trade.

Certain fixed-rate deductions can be made with respect to purchase of a vehicle for use in the trade and for the business use of a home, instead of using the normal trading income rules for such expenditure. These fixed-rate deductions are not examinable in the Principles of Taxation paper.

3.2 Capital expenditure

Capital expenditure is disallowable. Usually, accounting practice would exclude capital expenditure from the profit and loss account in any case. However, repairs and maintenance expenditure often requires careful review.

Maintenance (eg redecoration) and repairs (returning the asset to its original condition) are allowable.

Improvement or enhancement of the asset, however, is a capital expense and must be disallowed. This would include expenditure on an asset newly acquired in a dilapidated state, where expenditure is required to bring the asset into use in the business.

Depreciation of capital assets is also disallowable as are any profits or losses on the sale of fixed assets. For tax purposes depreciation and losses on disposals of fixed assets are added back to the net profit in the accounts, while profits on disposals of fixed assets are deducted from the net profit in the accounts.

3.3 Appropriations of profit

Appropriations of profit (such as the payment of a 'salary' to a sole trader or partner) are disallowable.

Payment of a salary to a family member which is not reasonable remuneration for the services provided to the business may also be treated as an appropriation of profit.

If a business pays the owner's personal income tax and national insurance contributions or any other personal expense on his behalf, these are also appropriations of profit (drawings) and are disallowable.

3.4 General provisions

The accounts may include a general provision for bad debts or a general stock provision.

The creation of, or increase in, a general provision is disallowable and must be added back to the accounting profit. Conversely, a decrease in a general provision must be deducted from the accounting profit.

The creation of, or increase in, a specific provision, for example relating to a specific debt, is allowable and does not require adjustment. A reduction in a specific bad debt provision is trading profit and so does not require adjustment.

3.5 Bad debts

Trade bad debts are allowable. Trade debts recovered are trading profit and do not require adjustment.

Non-trade bad debts are disallowable. These would include loans to employees unless either made in the course of trade or if the write-off is taxable as employment income for the employee.

Worked example: Bad debts

Jack's bad debts for the year to 30 April 2015 appear as follows:

	£		£
Written off		Balance b/f	
Trade debts	1,274	Specific provision	1,185
Loan to former employee	180	General provision	1,225
		Trade debts recovered	123
Specific provision	1,194		
General provision	1,260	Profit and loss a/c	1,375
	3,908		3,908

Requirement

What adjustments are required to arrive at Jack's taxable trading profits?

Solution

Loan to former employee written off – disallowable, add back £180

Increase in general bad debt provision – disallowable, add back (£1,260 – £1,225) = £35

Following changes in accounting standards, all reductions in the value of debtors are supposed to be specific in nature. This means that going forward, general provisions are less likely to be seen in practice. Instead of writing off or providing against a specific debt, debts will now be 'impaired'.

3.6 Entertainment and gifts

Expenditure on entertaining staff is allowable. All other entertaining expenditure (eg customer entertaining) is disallowable.

The following gifts are allowable:

- Gifts of trade samples (not for resale) which are given away in the ordinary course of the trade in order to advertise to the public generally

- Gifts to customers if they incorporate a conspicuous advertisement for the business, are not food, drink, tobacco or vouchers exchangeable for goods, and the total cost per customer is no more than £50

- Gifts to employees

All other gifts are disallowable.

3.7 Donations and subscriptions

Reasonably small donations to local charities are allowable if the gift enhances the public image of the trade.

Donations to national charities are disallowable.

Any charitable donations made within the Gift Aid Scheme are given tax relief in the income tax computation by extending the taxpayer's basic rate band (see earlier in this text). To ensure that tax relief is not given for these donations twice, any donations made with a Gift Aid declaration are disallowable in arriving at trading profits and must be added back to the net profit in the accounts.

Gifts of trading stock or used plant and machinery to charities or UK educational establishments are specifically allowable.

Political donations are generally disallowable.

Subscriptions to trade and professional associations are generally allowable.

3.8 Fines and penalties

The general rule is that fines and penalties are disallowable. Examples include parking fines incurred by a sole trader or partner and penalties for late payment of tax.

Parking fines incurred by an employee on a business activity are generally allowable by HMRC.

3.9 Interest

Interest paid on money borrowed for business purposes is allowable.

Interest on late payment of tax is disallowable.

3.10 Legal and professional fees

Legal and professional fees relating to income are allowable. Examples include collection of trade debts, employment issues, action for breach of contract, preservation of trading rights and preparation of accounts. Legal and professional fees incurred dealing with an HMRC enquiry or an appeal to HMRC are not allowable.

Legal and professional fees relating to capital expenditure are generally disallowable. Examples include costs of acquiring capital assets and drawing up a partnership agreement. However the following expenses relating to capital assets are specifically allowable:

- Legal costs relating to the **renewal** of a short lease (50 years or less)
- Costs of registration of a patent or copyright for trade use
- Incidental costs of raising long-term finance

3.11 Irrecoverable value added tax

Irrecoverable VAT is allowable for trading purposes only if the item of expenditure to which it relates is allowable.

3.12 Employment payments and pensions

Earnings paid to employees are generally allowable. If earnings are charged in the accounts but not paid within nine months of the end of the period of account, the cost is only allowable in the period in which the earnings are paid.

Redundancy payments and compensation for loss of office are generally allowable. However, on the cessation of trade, the deduction is restricted to additional payments of up to three times the amount of statutory redundancy pay.

The cost of educational courses for employees is allowable if incurred for trade purposes.

Employers' contributions to a registered pension scheme are allowable in the accounting period of payment, not when accrued.

Payments of employers' national insurance contributions in respect of employees are allowable.

3.13 Car leasing and rental costs

In principle, the costs of hiring, leasing or renting plant and equipment are allowable.

However for leases taken out on cars (not motorcycles) a flat rate disallowance of 15% of the lease payments applies for cars with CO_2 emissions above 130g/km for leases taken out on or after 6 April 2013 (1 April for companies). Thus from 6 April 2013 there is no disallowance if CO_2 emissions are less than or equal to 130g/km. For car leases taken out prior to 6 April 2013 (1 April for companies) the 15% disallowance applies only for CO_2 emissions above 160g/km.

Worked example: Leased car

Douglas leases a car with a retail price of £14,200 and CO_2 emissions of 151g/km on 1 June 2015. The leasing cost is £1,960 up to 31 December 2015.

Douglas prepares accounts to 31 December 2015.

Requirement

What is the disallowable amount which needs to be added back?

Solution

As the CO_2 emissions exceed 130g/km and the lease is taken out after 5 April 2013 there is a flat rate disallowance.

Disallowable amount 15% × £1,960   £294

If the sole trader or partner then uses the leased car partly for business and partly for private purposes a further adjustment is needed to disallow the private usage of the leased car.

Worked example: Leased car and private use by sole trader

Jane leases a car with a retail price of £16,000 and CO_2 emissions of 200g/km on 1 May 2015. Jane uses the car 60% for business and 40% for private purposes.

Jane prepares accounts to 31 December each year. The leasing cost up to 31 December 2015 was £1,600.

Requirement

What is the disallowed amount which needs to be added back?

Solution

Allowable amount

85% × £1,600 × 60% (business use) =	£816
Disallowable amount (£1,600 – £816) =	£784

Interactive question 1: Allowable or disallowable?   [Difficulty level: Exam standard]

Classify the following expenditure as allowable or disallowable and state how you would deal with it in the adjustment of profits computation.

Question	Fill in your answer
£1,000 on party for five employees	
Gift of desk diary to ten customers with trade logo costing £35 each	
£5,000 on new roof for workshop	
£500 increase in general bad debt provision	
£50 to local hospital, a registered charity, as sponsor for new scanner	
£150 debt to former employee written off	
£35 parking fines incurred by salesman on business	
£5,000 contribution to registered pension scheme	
Gift of bottle of wine to twenty customers with trade logo costing £25 each	
£1,000 donation to the Conservative Party, a political party	
£1,500 accountancy fees for preparing accounts	
£2,500 on redecoration of office	
£100 interest on late payment of tax	
£6,000 depreciation on capital assets	
£500 legal fees on grant of a new 25-year lease of shop	

See **Answer** at the end of this chapter.

4 Other adjustments

Section overview

- The sale price of goods taken from the business by the owner is trading profit.
- Non-trading income must be deducted.
- Business expenditure not shown in the accounts is deductible as an allowable expense.

4.1 Trading profits not shown in accounts

The main example of trading profit not shown in the accounts of the business arises when goods are taken from the business by the owner for personal use without reimbursing the business with the full value.

The owner must be taxed on the profit he would have made if the goods had been sold at market value.

The adjustment will depend on how the transaction has been shown in the accounts:

- If nothing is recorded in the accounts, add back the selling price
- If treated as drawings at cost, add back profit

Worked example: Goods taken for own use

Max took some goods from his business with a selling price of £160.

The cost of the goods was £90.

Requirement

What adjustments are required if:

(a) The transaction is not recorded in the accounts, or
(b) The transaction has been treated as drawings of £90?

Solution

(a) Add back selling price of £160
(b) Add back profit (£160 – £90) = £70

4.2 Non-trading income in accounts

Any non-trade income in the accounts must be deducted.

Examples include rental income, profits on the disposal of fixed assets and investment income. Sole traders may also include other miscellaneous income in their trade accounts.

4.3 Expenditure not shown in the accounts

The most common expenditure not shown in the accounts is business expenditure paid personally by the owner.

Such expenditure is allowable and should be deducted.

Summary

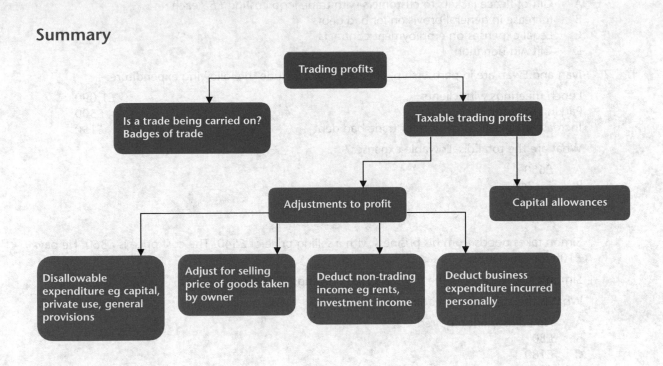

Self-test

Answer the following questions.

1   Which of the following is an allowable expense?

A   Gift of fleece jackets to customers with trade logo costing £55 each
B   Increase in general provision for bad debts
C   Legal expenses on employment contracts
D   Gift Aid donation

2   Ivan and Ewan are in partnership. Their accounts include the following expenditure:

Lunch meetings with clients   £1,090
Parking fines for Ivan   £500
Increase in specific provision for trade bad debt   £150

What are the total disallowable expenses?

A   £650
B   £1,240
C   £1,590
D   £1,740

3   Simon takes goods from his business with a selling price of £540. The cost price is £360. He pays £100 for the goods.

Simon's accounts show the transaction as drawings of £360.

What is the adjustment required?

A   No adjustment required
B   £80
C   £180
D   £540

4   Henry leases a car with a retail price of £20,000 and CO_2 emissions of 154g/km from 1 June 2015. The annual leasing charge is £5,000.

What adjustment needs to be made in his accounts for the year ended 31 May 2016?

A   No adjustment required
B   £750 added back
C   £4,250 added back
D   £5,000 added back

5   Patrick's accounts show £16,550 on repairs and maintenance during the year to 30 September 2015:

Demolishing out-house and building new toilets   £5,950
Repainting offices   £3,600
Installing new heating system   £7,000

How much should be added back to the accounting profit?

A   £9,550
B   £10,600
C   £12,950
D   £16,550

6   Janice leases a car with a retail price of £36,000 and CO_2 emissions of 120g/km from 1 July 2015. The annual leasing charge is £4,700. The car is for business use only.

What adjustment needs to be made in her accounts for the year ended 31 December 2015?

A   £1,998
B   £705
C   £353
D   £0

7 Paul Sarbanes is a self-employed garage proprietor in Leeds. On 22 December 2015 he made the following gifts.

Identify whether each gift is allowable or disallowable when calculating Paul's tax adjusted trading profit.

A case of wine costing £48 to a customer. Each bottle had the name of the garage on the label.

A   Allowable
B   Disallowable

Four bottles of spirits costing £90 to an employee.

C   Allowable
D   Disallowable

Cash bonus of £60 to each of his three junior employees.

E   Allowable
F   Disallowable

8 Manuel leased a car (CO_2 emissions 123g/km) for use in his business. Manuel took out the lease on 1 May 2015. The hire charges were £5,000 in his year ended 30 September 2015. Manuel used the car, which had a retail price when new of £30,000, 80% of the time for business.

The hire charge allowable as a deduction against trading profits is…

9 Niamh's accounts for the year ended 30 September 2015 showed legal and professional fees of £8,000.

Which **TWO** of the following costs are **NOT** allowable in calculating her tax-adjusted trading profit?

A   Fees incurred in the recovery of a trade bad debt
B   Legal fees for a successful appeal against a tax assessment
C   Renewal of a ten-year lease on business premises
D   Fees for preparation of the annual accounts
E   Cost of taking out a new five-year lease on business premises

10 The following sentences have been included in a draft letter to a client who is about to start a new business.

Identify whether each statement is correct or incorrect.

Expenditure shown in the profit and loss account is not always allowable for tax purposes. Disallowable expenditure must be added back when computing the taxable trading profits.

A   Correct
B   Incorrect

The building that you are acquiring is dilapidated and requires repair work. You are not able to use the building until this work has been completed. The additional expenditure incurred on this repair work is allowable when computing taxable trading profits.

C   Correct
D   Incorrect

11 Noah is a wine merchant with a year ended 31 March 2016.

Which **TWO** of the following are allowable expenses in calculating Noah's taxable trading profits?

A   A gift of a £10 bottle of wine to each of 200 potential new customers as a marketing method to entice them to buy more wine in the future

B   Gifts to his two employees of a wine hamper costing him £60 for each employee

C   Legal costs relating to the acquisition of a 25-year lease on new business premises

D   Donation to a national charity

12 Flynn has been a sole trader for many years. His profit and loss account to 31 January 2016 includes the following items of expenditure.

Which **TWO** are fully allowable in calculating Flynn's taxable trading profits?

A   Costs of registering a patent for trade use

B   Payment of a parking fine incurred by Flynn while travelling on business

C   Payment of £12,000 to his wife Freya for working as one of his shop assistants. The other assistants earn £8,000 per annum for working similar hours

D   The legal costs for renewing the ten-year lease on his shop premises

13 William Pitt is a self-employed tax adviser in Coventry. In the year ended 31 March 2016 he made the following gifts. All of the recipients are registered charities.

(i)   £50 to the renovation fund for Coventry Cathedral (a local charity)
(ii) £50 to the World Wide Fund for Nature (a national charity) via the Gift Aid Scheme
(iii) £25 to the National Trust (a national charity)

Select which of the following options shows the gift(s) allowed when computing William's trading profits assessment?

A   All of them
B   (iii) only
C   (i) and (ii) only
D   (i) only

14 Imogen is a sole trader and her accounts show £7,700 on repairs and maintenance during the year to 30 September 2015.

Repair to a newly acquired second hand machine to make it useable	£2,400
Repairs to the roof of the office damaged in a storm	£3,800
Redecorating the office	£1,500

How much should be added back to the accounting profit for tax purposes?

A   £2,400
B   £3,900
C   £5,300
D   £7,700

15 Marion has been trading as a shopkeeper for many years. Her latest accounts show the following expenditure.

	£
Annual salary to Peter, Marion's husband, who has worked in the shop on Saturdays (Note: other Saturday workers are paid £3,000 per annum)	14,000
Total motor expenses relating to Marion's car (business usage agreed at 60%)	800

How much should be added back to the accounting profit for tax purposes?

A   £14,800
B   £14,320
C   £11,800
D   £11,320

16 Barry's business has the following bad debt account for the year to 31 March 2016.

	£		£
Written off:		Balance brought forward	
Trade debts	3,600	– specific debts	4,600
Loan to former employee	500		
		Debt recovered – loan to	
		former employee	
Balance carried forward		previously written off	200
– specific debts	5,200	Profit & loss account	4,500
	9,300		9,300

Select which of the following is the adjustment required.

A   Add back £300
B   Add back £500
C   Add back £900
D   Deduct £300

17 Peter's accounts for the year ended 31 March 2016 include the following items within travel and entertaining:

	£
Flight to Aberdeen to visit a potential new customer. Peter delayed his return journey to spend a long weekend with friends at a ski resort close to Aberdeen.	250
Hospitality box at Aintree racecourse to entertain customers	4,050
Staff annual dinner dance (£200 per head)	3,800

How much should be added back in the accounts?

A   £4,050
B   £4,300
C   £7,850
D   £8,100

18 Bruce and Kieran are in partnership selling and repairing computers. Their accounts include the following expenditure.

Speeding fines for Bruce	£490
Gift of computer software to a local school	£1,200
Subscriptions to a computer trade magazine	£150

What are the total disallowable expenses?

A   £490
B   £640
C   £1,350
D   £1,690

19 Michelle's accounts include the following items.

Penalty for the late submission of VAT return	£270
Legal fees for the renewal of a short lease	£750
Employer's pension costs accrued (amount actually paid is £2,300)	£2,500

What are Michelle's total disallowable expenses?

A   £1,020
B   £950
C   £470
D   £270

20 Barbara is a sole trader and leases a car with a retail price of £16,000 and CO$_2$ emissions of 152g/km. The car is used 100% for business purposes by Barbara. The annual leasing charge, paid monthly, is £3,800. She took out the lease on 1 May 2015.

Select which of the following is the adjustment that Barbara needs to make in her accounts for tax purposes for the year ended 31 January 2016.

A   £3,230 added back
B   £428 added back
C   £570 added back
D   £3,372 added back

21 Paola is a sole trader. She has deducted the two items listed below in arriving at her draft tax adjusted profits of £46,223 for the year ended 28 February 2016.

Select whether an adjustment to profits should be made for each of the following items in order to determine Paola's final tax-adjusted trading profits.

A restaurant bill for £432 for a staff party attended by Paola and all three employees

A   Adjust
B   Do not adjust

Staff costs of £3,298 relating to work undertaken preparing the accounts for the business by Paola's husband

C   Adjust
D   Do not adjust

22 Andy is a sole trader and a higher-rate tax payer. His accounting profit for the year ended 31 March 2016 includes a deduction of £938, which is the amount of a donation made to a local hospital under the Gift Aid scheme on 1 February 2016.

Select whether the following statements are true or false relating to this donation.

An amount of £938 must be added back to the accounting profit to arrive at the adjusted trading profit

A   True
B   False

The basic rate band must be extended by £938 to correctly calculate Andy's tax liability

C   True
D   False

23 Donna owns a shoe shop that she has run as a sole trader for many years. In the year ended 31 December 2015 she took shoes for herself from the shop which had cost £220. The shoes retailed at a total of £450. No adjustment has been made in the accounts relating to the shoes.

The amount by which accounting profits need to be increased to arrive at trading profits, in relation to the shoes is...

24 Sam has a landscape gardening business, which he runs as a sole trader. In the year ended 31 March 2016 the salaries and wages account of the business is as follows.

	£
Salaries (including £27,000 for Sam)	55,000
Class 1 secondary contributions	745
Class 2 contributions	146
Pension contributions for Sam (all paid during the accounting period)	2,700
	60,609

The amount to be added back in calculating tax adjusted trading profit is

A   £27,000
B   £27,146
C   £29,700
D   £29,846

25 Paul and Jill set up in partnership on 1 April 2015. The partnership accounts for the year ended 31 March 2016 include legal and professional fees as follows.

	£
Accountancy fees	2,000
Legal fees on the preparation of the partnership agreement	800
Legal fees relating to the acquisition of a new 10-year lease on the office premises	1,500
Legal fees for recovery of trade debts	400
	4,700

The amount to be added back in calculating the tax adjusted profits is...

26 Jem is a VAT-registered sole trader. He has deducted the following two items listed below in calculating his draft tax adjusted profits of £92,421 for the year ended 31 December 2015.

Select whether an adjustment to profits should be made for each of the following items in order to determine Jem's final tax-adjusted trading profits.

A bill from a hotel for £480 (including VAT of £80) for a meal that Jem had with a major UK customer

A   Add back £480
B   Add back £400
C   Do not adjust

A bill from a hotel for £5,000 (excluding VAT) for the annual staff party costing £200 per head

D   Add back £5,000
E   Do not adjust

27 Sam is a sole trader with an accounting profit of £42,674 for the year ended 31 March 2016. The following two items are included in the accounts in arriving at the accounting profit.

Select what adjustment, if any, needs to be made to arrive at the tax-adjusted trading profit.

Bank interest received of £280 on the business bank account.

A   Deduct £280
B   Deduct £350
C   Do not adjust

Profit of £490 on disposal of a machine

D   Add £490
E   Deduct £490
F   Do not adjust

28 James is a sole trader drawing up accounts to 31 January. The motor expenses account for the year ended 31 January 2016 is as follows.

	£
Costs relating to James' car (70% business use)	2,000
Costs relating to the sales manager's car (80% business use)	1,800
Hire purchase interest payable on James' car	400
	4,200

How much should be added back when calculating the tax adjusted trading profit?

A   £600
B   £720
C   £960
D   £1,080

29   Caroline is a sole trader and identified the following amounts which have not been included in her accounts.

Select how each item should be treated in the adjustment to profits working in order to determine Caroline's tax adjusted trading profit.

Caroline has personally paid for her home telephone bills which include calls of £1,000 of which 30% relates to business

A   Increase trading profits by £300
B   Reduce trading profits by £300
C   Do not include in calculating tax adjusted trading profits

Caroline made a £200 donation to a local hospice, this was not paid under the Gift Aid scheme

D   Increase trading profits by £200
E   Reduce trading profits by £200
F   Do not include in calculating tax adjusted trading profits

30   Soria deducted the following amounts in arriving at her taxable trading profits of £65,329 for the year ended 31 March 2016.

Select whether an adjustment to profits should be made for each of the following items in order to determine Soria's final tax adjusted trading profit.

£10,000 as salary to her husband who works two days per week as a bookkeeper for her business

A   Adjust
B   Do not adjust

Irrecoverable VAT of £3,500 on a company car purchased for an employee

C   Adjust
D   Do not adjust

31   Tariq charged the following items in arriving at his net trading profit for the year to 31 March 2016:

	£
Amount written off debtors relating to a client who is in liquidation	4,800
Interest on late payment of income tax	1,234

How much should be disallowed when calculating Tariq's tax adjusted trading profits for the year?

A   £0
B   £1,234
C   £4,800
D   £6,034

32   Peri is self-employed and in December 2015 he made the following gifts.

Select whether each of the following gifts is allowable or disallowable when calculating Peri's tax adjusted trading profit.

A food hamper costing £35 to each client. Each hamper basket had the name of the business on the outside.

A   Allowable
B   Disallowable

A food hamper costing £60 to each employee. Each hamper basket had the name of the business on the outside.

C   Allowable
D   Disallowable

33   On 1 June 2015 Nadav leased a car (CO_2 emissions 135g/km) for use in his business, incurring hire charges of £3,500 in his year ended 31 March 2016. Nadav's sales manager will use the car, which had a retail price when new of £20,000, 60% of the time for business.

The hire charge allowable as a deduction against trading profits is ...

34 On 1 June 2015 Nadav leased a car (CO_2 emissions 125g/km) for use in his business. During his year ended 31 March 2016 he incurred hire charges of £2,450. Nadav uses the car 45% of the time for business.

The hire charge allowable as a deduction against trading profits is ...

35 Nuala's impairment losses account for the year ended 31 October 2015 is as follows.

	£		£
Trade debts written off	1,000	Balance b/f	
Balance carried forward		Specific provision	2,000
Specific provision	1,800	General provision	150
General provision	280	Profit and loss account	930
	3,080		3,080

The adjustment required to the net profit per the accounts to arrive at the taxable trading profits is

A   Add back £130
B   Deduct £130
C   Add back £200
D   Deduct £200

36 Huckleberry, a sole trader, has calculated the following amounts which have yet to be included in his final taxable trading profits.

Select how each item should be treated in order to determine Huckleberry's final taxable trading profits.

Huckleberry has calculated his irrecoverable VAT on UK client entertaining to be £4,656

A   Increase taxable trading profits by £4,656
B   Reduce taxable trading profits by £4,656
C   Do not include in taxable trading profits

Huckleberry gave his customers calendars worth £35 each bearing the business logo. In total he spent £3,500 on the calendars.

D   Increase taxable trading profits by £3,500
E   Reduce taxable trading profits by £3,500
F   Do not include in taxable trading profits

37 Leo, a sole trader, allowed the following amounts in arriving at his draft taxable trading profits of £180,000 for the year ended 31 March 2016.

Select how each item should be treated in the adjustments to profits working in order to determine Leo's final taxable trading profits.

Leo included £550 relating to the write off of a loan to an employee who left the business some time ago.

A   Add back £550
B   Deduct £550
C   Do not adjust

Leo deducted £600 relating to charitable donations to Oxfam (a national registered charity). A Gift Aid declaration had been made in respect of the donation.

D   Add back £600
E   Do not adjust

38 Tom has traded as a greengrocer for many years. In his year ended 30 April 2015 he took fruit and vegetables from the business which cost £350. He could have sold the goods for £600. Tom has not recorded this transaction in his accounts.

The amount to be added back to the net profit per the accounts to arrive at taxable trading profits for the year ended 30 April 2015 is

A £600
B £350
C £250
D £0

39 Which of the following is an allowable expense for a sole trader?

A Repairs to a newly purchased second-hand machine. The repairs were essential before the machine could be used

B Write-off of a loan to a former employee

C Legal fees for the renewal of a 20-year lease

D Donation to a small local charity, under the Gift Aid scheme

40 Tadzio, a sole trader, has included the following amounts in arriving at his draft taxable trading profits.

Select how each amount should be treated in the adjustments to profits working in order to determine Tadzio's final taxable trading profits.

Tadzio has calculated a profit on disposal of a machine to be £3,250.

A Add back £3,250
B Deduct £3,250
C Do not adjust

Tadzio and his salesman incurred parking fines of £200 and £100 respectively while on business.

D Add back £200
E Add back £300
F Do not adjust

41 Nikita's accounts include gifts of £2,200 for the year ended 30 June 2015.

	£
Food hamper with business logo to 10 customers	400
Food hamper with business logo to 25 employees	1,000
Computers no longer used by the business, to a local school	800

The amount to be added back to the net profit per the accounts to arrive at taxable trading profits for the year ended 30 June 2015 is

A £2,200
B £1,400
C £800
D £400

42 Naoko's accounts include staff costs for the year ended 31 October 2015 as follows.

	£
Wages and salaries (including £8,000 for Naoko's son)	49,650
National insurance contributions (including Naoko's £4,254 Classes 2 and 4)	10,453
	60,103

Naoko's son works on Saturdays. Other Saturday workers are paid £5,000 pa.

The amount to be added back to the net profit per the accounts to arrive at taxable trading profits for the year ended 31 October 2015 is …

Now, go back to the Learning objectives in the Introduction. If you are satisfied you have achieved these objectives, please tick them off.

Technical reference

Legislation

References relate to Income Tax (Trading and Other Income) Act 2005 (*ITTOIA 2005*)

Charge to tax on trade profits	s.5
Accounting practice	s.25

Disallowable expenditure

• Capital	s.33
• Wholly and exclusively	s.34
• Bad debts	s.35
• Unpaid remuneration	s.36
• Employee benefits	ss.38-44
• Business entertainment and gifts	ss.45-47
• Car hire	ss.48-50
• Penalties etc	s.54

Allowable expenditure

• Incidental costs of finance	s.58
• Redundancy payments	ss.76-80
• Incidental expenses re patents	s.89
• Gifts to charities etc of stock	s.108

HMRC manuals

Business income manual (Found at http://www.hmrc.gov.uk/manuals/bimmanual/index.htm)

Trade: badges of trade: summary	BIM20205
Measuring the profits (general rules)	BIM30000
The relationship between tax and accountancy	BIM 31000
Capital/revenue divide: introduction: overview of the guidance	BIM35001
Wholly & exclusively	BIM37000

This technical reference section is designed to assist you. It should help you to know where to look for further information on the topics covered in this chapter. **You will not be examined on the contents of this section in your examination**.

Answer to Interactive question 1

Question	Fill in your answer
£1,000 on party for five employees	Allowable as the £150 limit applies to employment income not trading profits (NB taxable benefit for employees)
Gift of desk diary to ten customers with trade logo costing £35 each	Allowable (advert, £50 or less)
£5,000 on new roof for workshop	Disallowable (capital), add back £5,000
£500 increase in general bad debt provision	Disallowable, add back £500
£50 to local hospital, a registered charity, as sponsor for new scanner	Allowable (small, local, public image)
£150 debt to former employee written off	Disallowable, add back £150
£35 parking fines incurred by salesman on business	Allowable
£5,000 contribution to registered pension scheme	Allowable
Gift of bottle of wine to twenty customers with trade logo costing £25 each	Disallowable (drink), add back £500 (20 × £25)
£1,000 donation to the Conservative Party, a political party	Disallowable (political donation), add back £1,000
£1,500 accountancy fees for preparing accounts	Allowable
£2,500 on redecoration of office	Allowable (maintenance)
£100 interest on late payment of tax	Disallowable, add back £100
£6,000 depreciation on capital assets	Disallowable add back £6,000
£500 legal fees on grant of a new 25 year lease of shop	Disallowable (not renewal), add back £500

1   C – legal expenses on employment contracts – allowable

Gift of fleece jackets to customers with trade logo costing £55 each – disallowable as exceeds £50 per customer

General provision for bad debts – disallowable

Gift Aid donation – disallowable, take into account in income tax computation

2   C – £1,590

Lunch meetings with clients – disallowable as entertaining

Parking fines for Ivan – disallowable as incurred by partner

Specific provision for trade bad debt – allowable as specific and for trade debt

3   B – £80

Add back profit (£540 – £360) = £180 – £100 (paid by Simon) = £80

4   B – £750 added back

Disallowable amount (15% × £5,000)   £750

5   C – £12,950

Demolishing out-house and building new toilets: disallowable, capital

Repainting offices: allowable

Installing new heating system: disallowable, capital

6   D – £0

As the CO_2 emissions are below 130g/km there is no disallowance.

Note: Only (6/12 × £4,700) £2,350 leasing charge would be in the accounts for the year ended 31 December 2015.

7   A case of wine costing £48 to a customer. Each bottle had the name of the garage on the label.

B   Disallowable

Gifts to customers of alcohol

Four bottles of spirits costing £90 to an employee.

C   Allowable

Gifts to employee are allowable as part of staff costs (but benefit on employee)

Cash of £60 to each of his three junior employees.

E   Allowable

Cash bonus to employee is simply remuneration, ie part of staff costs (but taxable on employee)

8   The hire charge allowable as a deduction against trading profits is £4,000

£5,000 × 80% (private use)

There is no flat rate disallowance as CO_2 emissions do not exceed 130g/km.

9   B   Legal fees of a successful appeal against a tax assessment

E   Cost of taking out a new five-year lease on business premises

10 Expenditure shown in the profit and loss account is not always allowable for tax purposes. Disallowable expenditure must be added back when computing the taxable trading profits.

   A   Correct – the profit in the P&L account has been reduced by this amount therefore it should be added back.

   The building that you are acquiring is dilapidated and requires repair work. You are not able to use the building until this work has been completed. The additional expenditure incurred on this repair work is allowable when computing taxable trading profits.

   D   Incorrect – the expenditure on the second hand asset makes it fit for purpose, so is capital expenditure and is not allowable.

11 A   A gift of a £10 bottle of wine to each of 200 potential new customers as a marketing method to entice them to buy more wine in the future, ie a trade sample.

   B   Gifts to his two employees of a wine hamper costing him £60 for each employee.

   A sample of trading stock to potential customers is allowable – it is irrelevant that it is alcohol.

   Gifts to employees are allowable.

   The legal fees on a **new** short lease are disallowable.

   Donations to national charities are disallowable.

12 A   Costs of registering a patent for trade use.

   D   The legal costs for renewing the ten-year lease on his shop premises.

   Costs of registering a patent for trade use are specifically allowable.

   Fees for **renewal** of a short lease are allowable.

   Parking fines incurred by a sole trader are always disallowable.

   The payment to his wife is only partly allowable.

13 D   (i) only

   Only gifts to local charities are allowable.

14 A   £2,400

   Repairs to a newly acquired second hand asset are not allowable if the repair is required in order to make it fit for purpose.

   Roof repairs and redecorating are maintenance in order to take an asset back to its original condition hence allowable.

15 D   £11,320

   Only a reasonable payment to a family member is allowable, so add back Peter's excess salary of £11,000 (£14,000 – £3,000)

   The private proportion of Marion's motor expenses is not allowable 40% × £800 = £320

16 A   Add back £300

	£
The write off of the former employee loan needs to be added back	500
The recovery of the former employee loan must be deducted	(200)
Net effect	300

   The write off of trade debts is allowable, as is the movement on specific provisions.

17 B £4,300

The flight must be added back as it is not wholly and exclusively for business purposes (duality).

Entertaining of customers must always be disallowed ie added back.

The staff entertaining is allowable for the business as long as it is reasonable (the individuals will however have a taxable benefit for employment income purposes as it exceeds the limit permitted for employment income purposes of £150 pa).

18 A £490

Fines of the proprietor are merely an appropriation of profits and disallowed.

Gifts out of stock to a UK educational establishment are specifically allowable.

Trade subscriptions are allowable.

19 C £470

Fines or interest relating to tax are specifically disallowed for individuals so £270 is disallowed.

The renewal costs of a short lease are allowable.

The employer's pension contributions are allowable in the year actually paid so £200 is disallowed.

20 B £428 added back

The amount to be added back/disallowed is 15% × £3,800 × 9/12 = £428

There is a 15% disallowance as the car has CO_2 emissions that exceed 130g/km.

21 B Restaurant bill – do not adjust

D Staff costs – do not adjust

22 A An amount of £938 must be added back   – True

D The basic rate band must be extended by £938   – False

The basic rate band must be extended by the gross amount of £1,173 (£938 × 100/80)

23 The amount by which accounting profits need to be increased to arrive at trading profits, in relation to the shoes is £450

As no adjustment has been made in the accounts the profits must be increased by the full retail price.

If the accounts had already been adjusted for the cost element then the only adjustment required would be for the profit of £230 (£450 – £220).

24 D £29,846

The disallowable elements to be added back are those relating directly to Sam (ie his drawings).

	£
Sam's salary	27,000
Class 2 contributions (for Sam)	146
Sam's pension contributions	2,700
	29,846

25 The amount to be added back in calculating the tax adjusted profits is £2,300

There are two amounts that are specifically disallowed by legislation:

	£
Legal fees on the preparation of the partnership agreement	800
Legal fees relating to a new 10 year lease on the office premises	1,500
	2,300

26 A   A bill from a hotel for £480 (including VAT of £80) for a meal   – Add back £480

    E   A bill from a hotel for £5,000 (excluding VAT) for the annual staff party   – Do not adjust

         Entertaining customers is disallowable expenditure but entertaining staff is allowable. Furthermore irrecoverable VAT (on UK client entertaining) is allowable only if the expenditure to which it relates is allowable. As the client entertaining is disallowable the VAT on this is also disallowable.

27 A   Bank interest received of £280 on the business bank account   – Deduct £280

    E   Profit of £490 on disposal of a machine   – Deduct £490

    Both of these amounts have increased accounting profit but neither are trading income, so a deduction must be made for each one.

28 B   £720

         The disallowable amounts to be added back are

	£
Relating to James' car (30% × £2,000)	600
Relating to the sales manager's car – all allowable	–
Hire purchase interest payable on James' car (30% × £400)	120
	720

29 B   Caroline has personally paid for her home telephone bills   – Reduce trading profits by £300

    E   Caroline made a £200 donation to a local hospice   – Reduce trading profits by £200

30 B   £10,000 of salary to her husband who works two days per week as a bookkeeper – Do not adjust

    C   Irrecoverable VAT of £3,500 on a company car purchased for an employee   – Adjust

         As Soria's husband is being paid a reasonable salary for the work done no adjustment is required.

         VAT cannot be recovered on motor cars as the VAT legislation forbids this recovery. Irrecoverable VAT is added to the overall cost of the car for the business. As the purchase of a car is capital expenditure it is disallowable and the VAT on this is also disallowable. The VAT should be included as part of the cost of the car in the capital allowances computation.

31 B   £1,234

         Specific bad debts written off are an allowable deduction.

         Interest on late payment of income tax is a disallowable expense.

32 The correct answer is B, C

    Gifts to customers of food are disallowable

    Gifts to employees are allowable for company as part of staff costs, but a taxable benefit for employees

33 The correct answer is £2,975

    Flat rate disallowance of 15% as CO_2 emissions exceed 130g/km and lease taken out after 5 April 2013.

    Private use by an employee is irrelevant.

    15% × £3,500 = £525

    Allowable deduction = £3,500 – £525 = £2,975

34 The correct answer is £1,103

No flat rate disallowance as CO_2 emissions do not exceed 130g/km.

Private use by the sole trader is disallowable and only the business use proportion of the hire charge is allowable.

Allowable deduction = £2,450 × 45% = £1,103

35 The correct answer is A

Add back £130

The general provision has increased by £130 so there must be an expense in the accounts relating to this – so add it back.

36 The correct answer is C, E

Irrecoverable VAT – do not include

Gifts – reduce taxable trading profits

Irrecoverable VAT is only allowed as a business expense if the item to which it relates (ie the client entertaining) is itself allowable for income tax. As client entertaining is disallowed, so too is the associated VAT.

Gifts to customers are allowed as long as they cost less than £50 each, bear the business logo and are not food, tobacco or alcohol.

37 The correct answer is A, D

Loan write off – add back £550, Donations – add back £600.

The loan write off is not trade related as it is not part of its trade to lend money, and it is not part of employee remuneration. The loan write off cannot be taxed as a benefit on the employee as he left the business some time ago. As it would originally have been deducted in arriving at the draft taxable trading profits figure, it needs to be added back to eliminate it.

The charitable donation is a Gift Aid donation, not a trading expense. Therefore £600 included in the draft trading profits figure should be added back.

38 The correct answer is A

If the transaction has not been recorded in the accounts the full selling price must be added back.

Alternatively if the cost of the goods had been recorded as drawings the profit of £250 would have to be added back.

39 The correct answer is C

The fees for renewal of a short lease are allowable (fees for a new short lease would be disallowable).

As the second-hand machine was not fit for purpose when purchased, the repairs are deemed to be capital, so not allowable. The repairs will be included as part of the capital cost within capital allowances.

Former employee loans are not for trade purposes therefore not allowable.

Donations to small local charities are allowable if not under the Gift Aid scheme. Where donations are made under the Gift Aid scheme, tax relief is given via the income tax computation instead.

40 The correct answer is B, D

The profit on disposal of the machine is shown in the accounts but is dealt with by capital allowances for tax purposes. The profit on disposal must be deducted.

Parking fines of employees whilst on business are an allowable expense, but parking fines of the proprietor are not allowable. Therefore Tadzio's fines of £200 must be added back.

41   The correct answer is D

Gifts of food to customers are disallowable, so add back £400.

The gifts to the employees are allowable, so no adjustment is required.

Donations of used plant and machinery to UK educational establishments are allowable, so no adjustment is required.

42   The correct answer is £7,254

	£
Excess salary paid to Naoko's son (£8,000 – 5,000)	3,000
Naoko's Class 2 and 4 NICs (only employer contributions are allowable)	4,254
	7,254

CHAPTER 6

Capital allowances

Introduction
Examination context
Topic List

Learning objective

- Calculate the adjusted trading profits after capital allowances on plant and machinery of a sole trader or partnership

The specific syllabus reference for this chapter is 3e.

Syllabus links

Capital allowances are an important area of taxation and are examinable at all levels.

You will be expected to be thoroughly conversant with the topics covered in this chapter in the Tax Compliance paper and in the Business Planning: Taxation paper, so it is vital that you make sure you learn the material in this chapter very well.

Examination context

In the examination, in the objective test questions relating to unincorporated businesses and in the scenario-based question for corporation tax, candidates may be required to:

- Identify which assets qualify as plant and machinery

- Calculate writing down allowances at the correct rate and deal with disposals of plant and machinery

- Identify which assets are eligible for first year allowances

- Correctly apply the annual investment allowance

- Correctly treat cars and other assets with private use by the sole trader or partner

- Determine the amount of any balancing adjustment

- Calculate capital allowances for periods shorter or longer than 12 months

For extra question practice on these topics go to the section of the Question Bank covering this chapter. There is further practice of capital allowances in the section of the Question Bank containing scenario-based questions for corporation tax. However, you will need to study Chapter 10 before attempting these scenario-based questions.

A methodical approach is required to calculate capital allowances. This can be an unnecessarily time-consuming area if such an approach is not adopted.

1 Introduction

Section overview

- Capital allowances give tax relief for expenditure on capital assets such as plant and machinery.

- Plant includes assets which perform an active function in a business and some other expenditure specified in legislation.

- Sole traders, partners and companies qualify for capital allowances on assets used in their businesses.

- The acquisition cost of an asset is usually the cost of the asset to the business.

- The disposal value of assets in the capital allowances computation cannot exceed original cost.

1.1 What are capital allowances?

This chapter covers the second step in computing taxable trading profits which is the calculation of capital allowances. These are deducted from the adjusted accounting profit as described in the previous chapter.

Capital allowances are tax allowances for certain types of capital expenditure. Depreciation on assets is not allowable for tax purposes. Instead, capital allowances give tax relief by allowing part of the cost of capital assets each year.

Capital allowances must be claimed by a taxpayer. A taxpayer may claim less than the full amount of the capital allowances, for example if trading profits are not sufficient to absorb the full allowances. This will mean that larger allowances will be available in future periods of account.

In your examination, you are only required to deal with one type of capital allowance which is the allowance for expenditure on plant and machinery.

Machinery includes all machines, motor vehicles and computers. Plant includes such things as office furniture and equipment.

The definition of plant can be problematic. In general, if an asset performs an active function in the business it is considered to be plant whereas if an asset is passive and merely part of the setting in which the business is carried on it does not qualify as plant.

This definition can cause difficulties with expenditure related to buildings. For example, moveable partitions are deemed to be plant since they perform an active function in the business whereas fixed partitions are not deemed to be plant since they are just part of the business setting.

There are also some types of expenditure which are specified in legislation as qualifying for capital allowances on plant and machinery. These include:

- Building alterations incidental to the installation of plant and machinery
- Licence to use computer software

1.2 Who is entitled to capital allowances?

Capital allowances are available to a taxable person who incurs capital expenditure on assets to be used for the purposes of a trade carried on by that person.

Taxable person here means a sole trader, a partner in a partnership, or a company. In this chapter, we will concentrate on trades carried on by a sole trader or a partnership.

It is important to remember that capital allowances for a sole trader or a partnership are calculated for each period of account, not for each tax year.

Companies are dealt with later in this text. Most of the rules in this chapter apply in a similar way for companies, but you will see that there are certain key differences. In particular, companies can never have a capital allowances computation for more than a 12-month period.

1.3 Acquisition cost

You will need to identify the acquisition cost of assets qualifying for capital allowances as the allowances will be based on this amount.

In most cases, you will simply be given a figure for the cost of the asset and will use this in your computation.

The owner may bring personally-owned assets into the business. This may happen when a business starts. Here, the acquisition cost for capital allowances is the market value of the asset when it is brought into the business.

1.4 Disposal value

You may also need to know the disposal value of an asset to work out capital allowances.

The general rule is that the disposal value is the sale proceeds of the asset. However, this cannot exceed the original cost of the asset.

If the asset is given away or sold for less than market value, the disposal value will be the market value on the date of disposal.

If the asset is scrapped or destroyed, the disposal value is the scrap value or the compensation received, as appropriate.

If a business ceases, a disposal value must be brought into the capital allowances calculation and balancing adjustments calculated (see later in this chapter). The disposal value will be the proceeds received or the scrap value (which may be nil). Note that no other allowances are given in the period a trade ceases.

1.5 Overview of capital allowances on plant and machinery

	FYA £	Main pool £	Each private use asset £	Allowances £
Per period of account				
TWDV b/f		X	X	
Acquisitions – low emission car	X			
FYA @ 100%	(X)			X
	—			
Acquisitions – ECA	X			
FYA @ 100%	(X)			X
	—			
Disposals		(X)		
Acquisitions (AIA)		X		
AIA		(X)		X
Acquisitions (non AIA & FYA) cars		X		
		‾X‾		
WDA @ 18%		(X)	(X)	X*
TWDV c/f		X	X	
Total allowances				‾X‾

* Only the business use percentage of the WDA on private use assets is taken to the capital allowances column.

AIA: annual investment allowance

FYA: first year allowance

Private use asset: used partly for non-business purposes by a sole trader or partner

2 Main pool: writing down allowances

Section overview

- Most expenditure on assets is pooled in the main pool.

- For each period of account, acquisition costs are added to the pool and disposal costs deducted from the pool.

- A writing down allowance (WDA) is given on the balance of the pool at the end of the period of account.

- The tax written down value (TWDV) of the pool is carried forward to the start of the next period of account.

2.1 Assets in the main pool

In most cases, capital allowances are not calculated for expenditure on a single asset, but on a pool of expenditure, ie on a number of assets. For each period of account, the cost of assets acquired is added to the pool and the value of any disposals deducted from the pool.

Expenditure on assets in the main pool includes:

- All machinery, fixtures and fittings and equipment

- Vans, forklift trucks, lorries, motorcycles

- Cars with CO_2 emissions of not more than 130g/km purchased on or after 6 April 2013 (1 April for companies) and those of not more than 160g/km purchased before 6 April 2013 (1 April for companies). The capital allowances available on expenditure on cars are summarised later in this Chapter.

2.2 Writing down allowance

A **writing down allowance** (WDA) is given on the balance of the main pool at the end of the period of account.

The WDA is a percentage of the pool balance for a period of account.

The WDA is currently 18% per annum.

If the period of account is not 12 months, the WDA is scaled up or down accordingly.

The WDA is claimed as a capital allowance and is deducted from the pool balance. The remainder of the value of the pool is then carried forward to the start of the next period of account. This amount is called the **tax written down value** (TWDV). It continues to be written down on a reducing balance basis.

Certain assets are pooled in a 'special rate pool' and receive a WDA at a lower rate. These are not within your syllabus.

Worked example: Writing down allowances

Trump started in business on 1 June 2014. He decided to make up his accounts to 31 December each year. He makes the following acquisitions:

1.6.14   Brings Volvo car into business, market value £5,500 (actual cost two years ago £7,000) with CO_2 emissions of 125 g/km

1.9.14   Buys Nissan car costing £6,500, with CO_2 emissions of 123g/km

He makes the following disposals:

1.9.15   Sells Volvo for £4,000

1.11.15   Nissan car is involved in an accident and is scrapped. Trump receives compensation of £250.

Neither car is used for Trump's non-business journeys and neither car is a qualifying low emission car.

Requirement

Show the maximum capital allowances available for Trump's first two periods of account.

Solution

	Main pool £	Allowances £
Period of account – 1.6.14 to 31.12.14 (7 months)		
Acquisitions		
1.6.14 Volvo (MV)	5,500	
1.9.14 Nissan	6,500	
	12,000	
No disposals		
WDA: £12,000 × 18% × 7/12 (time apportioned for 7 month period)	(1,260)	1,260
TWDV c/f	10,740	
Period of account – 1.1.15 to 31.12.15 (12 months)		
Acquisitions		
No acquisitions		
Disposals		
1.9.15 Volvo	(4,000)	
1.11.15 Nissan (scrap proceeds)	(250)	
	6,490	
WDA £6,490 × 18%	(1,168)	1,168
TWDV c/f	5,322	

3 Main pool: first year allowances

Section overview

- First year allowances (FYAs) may be given in the period of account in which expenditure is incurred.

- All businesses may claim a 100% FYA on certain energy-saving expenditure, low emission cars and zero emission goods vehicles.

3.1 What are first year allowances?

As its name suggests, a first year allowance (FYA) is given in the period of account in which the expenditure is incurred.

A FYA is always available in full, regardless of the length of the period of account. Where the full 100% FYA is claimed, there are no further WDAs on such expenditure.

3.2 100% first year allowances

There is a 100% FYA for expenditure on new and unused zero emission goods vehicles where expenditure is incurred on or after 6 April 2010 (1 April for companies).

There is also a 100% FYA for expenditure on designated energy saving technologies, such as equipment that generates heat and power.

In addition, a 100% FYA applies to expenditure on new qualifying low emission cars. To qualify as a low emission car it must be electrically propelled or emit not more than:

- 75g/km of CO_2 for cars purchased on or after 1 April 2015
- 95g/km of CO_2 for cars purchased on or after 1 April 2013
- 110g/km of CO_2 for cars purchased before 1 April 2013

The capital allowances available for cars generally are summarised later in this Chapter.

3.3 Disposal of assets attracting first year allowances

In the year of disposal of an asset previously qualifying for first year allowances, or in the accounting period of cessation, the disposal proceeds (limited to cost) must be deducted from the relevant pool.

4 Annual investment allowance

Section overview

- An annual investment allowance (AIA) is available for expenditure on plant and machinery, except cars.

- The AIA is given for a 12 month period of account. From 6 April 2014 (1 April 2014 for companies) until 31 December 2015 the AIA is £500,000 for a 12-month period.

- Any balance of expenditure in excess of the AIA receives a WDA at the end of the accounting period.

4.1 Annual Investment Allowance

An Annual Investment Allowance (AIA) is available to a sole trader, partnership or company. It can be used against qualifying expenditure, which includes most plant and machinery, except cars.

The maximum allowance is £500,000 per annum for expenditure incurred on or after 6 April 2014 (1 April 2014 for companies) and until 31 December 2015. It must be set against expenditure in the accounting period in which it is incurred.

For accounting periods ending after 31 December 2015, the AIA available may vary because the maximum allowance from 1 January 2016 onwards is subject to change. For your exam, in questions involving the AIA, accounting periods will end on or before 31 December 2015. You will therefore only need to deal with the maximum allowance of £500,000.

For accounting periods which are not 12 months long, the maximum AIA is scaled up or down accordingly.

Any balance of expenditure incurred within an accounting period on which the AIA is not given is eligible for a WDA.

Worked example: Annual investment allowance

Jose has been trading for many years and makes up accounts to 31 December each year. His capital allowances pool brought forward at 1 January 2015 is £6,560. He makes the following acquistions and disposals:

1.6.15	Sells for £480 plant which cost £900 two years earlier
24.8.15	Buys a printing press for £40,000

Requirement

What are the maximum capital allowances available to Jose for the year ended 31 December 2015?

Solution

	Main pool	Allowances
Period of account – Year ended 31 December 2015	£	£
TWDV b/f	6,560	
Acquisitions		
24.8.15 Press	40,000	
Less AIA	(40,000)	40,000
Disposals		
1.6.15 Plant	(480)	
	6,080	
WDA @ 18%	(1,094)	1,094
TWDV c/f	4,986	41,094

Interactive question 1: Annual investment allowance   [Difficulty level: Exam standard]

Wolfgang commences to trade on 1 January 2015 and draws up accounts to 31 December each year. During his first year to 31 December 2015, he incurs the following expenditure:

6.4.15	Machinery	£512,000
6.7.15	Car with emissions of 53g/km	£8,000
31.10.15	Car with emissions of 125g/km	£10,500

Requirement

Using the standard format below, compute the maximum capital allowances available to Wolfgang for the year ended 31 December 2015.

	FYA £	Main pool £	Allowances £
Period of Account year ended....			
Acquisitions (FYA): FYA	8,000 (8,000)		8,000
	0		
Acquisitions (AIA): AIA		512,000 (500,000)	500,000
Acquisitions (non AIA or FYA):		10,500 22,500	
WDA	0	(4050)	4050
TWDV c/f	0	18450	
Total allowances	0	18450	512,050

See **Answer** at the end of this chapter.

5 Small plant and machinery pools

Section overview

- Businesses may write off small balances remaining at the end of the accounting period in the main pool.

- This applies where the tax written down value at the end of the accounting period is £1,000 or less.

- The £1,000 limit is scaled up or down for long or short accounting periods.

5.1 WDA for small pools

If the balance on the main pool is less than the small pool limit at the end of the accounting period, a WDA can be claimed up to the value of the small pool limit. This means that the main pool may be written down to nil, rather than a small balance being carried forward on which allowances have to be claimed each year.

The small pool limit is £1,000 for a 12-month period of account. It is available to businesses of any size – sole traders, partnerships and companies. The write-off does not apply to single-asset pools for private-use assets (see next section).

The £1,000 limit is scaled up or down where the period of account is not 12 months.

6 Cars and assets with private use

Section overview

- There are special rules for capital allowances on cars.

- Some assets, including some cars, are not put in the main pool but have a separate pool for each asset.

- This applies to assets with private use by the sole trader or partner.

6.1 Cars

The treatment of cars depends on when they were purchased and their level of CO_2 emissions.

If the car is one with private use by a sole trader or partner it goes into a single asset pool, however the allowances received are based on the emissions of the car (see below).

Cars are not eligible for the annual investment allowance.

Cars in the main pool which are not low emission cars receive a WDA of 18% per annum:

Date of acquisition	Main Pool
6 April 2009 to 5 April 2013 (1 April 2009 to 31 March 2013 for companies)	≤ 160g/km
6 April 2013 onwards (1 April 2013 onwards for companies)	≤ 130g/km

Cars which are treated as low emission cars receive a FYA of 100% instead of a WDA of 18%:

Date of acquisition	Low Emission Car
1 April 2009 to 31 March 2013	≤ 110g/km
1 April 2013 to 31 March 2015	≤ 95g/km
On or after 1 April 2015	≤ 75g/km

The rules applying to cars purchased before April 2009 are not within your syllabus.

Worked example: Cars

Gordon prepares accounts to 31 March each year. He had a main pool balance of £7,600 brought forward at 1 April 2015. He made purchases during May 2015 as follows:

Toyota car – emissions 130g/km, business use only £16,000
Honda car – emissions 65g/km, business use only £10,300

Requirement

What are the maximum capital allowances available to Gordon for the year ended 31 March 2016?

Solution

	Main pool £	Allowances £
Period of account		
Year ended 31.3.16		
TWDV b/f	7,600	
Acquisitions		
Car – 65g/km (100% FYA)	10,300	
FYA	(10,300)	10,300
Car – 130g/km (main pool, no FYA)	16,000	
	23,600	
WDA @ 18%	(4,248)	4,248
TWDV c/f	19,352	
Total allowances		14,548

6.2 Assets with private use by sole trader or partner

Any asset that is partly used privately by a sole trader or partner is kept in a separate pool. The AIA or FYA where applicable, or otherwise the WDA, is still calculated in full and deducted from the single asset pool, but the trader can only claim the business element of the allowance.

Worked example: Assets with private use

Jasper has been in business for many years making up accounts to 30 April each year. The only asset he owns for capital allowances purposes is computer equipment which he uses 20% privately and which has a tax written down value at 1 May 2015 of £2,000.

On 1 August 2015, he buys a car with CO_2 emissions of 122g/km for £16,000 which he uses 30% privately.

Requirement

What are the maximum capital allowances that Jasper can claim for the year to 30 April 2016?

Solution

	Computer £	Car £	Allowances £
Period of account			
Year ended 30.4.16			
TWDV b/f	2,000		
Acquisition (no FYA or AIA)		16,000	
WDA @ 18%	(360) × 80%		288
WDA @ 18%		(2,880) × 70%	2,016
TWDVs c/f	1,640	13,120	
Allowances			2,304

Interactive question 2: Assets with private use [Difficulty level: Exam standard]

Jolene started trading on 1 July 2015. Her first set of accounts were made up to 31 March 2016.

On 1 December 2015, Jolene purchased a car with CO_2 emissions of 125g/km for £21,000 which she uses 70% for business purposes.

Requirement

Using the standard format below, compute the maximum capital allowance for Jolene for the period ended 31 March 2016.

	Car £	Allowances £
Period of account .....01/07/15...... to ....31/03/16....		
Acquisition	21,000	
WDA	(2835) × 70 %	1985
TWDV c/f	~~19018~~ 18165	
Allowances		1985

See **Answer** at the end of this chapter.

The rules above apply only to assets purchased and used by owners of unincorporated businesses. Private use by an employee does not restrict the allowances available.

Companies are dealt with later in this text. You will see that there are no private-use restrictions for companies where assets are used partly for private purposes.

7 Balancing adjustments

Section overview
- A balancing charge arises on disposal if too many capital allowances have been given.
- A balancing allowance arises on disposal if too few capital allowances have been given.

7.1 Balancing charge

If too many capital allowances have been given on an asset over its lifetime, a balancing charge arises. This might happen if an asset is sold for an amount in excess of its tax written down value.

The balancing charge will be taxed either by using it to reduce the capital allowances in the period of account or by adding it to the adjusted trading profits computation.

If the asset is one with private use, only the business use element is actually chargeable.

A balancing charge can occur on the main pool and on single asset pools even when the trade has not ceased.

7.2 Balancing allowance

If too few capital allowances have been given on an asset over its lifetime, a balancing allowance may arise. This might happen if an asset is sold for an amount less than its tax written down value.

The balancing allowance will be added to the capital allowances otherwise available for the period of account.

If the asset is one with private use, only the business use element is allowable as for all capital allowances.

A balancing allowance can only arise on the main pool if the business comes to an end. Balancing allowances can arise on single asset pools when the asset is sold, even when the business has not ended.

Capital allowances 133

Remember that in the period a trade ceases, no AIAs, FYAs or WDAs are given, only balancing adjustments.

Worked example: Balancing adjustments

Philip has carried on a trade for many years making up accounts to 31 March.

At 1 April 2015, Philip had a main pool with a tax written down value of £6,250, and a Ford car with 20% private use with a tax written down value of £10,000.

On 1 December 2015, Philip sold office equipment for £7,200 (original cost £10,000).

On 1 February 2016, Philip sold his Ford for £7,500. On the same day Philip bought an Audi car with CO_2 emissions of 125g/km for £17,500. The Audi also has 20% private use.

Requirement

What are the maximum capital allowances available to Philip for the year ended 31 March 2016?

Solution

	Main pool £	Ford £	Audi £	Allowances £
Period of account				
Year ended 31.3.16				
TWDV b/f	6,250	10,000		
Acquisition (no AIA or FYA)				
1.2.16			17,500	
Disposals				
1.12.15	(7,200)			
	(950)			
Balancing charge	950			(950)
	——			
1.2.16		(7,500)		
		2,500		
Balancing allowance		(2,500) × 80%		2,000
		——		
WDA @ 18%			(3,150) × 80%	2,520
TWDV c/f			14,350	
Allowances				3,570

If the balancing charge had exceeded the allowances, the excess charge would have been added to the adjusted trade profit for the year.

Summary and Self-test

Summary

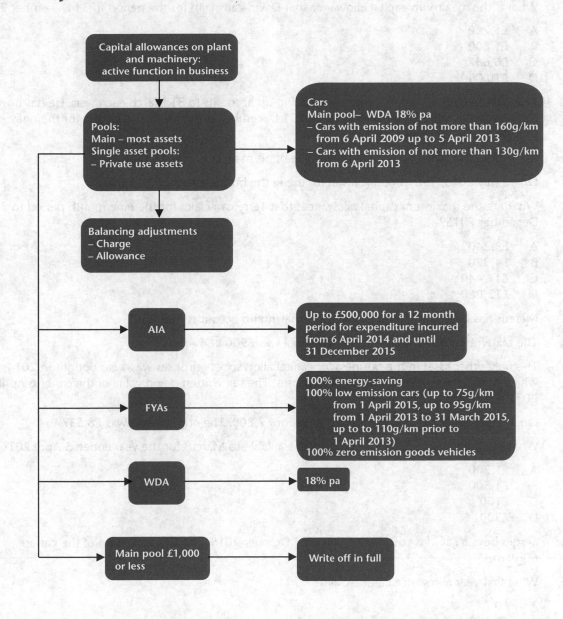

Capital allowances on plant and machinery: active function in business

Pools:
Main – most assets
Single asset pools:
– Private use assets

Cars
Main pool– WDA 18% pa
– Cars with emission of not more than 160g/km from 6 April 2009 up to 5 April 2013
– Cars with emission of not more than 130g/km from 6 April 2013

Balancing adjustments
– Charge
– Allowance

AIA
Up to £500,000 for a 12 month period for expenditure incurred from 6 April 2014 and until 31 December 2015

FYAs
100% energy-saving
100% low emission cars (up to 75g/km from 1 April 2015, up to 95g/km from 1 April 2013 to 31 March 2015, up to to 110g/km prior to 1 April 2013)
100% zero emission goods vehicles

WDA
18% pa

Main pool £1,000 or less
Write off in full

Self-test

Answer the following questions.

1   David began trading on 1 May 2015. On that date he brought a car into the business (business use only) valued at £10,000. The car has CO_2 emissions of 128g/km

David made up his first accounts to 31 December 2015.

What is the maximum capital allowance that David can claim for the period to 31 December 2015?

A   £1,200
B   £1,800
C   £6,667
D   £10,000

2   Terry has been trading for many years making up accounts to 31 March each year. He has however decided to change his accounting date to 31 December and makes up accounts for the nine months to 31 December 2015.

At 1 April 2015, the tax written down value of his main pool was £8,000.

On 12 July 2015, Terry bought a van for use in the business costing £16,000.

What are the maximum capital allowances that Terry can claim for the nine month period to 31 December 2015?

A   £3,240
B   £4,320
C   £17,440
D   £17,080

3   Marcus has been trading for many years, making up accounts to 5 April.

The tax written down value of the main pool was £900 at 6 April 2015.

The only other asset in the business for capital allowances purposes was a car bought in 2014, which Marcus uses 75% for business purposes. The tax written down value of the car at 6 April 2015 was £7,000.

On 1 September 2015 Marcus sold the car for £7,800. The original cost was £8,537.

What are the maximum capital allowances available to Marcus for the year ended 5 April 2016?

A   £1,700
B   £1,500
C   £100
D   £300

4   Sergio buys a car at a cost of £14,000 on 7 October 2015. The CO_2 emissions of the car are 60g/km.

What first year allowance can he claim?

A   £0
B   £1,120
C   £2,520
D   £14,000

5   Nadia starts trading on 1 January 2015. On 1 November 2015 she buys a single item of machinery for £514,000.

What is the maximum capital allowance Nadia can claim for the year ended 31 December 2015?

A   £92,520
B   £514,000
C   £500,000
D   £502,520

6   Aimee starts trading on 1 April 2015. On 1 July 2015 she buys a single item of plant for £400,000.

What is the maximum capital allowance Aimee can claim for the nine months to 31 December 2015?

A   £400,000
B   £375,000
C   £379,500
D   £378,375

7   Jacob has been trading for many years,, making up accounts to 31 December.

Jacob had tax written down values at 1 January 2015 of:

Main pool	£11,800
Car (purchased 2011 with CO_2 emissions of 135g/km – 40% private use by Jacob)	£14,000

On 15 May 2015 Jacob purchased a car for 50% business, 50% private use by an employee, with CO_2 emissions of 125g/km at a cost of £7,600.

What are the maximum capital allowances that Jacob can claim for the year to 31 December 2015?

A   £4,244
B   £5,004
C   £6,012
D   £11,236

Now go back to the Learning objective in the Introduction. If you are satisfied you have achieved this objectives, please tick it off.

Technical reference

Legislation

References relate to Capital Allowances Act 2001 (*CAA 2001*)

Qualifying activities	ss.15 – 20
Qualifying expenditure: general	ss.21 – 38
Qualifying expenditure: first year allowances	ss.39 – 49
Pooling	ss.53 – 54
Writing down allowances	s.55
First year allowances	s.52
Main rate cars	s.104AA
Private use assets	ss.205 – 208
Balancing adjustments	s.56
Annual investment allowance	ss.38A – 38B
	ss.1A – 1N
Small pools	s.56A

HMRC manual

Capital allowances manual (Found at http://www.hmrc.gov.uk/manuals/camanual/index.htm)

Plant and machinery allowances (PMAs): Introduction: Outline	CA20006
General: Definitions: Chargeable period, accounting period and period of account	CA11510
PMA: FYA: Expenditure on which available and rates	CA23110

This technical reference section is designed to assist you. It should help you to know where to look for further information on the topics covered in this chapter. **You will not be examined on the contents of this section in your examination.**

Answers to Interactive questions

Answer to Interactive question 1

	FYA £	Main pool £	Allowances £
Period of account			
Year ended 31 December 2015			
Acquisitions (FYA)			
6.7.15 car (< 75g/km)	8,000		
FYA @ 100%	(8,000)		8,000
	–		
Acquisitions (AIA)			
6.4.15 Machinery		512,000	
AIA		(500,000)	500,000
Acquisitions (non AIA or FYA)			
31.10.15 car		10,500	
		22,500	
WDA @ 18%		(4,050)	4,050
TWDV c/f		18,450	
Total allowances			512,050

Answer to Interactive question 2

	Car £	Allowances £
Period of account		
1 July 2015 to 31 March 2016 (9 months)		
Acquisitions	21,000	
WDA @ 18% × 9/12	(2,835) × 70%	1,985
TWDV c/f	18,165	
Allowances		1,985

Answers to Self-test

1   A – £1,200

	Main pool £	Allowances £
Period of account		
1 May 2015 to 31 December 2015 (eight months)		
1 May 2015 Acquisition	10,000	
WDA: 18% × 8/12	(1,200)	1,200
TWDV c/f	8,800	
Allowances		1,200

2   D – £17,080

	Main pool £	Allowances £
Period of account		
1 April 2015 to 31 December 2015		
TWDV b/f	8,000	
Acquisition (AIA)		
12 July 2015 Van	16,000	
AIA	(16,000)	16,000
WDA @ 18% × $\dfrac{9}{12}$	(1,080)	1,080
TWDV c/f	6,920	
Allowances		17,080

3   D – £300

	Main pool £	Car £	Allowances £
Period of account			
6 April 2015 to 5 April 2016			
TWDV b/f	900	7,000	
Disposal			
1 September 2015		(7,800)	
Balancing charge		(800) × 75%	(600)
WDA ≤ £1,000 (note)	(900)		900
TWDV c/f	0		
Allowances			300

Note: The pool is written off in full as it does not exceed £1,000

4   D – £14,000

The car is a qualifying low emission car (CO_2 emissions 75g/km or less). 100% FYA for such cars.

5   D – £502,520

	£
AIA in full	500,000
WDA (£514,000 – £500,000) @ 18%	2,520
Total capital allowance	502,520

6   D – £378,375

9 month period of account.

AIA and WDA are pro rated for short period of account. (Note though that a FYA is never pro rated.)

	£
AIA in full (£500,000 × 9/12)	375,000
WDA (400,000 – 375,000) × 18% × 9/12	3,375
Total capital allowance	378,375

7   B – £5,004

	Main pool £	Car £	Allowances £
Period of account			
Year ended 31 December 2015			
TWDV b/f	11,800	14,000	
Acquisition – car (no FYA or AIA)	7,600		
	19,400		
WDA @ 18% (employee private use ignored)	(3,492)		3,492
WDA @ 18% (restricted for Jacob's private use)		(2,520) × 60%	1,512
	15,908	11,480	
			5,004

Principles of Taxation

CHAPTER 7

Trading profits – basis of assessment

Introduction

Examination context

Topic List

    1   Current year basis

    2   Opening years

    3   Overlap profits

    4   Closing years

    5   Partnerships

    6   Cash basis for small businesses

Summary and Self-test

Technical reference

Answers to Interactive questions

Answers to Self-test

Learning objectives

- Calculate the assessable trading profits for a new unincorporated business and identify the overlap profits on the commencement of trade ☐

- Calculate the assessable trading profits for a continuing business ☐

- Calculate the final assessable trading profits for an unincorporated business ceasing to trade ☐

- Allocate the tax-adjusted profits of a partnership to each partner and calculate the final assessable profits for each partner for any given tax year ☐

- Calculate the adjusted trading profits of a sole trader or partnership using the cash basis of accounting ☐

Specific syllabus references for this chapter are: 3e, 3f, g, h, i.

Syllabus links

The topics covered in this chapter are very important to your knowledge of how an unincorporated business is taxed.

When you tackle the Tax Compliance paper later on in the Professional Level, you will be expected to be very familiar with the concepts in this chapter.

Examination context

In the examination, in the objective test questions, candidates may be required to:

- Correctly apply the current year basis for taxing trading profits

- Calculate the taxable trading profits in the opening years of a business, including overlap profits

- Determine the taxable trading profits in the final tax year of a business

- Understand how partnership profits are allocated to individual partners and are taxed on them individually

- Determine taxable trading profits using the cash basis of accounting

For extra question practice on these topics go to the section of the Question Bank covering this chapter.

A significant amount of practice is required by candidates in order to be able to deal efficiently with opening year rules for sole traders and partnerships.

1 Current year basis

Section overview

- Rules are needed to link a period of account of an unincorporated business to a tax year.

- Under the current year basis, the basis period for the tax year is the 12-month period of account ending in that tax year.

1.1 Basis periods and tax years

In the previous two chapters, you learned how to calculate the taxable trading profits of an unincorporated business. In this chapter you will learn how the taxable trading profits for a period of account are taxed in a particular tax year.

The tax year runs from 6 April to 5 April. Many businesses do not have periods of account ending on 5 April. Rules are needed to link a period of account of a business with a tax year to find the amount of taxable trading profits for that year. The period which is taxable in a particular tax year is called a **basis period** because it is the basis of assessment for that tax year.

The basic rule is called the **current year basis** (CYB). Under the current year basis, the basis period for the tax year is the taxable trading profits for **the 12-month period of account ending in that tax year**.

Worked example: Basis period

Sasha has been trading for many years, making up accounts to 31 December each year.

Her recent taxable trading profits have been as follows:

y/e 31 December 2014	£12,000
y/e 31 December 2015	£15,000

Requirement

What is the amount of taxable trading profit assessable in 2015/16?

Solution

The basis period for 2015/16 is the period of account ending 31 December 2015.

Sasha's taxable trading profit for 2015/16 is therefore   £15,000

2 Opening years

Section overview

- Special rules are needed in the opening years of a business.

- In the first tax year, the actual basis applies.

- In the second tax year, the basis period depends on the length of any period of account ending in that tax year.

- By the third tax year, the current year basis usually applies.

2.1 Introduction

Special rules are needed for the opening years of a business. This is because there will not usually be a 12-month period of account ending in the tax year in which the business starts.

For example, a business may start on 1 July 2015, preparing accounts to 30 June 2016. The first tax year in which the business operates is 2015/16, as this is the tax year in which the date of commencement falls, but there is no 12-month period of account ending in that tax year.

The opening year rules ensure that there is an amount of taxable trading profit for each tax year that the business is trading.

2.2 First tax year

The basis of assessment in the first tax year that a business operates is the **actual basis**. This means that the taxable trading profits for the first tax year are the taxable trading profits of the business from the date of commencement **to the following 5 April**.

It will usually be necessary to time apportion the taxable trading profits in the first (and sometimes the second) period of account to find this amount. For examination purposes, time apportionment should be made to the nearest month. In practice, apportionment is made on a daily basis.

Worked example: First tax year

Ahmed started trading on 1 October 2015. He decided to make up his accounts to 30 September each year and his results to 30 September 2016 show taxable trading profits of £18,000.

Requirement

What is the amount of taxable trading profit taxed in 2015/16?

Solution

The first tax year is 2015/16 as 1 October 2015 falls within this tax year.

The basis period runs from 1 October 2015 to 5 April 2016 (six months).

The taxable trading profit taxed in 2015/16 is therefore £18,000 x 6/12 =   £9,000

2.3 Second tax year

The basis of assessment in the second tax year depends on the length of the period of account ending in the second tax year. There are four possibilities:

Period of account ending in tax year	Basis period
Less than 12 months long	First 12 months of trading
12 months long	That 12-month period of account
More than 12 months long	12 months to the end of the period of account ending in the second tax year
No such period of account	Actual basis (6 April to 5 April)

Worked example: Second tax year

Ernest started trading on 1 January 2015. He decided to make up accounts to 31 December. His taxable trading profit for the period of account for the year ended 31 December 2015 is £12,000.

Requirement

What are the amounts of taxable trading profits taxed in the first two tax years of trading?

Solution

First tax year (2014/15)
Actual basis
Basis period 1 January 2015 to 5 April 2015
$3/12 \times £12,000$ **£3,000**

Second tax year (2015/16)
12-month period of account ending in 2ⁿᵈ tax year
Basis period 1 January 2015 to 31 December 2015
y/e 31 December 2015   **£12,000**

Interactive question 1: First and second tax years   [Difficulty level: Exam standard]

Scott started trading on 1 November 2014. He decided to make up his accounts to 31 July. His taxable trading profit for the 9-month period of account to 31 July 2015 is £18,000 and for the year ended 31 July 2016 is £48,000.

Requirement

Using the standard format below, compute the amounts of taxable trading profit taxed in the first two tax years of trading.

First tax year (20...../.....)

Basis period .... to ....

     £ _____

Second tax year (20...../.....)

Basis period .... to ....

     £ _____

See the **Answer** at the end of this chapter.

2.4 Third tax year

Usually, the current year basis applies to the third tax year of trading because there will be a 12-month period of account ending in that tax year.

Occasionally, there will not be a 12-month period of account ending in the third tax year. In this case the basis period will be the 12 months to the end of the period of account ending in the third tax year.

Worked example: Third tax year

Sergio started trading on 1 February 2014. He decided to make up his accounts to 30 April each year.

Sergio has taxable trading profits of £30,000 for the 15-month period ended 30 April 2015 and £12,000 for the year ended 30 April 2016.

Requirement

What are the amounts of taxable trading profits taxed in the first three tax years of trading?

Solution

First tax year (2013/14)
Actual basis
Basis period 1 February 2014 to 5 April 2014
2/15 × £30,000   **£4,000**

Second tax year (2014/15)
No period of account ending in 2nd tax year
Basis period 6 April 2014 to 5 April 2015
12/15 × £30,000   **£24,000**

Third tax year (2015/16)
Period of account ending in 3rd tax year more than 12 months
Basis period 1 May 2014 to 30 April 2015
12/15 × £30,000   **£24,000**

3 Overlap profits

Section overview

- The application of the opening year rules means that some taxable trading profits may be taxed twice.
- Such profits are called overlap profits.

3.1 Overlap profits

You may have noticed that the way the opening year rules apply means that some taxable trading profit is taxed in more than one tax year.

Choosing a period of account which ends on a date other than 5 April will result in this double counting and any trading profits taxed more than once are called **overlap profits**.

Overlap profits are carried forward to be relieved in the future, as we will see later in this chapter.

Worked example: Overlap profits

Maureen starts trading on 1 June 2014. She decides to make up accounts to 31 July.

For the 14-month period of account ended 31 July 2015, her taxable trading profit is £20,160.

Requirement

What amounts of taxable trading profits are taxed in the first two tax years of trading and what is the amount of overlap profits?

Solution

First tax year (2014/15)
Actual basis
Basis period 1 June 2014 to 5 April 2015
10/14 × £20,160   **£14,400**

Second tax year (2015/16)
Period of account in 2nd tax year exceeds 12 months
Basis period 1 August 2014 to 31 July 2015
12/14 × £20,160   **£17,280**

Overlap profits
Period of overlap 1 August 2014 to 5 April 2015
Overlap profits
8/14 × £20,160   **£11,520**

Interactive question 2: Opening years   [Difficulty level: Exam standard]

Connie starts a trade on 1 January 2014 and has the following taxable trading profits:

6 months to 30 June 2014	£28,500
12 months to 30 June 2015	£48,000

Requirement

Using the standard format below, show the amounts of taxable trading profits taxed in the first three tax years of trading and the amount of overlap profits.

First tax year (20......./.......)

Basis period .... to ....

£ _____

Second tax year (20......./.......)

Basis period .... to ....

£ _____

Third tax year (20...../.....)

Basis period .... to ....

£ _____

Overlap profits
Period of overlap............. to .... and .... to ....
Overlap profits

£ _____

See the **Answer** at the end of this chapter.

4 Closing years

Section overview

- The final tax year is the tax year in which the business ceases to trade.

- The basis period for the final tax year is from the end of the basis period for the previous tax year to the date of cessation.

- Any overlap profits are deducted from taxable trading profits in the final tax year.

4.1 Final tax year

The final tax year for a business is the tax year in which the business ceases to trade, ie the tax year in which the date of cessation of trade falls.

The basis period for the final tax year is from the end of the basis period for the penultimate tax year to the date of cessation. Different rules apply if a business ceases within the first two tax years of trading, but these are not in the syllabus.

Worked example: Final tax year

Darren started trading on 1 May 2012. He chose to make up his accounts to 31 December each year. He had taxable trading profits of £10,000 for the year ended 31 December 2014.

Darren ceased trading on 30 November 2015. His final accounting period was the 11 months to 30 November 2015 and his taxable trading profits for that period were £6,000.

Requirement

What amounts of taxable trading profits are taxed in the final two tax years of trading?

Solution

Final tax year (2015/16)
End of previous basis period to cessation = Basis period 1 January 2015 to 30 November 2015
11 month p/e 30 November 2015   £6,000

Penultimate tax year (2014/15)
CYB = Basis period 1 January 2014 to 31 December 2014
y/e 31 December 2014   £10,000

4.2 Penultimate tax year

Usually, the current year basis will apply to the penultimate tax year (ie 12-month period of account ending in the penultimate tax year).

If the final period of account exceeds 12 months, there may be no period of account ending in the penultimate tax year. In this case, the basis period for the penultimate tax year will be the 12 months to the normal year-end date falling in that tax year.

4.3 Relief for overlap profits

Overlap profits arising in the opening years are deducted from the taxable trading profits in the final tax year.

Interactive question 3: Opening and closing years   [Difficulty level: Exam standard]

Ian started trading on 1 August 2011. He chose to make up his accounts to 31 May each year.

Ian had the following taxable trading profits:

10 months to 31 May 2012	£24,000
y/e 31 May 2013	£31,000
y/e 31 May 2014	£44,000

Ian's business ceased on 30 April 2015. His taxable trading profits for the last eleven months of the business were £38,000.

Requirement

Using the standard format below, show the amounts of taxable trading profits taxed in all tax years.

First tax year (20...../.......)
Basis period .... to ....

                                                                                    £_____

Second tax year (20...../.......)
Basis period .... to ....

                                                                                    £_____

Third tax year (20...../......)
Basis period .... to ....

                                                                                    £_____

Overlap profits
Period of overlap .... to .... and .... to ....
Overlap profits

                                                                                    £_____

Penultimate tax year (20...../........)
Basis period .... to ....

                                                                                    £_____

Final tax year (20...../.....)
Basis period .... to ....
Less: overlap profits

                                                                                    £_____

See the **Answer** at the end of this chapter.

---

5 Partnerships

Section overview

- A partnership itself is not a taxable person.
- Each partner is liable to income tax on his share (and only his share) of the partnership's taxable trading profits.
- The current year basis applies to continuing partnerships.
- Opening and closing year rules apply to partners who join and leave the partnership but the continuing partners remain on the current year basis.

5.1 How partners are taxed

A partnership is a collection of one or more individuals carrying on a business with a view to profit. Usually, partnerships are based on unlimited liability of the partners. It is also possible to form a limited liability partnership (LLP). Both types of partnership are taxed in the same way.

The partnership itself is not a taxable person for income tax purposes. Instead, the partners will be liable to tax on their individual shares of the taxable trading profits of the partnership on the same basis as a sole trader. Therefore, for a continuing partnership, the basis of assessment for a tax year will be the current year basis. Opening and closing year rules also apply to each partner.

The partnership accounts will be produced in a similar way to those for a sole trader. As for a sole trader, adjustments will need to be made to the accounting profit and capital allowances deducted to produce a figure for taxable trading profits. In this section we will see how that figure is then divided between the partners to calculate the taxable trading profit taxable on each partner.

5.2 Allocation of partnership profits

The taxable trading profits of the partnership are allocated between the partners according to the profit-sharing agreement for the period of account.

The agreement may specify that one or more of the partners is entitled to a 'salary' (in fact, simply an allocation of profits) and/or interest on capital introduced into the partnership. These amounts should be allocated first and then the remaining amount of taxable trading profits should be allocated in accordance with the agreed profit-sharing ratio (PSR).

After allocation, assessments are calculated for the partners using the same rules as for sole traders.

Worked example: Partnership

Erin and Cassandra have been in partnership for several years. The taxable trading profit of the partnership for the year ending 31 March 2016 is £55,000.

The profit-sharing agreement for the partnership provides for Erin to be paid a salary of £10,000 a year and Cassandra to be paid a salary of £15,000 a year. Any remaining profits are divided between Erin and Cassandra in the ratio 2:1.

Requirement

What is the taxable trading profit for Erin and Cassandra for 2015/16?

Solution

	Total £	Erin £	Cassandra £
Salary	25,000	10,000	15,000
Balance 2:1	30,000	20,000	10,000
Totals	55,000	30,000	25,000

For the year ended 31 March 2016 Erin has taxable trading profits of £30,000 and Cassandra has taxable trading profits of £25,000. As the partnership is not new this will be taxed on each partner on a CYB in 2015/16.

You need to be particularly careful where there is a change in the profit-sharing agreement during the period of account. The best way of tackling such questions is to divide the period of account into the periods of the different profit-sharing agreements. Make sure that you time-apportion any salaries and interest on capital as appropriate.

Interactive question 4: Partnership profit allocation   [Difficulty level: Exam standard]

Calder, Scott and Tim have been in partnership for several years. Partnership accounts are made up to 31 May. The partnership had taxable trading profits of £136,000 for the year ended 31 May 2015.

Until 30 September 2014, the partnership had shared profits equally. From 1 October 2014 it was agreed that the partners should be paid a salary and the profit-sharing ratio (PSR) was amended as follows:

	Calder	Scott	Tim
Salary per year	£50,000	£40,000	£30,000
PSR	25%	35%	40%

Requirement

Using the standard format below, compute the amount of taxable trading profit for each partner in 2015/16.

	Total £	Calder £	Scott £	Tim £
First PSR period				
.... to				
PSR				
Second PSR period				
.... to				
Salaries				
PSR				
Totals				

See the **Answer** at the end of this chapter.

6 Cash basis for small businesses

Section overview

- Unincorporated businesses whose receipts for the tax year do not exceed the relevant threshold may elect to use the cash basis when calculating their taxable trading income.

- The profit per the accounts must still be adjusted for tax purposes. The main differences between cash basis and accruals accounting relate to capital expenditure and interest payments.

- The basis of assessment rules which determine in which tax year the profits of an accounting period are taxed apply in the same way as for accruals accounting traders.

6.1 Introduction

Certain small unincorporated businesses may elect to use the cash basis rather than accruals accounting for the purposes of calculating their taxable trading income.

The cash basis is intended to simplify the tax reporting system for many small businesses who do not need to prepare accruals-based accounts in order to effectively manage their business.

Under the cash basis, a business is taxed on its cash receipts less any cash payments of allowable expenses.

In the exam you will be told if a business is using the cash basis. If so, unless told otherwise, you should assume that the business has also used a cash basis for its financial accounts.

6.2 Which businesses can use the cash basis?

The cash basis can only be used by unincorporated businesses (sole traders and partnerships) with receipts for the tax year that do not exceed the VAT registration threshold (currently £82,000). The limit is increased to twice the VAT registration limit (£164,000) for recipients of Universal Credit.

A trader must leave the scheme if his receipts in the previous tax year exceeded twice the VAT registration threshold for that previous year and receipts for the current year exceed the VAT registration threshold for the current year (currently £82,000).

A trader may leave the scheme if his 'commercial circumstances' change such that the scheme is no longer appropriate for him (see below).

The above limits are proportionately reduced for accounting periods of less than 12 months.

The combined receipts of all the trader's businesses must be considered in deciding whether a trader can use the scheme.

Companies are specifically excluded from using the cash basis.

6.3 Calculation of taxable profits

The taxable trading profits are calculated as:

Total cash receipts less total allowable business expenses paid

subject to adjustments required by tax law.

As we saw earlier in this text for accruals accounting traders, the starting point for calculating the taxable profit is the net profit per the accounts. A number of adjustments to this net profit are then required for tax purposes.

The same approach applies when using the cash basis. Many of the tax adjustments are the same as for accruals accounting, eg expenditure not wholly and exclusively for the purposes of the business is still a disallowable expense.

There are however a number of differences. The main special rules which only apply to the cash basis relate to:

- Capital expenditure
- Interest paid

These are covered below.

6.3.1 Taxable receipts

Taxable receipts include all amounts received including cash, card receipts, cheques and payments in kind. They also include amounts received from the sale of plant and machinery (but not cars) which qualify for capital allowances.

As for accruals accounting traders, the net profit per the accounts must be adjusted for:

• Receipts which have not been included in the accounts but which are taxable as trade profits eg where the trader takes goods for his own use	Added to net profit

And

• Receipts included in the accounts which are not taxable as trade profits eg interest income, capital receipts	Deducted from net profit

Whilst in principle the adjustments required are the same as for accruals accounting, they are adapted as follows for the cash basis:

- Where a trader takes stock out of the business for his own use without paying an arm's length price a 'just and reasonable' amount (for example the cost of the stock) should be added to the taxable profit (rather than treating the goods as sold at market value).

- Not all capital receipts are deducted from the net profit. Only deduct the capital receipts from the sale of cars and other assets which are not classed as plant and machinery eg land and buildings.

In addition the following adjustments, which are specific to the cash basis are required:

- Where a trader ceases to use a capital asset for the purposes of the trade, the market value of the asset at that date is treated as a taxable receipt.

- When a trader ceases to trade, the value of stock and work in progress is treated as a taxable receipt in the final period of account.

6.3.2 Allowable expenses payments

Business expenses are deductible when they are paid and include capital expenditure on plant and machinery (but not cars).

The majority of the specific tax rules covered earlier in this Text concerning the deductibility of expenditure also apply to the cash basis.

However, some of the tax adjustments required in arriving at taxable trading profits for an accruals accounting trader are not applicable to the cash basis and there are other adjustments which are specific to the cash basis.

The main provisions which are specific to the cash basis are:

- Capital expenditure on plant and machinery: Expenditure on plant and machinery (but not cars) is an allowable expense for the cash basis (see below).

- Bad debts: Not an allowable deduction for the cash basis as income is only taxed when it is received.

- Leased cars: The 15% restriction does not apply; ie amounts paid are allowable in full.

6.3.3 Capital expenditure

Under the normal accruals basis (see earlier in this Text) capital expenditure is disallowed in computing taxable trading profits and instead capital allowances are available on plant and machinery. In addition, capital receipts are not taxable as trading receipts (unless capital allowances have been claimed in which case the proceeds are brought into the capital allowances computation) but may be subject to capital gains tax.

For traders using the cash basis, payments made to acquire plant and machinery (except cars) which would otherwise qualify for capital allowances are instead allowable expenses when they are made, and capital allowances are not available. This includes the acquisition cost of vans and motor cycles. Similarly, capital receipts from the sale of plant and machinery (except cars) are taxable when received.

For other assets eg land and buildings and cars, the same rules apply as for accruals accounting traders. Thus capital payments are disallowed (along with legal fees on such acquisitions) but capital allowances can be claimed on cars in the normal way.

If an item of plant and machinery is used for both business and private purposes, only the proportion of expenditure related to business use is deductible ie add back the private use proportion to the profit per the accounts.

6.3.4 Interest paid

Interest paid on a loan is a deductible expense from trading profits (even if the loan is not wholly and exclusively for the purposes of the trade) subject to a maximum of £500 for a 12-month period.

Note that this restriction only applies to loan interest ie it does not apply to interest charges for leasing assets; interest charged by suppliers of goods or services; or credit card interest on allowable purchases.

Worked example: Cash basis for small businesses

Siobhan started to trade as a sole trader on 1 May 2015 and has elected to use the cash basis for income tax purposes. The receipts figure in her accounts for the year to 30 April 2016 is analysed as follows:

	£
Cash receipts from customers	30,000
Bank transfers received from customers	26,000
Cash receipt from sale of a van	4,000
Cash receipt from sale of a car	2,000
Interest credited to business bank account	400
Total receipts	62,400

In addition, Siobhan took goods out of the business for her own use which had cost £350.

The expense payments figure in her accounts for the year to 30 April 2016 is analysed as follows:

	£
Cheque payments to suppliers of goods for resale	20,200
Cheque payments to other suppliers	9,000
Cheque payment for purchase of machinery	5,000
Bank transfer for purchase of car (50% business use)	6,000
Interest paid on bank loan to acquire machinery and car	700
Total payments	40,900

As at 30 April 2016 Siobhan still had a third of the goods paid for during the year, in stock.

The payments made to other suppliers include £80 paid to a restaurant where Siobhan entertained a potential supplier.

Requirement

Calculate the taxable trading profit for Siobhan for the year ended 30 April 2016 under the cash basis rules.

Solution

	£	£
Total receipts per the accounts	62,400	
Deduct receipts not taxable as trading income:		
– Receipt from sale of car	(2,000)	
– Interest received	(400)	
Add goods for own use	350	
Taxable trading receipts		60,350
Total payments per the accounts	(40,900)	
Disallowable entertaining	80	
Machinery (allowable expense)	–	
Car purchase – disallowable capital addition	6,000	
Interest paid on bank loan (maximum allowed £500)	200	
		(34,620)
Less capital allowances (WDA for car = £6,000 × 18% × 50% BU)		(540)
Taxable trading profit		25,190

Note: No adjustment is made for the year end stock as it is the actual payments made in the year that are deductible.

6.4 Basis of assessment

A trader using the cash basis can, like any other trader, prepare his accounts to any date in the year. The basis of assessment rules which determine in which tax year the profits of an accounting period are taxed, apply in the same way for the cash basis as they do for accruals accounting traders.

6.5 Election

An election to join the scheme is made by ticking the 'cash basis' box in the self assessment tax return. The election applies to all the businesses run by the trader.

The election is effective for the tax year for which it is made and all subsequent tax years unless:

(i) The trader's receipts exceed the eligibility limit (see above); or

(ii) (a) There is a change of circumstances which makes it more appropriate to prepare accounts using UK GAAP, and

    (b) The trader elects to calculate profits using UK GAAP.

Summary and Self-test

Summary

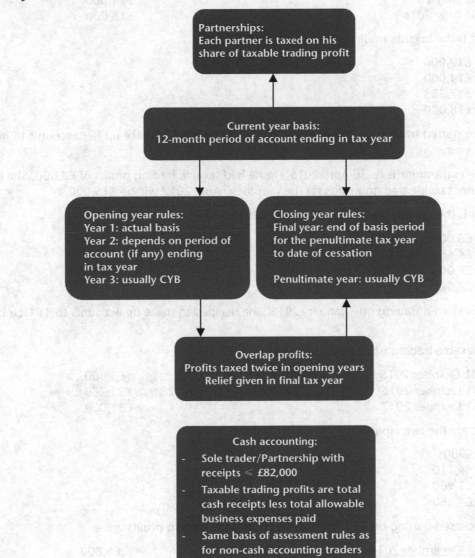

Partnerships:
Each partner is taxed on his share of taxable trading profit

Current year basis:
12-month period of account ending in tax year

Opening year rules:
Year 1: actual basis
Year 2: depends on period of account (if any) ending in tax year
Year 3: usually CYB

Closing year rules:
Final year: end of basis period for the penultimate tax year to date of cessation

Penultimate year: usually CYB

Overlap profits:
Profits taxed twice in opening years
Relief given in final tax year

Cash accounting:
- Sole trader/Partnership with receipts ≤ £82,000
- Taxable trading profits are total cash receipts less total allowable business expenses paid
- Same basis of assessment rules as for non-cash accounting traders

Self-test

Answer the following questions.

1   Gordon has been trading for many years making up his accounts to 31 May each year. His taxable trading profits are as follows:

y/e 31 May 2014	£12,000
y/e 31 May 2015	£14,000
y/e 31 May 2016	£18,000

What is the taxable trading profit taxed in 2015/16?

A   £12,000
B   £14,000
C   £17,333
D   £18,000

2   Florrie started trading on 1 September 2015. She decided to make up her accounts to 30 April each year.

In the eight months to 30 April 2016, Florrie had taxable trading profits of £8,000. She estimates that her taxable trading profits for the year to 30 April 2017 will be £15,000.

What is the taxable trading profit taxed in 2015/16?

A   £6,000
B   £4,667
C   £7,000
D   £8,000

3   Ursula started trading on 1 January 2015. She decided to make up accounts to 31 October each year.

Her taxable trading profits are as follows:

p/e 31 October 2015	£3,000
y/e 31 October 2016	£23,760
y/e 31 October 2017	£31,000

What are the overlap profits?

A   £900
B   £4,710
C   £3,960
D   £4,860

4   Ross ceased trading on 31 March 2016. His taxable trading profits were:

y/e 31 December 2014	£6,800
y/e 31 December 2015	£5,600
p/e 31 March 2016	£4,500

Ross had £2,300 of overlap profits on commencement.

What is the taxable trading profit for 2015/16?

A   £10,100
B   £7,800
C   £6,400
D   £2,200

5   Anne and Jane have been in partnership for many years making up accounts to 30 November. The profit-sharing agreement of the partnership is that Anne is entitled to an annual salary of £10,500 and Jane is entitled to an annual salary of £12,300. They are also entitled to interest at 5% on capital introduced to the partnership. Anne has capital of £52,500 and Jane has capital of £34,500. Any remaining profits are shared equally.

For the year ended 30 November 2015, the taxable trading profit of the partnership is £147,750.

What is the taxable trading profit of the partners for 2015/16?

A   Anne £60,300, Jane £60,300
B   Anne £73,425, Jane £74,325
C   Anne £73,875, Jane £73,875
D   Anne £87,000, Jane £87,900

6   Andrew is a sole trader who uses the cash basis for income tax purposes. His accounts for the year to 31 December 2015 include a deduction of £10,000 for the purchase of a car on 1 July 2015. The car has CO_2 emissions of 125g/km and is used only for business. The accounts also include a deduction of £6,000 for a new machine on 15 October 2015.

What adjustment to Andrew's accounting profit for the year to 31 December 2015 is required to arrive at his taxable trading profit after capital allowances?

A   Add back £16,000; deduct capital allowances of £1,800
B   Add back £10,000; deduct capital allowances of £1,800
C   Add back £16,000; deduct capital allowances of £7,800
D   Add back £10,000; deduct capital allowances of £7,800

Now go back to the Learning objectives in the Introduction. If you are satisfied you have achieved these objectives, please tick them off.

Technical reference

Legislation

References relate to Income Tax (Trading and Other Income) Act 2005 (*ITTOIA 2005*) unless otherwise stated.

Current year basis	s.198
Opening years	ss.199-201
Overlap profits	ss.204-205
Closing years	ss.201-202
Partnerships	ss.846-856

HMRC manual

Business income manual (Found at http://www.hmrc.gov.uk/manuals/bimmanual/index.htm)

Computation of liability: basis periods - general rule	BIM81010
Computation of liability: basis periods – commencement years	BIM81015
Computation of liability: overlap relief - introduction	BIM81075
Computation of liability: basis periods – year of cessation	BIM81025
Cash basis: receipts: overview	BIM70015
Cash basis: receipts: capital receipts	BIM70020
Cash basis: expenses: overview	BIM70030
Cash basis: expenses: capital expenditure	BIM70035
Cash basis: expenses: interest payments and incidental costs of obtaining finance	BIM70040
Partnerships: Computation & assessment: Profits and Losses Computed at Partnership Level	BIM82210
Partnerships: Computation & assessment: Allocation of Profits and Losses	BIM82240

> This technical reference section is designed to assist you. It should help you to know where to look for further information on the topics covered in this chapter. **You will not be examined on the contents of this section in your examination.**

Answers to Interactive questions

Answer to Interactive question 1

First tax year (2014/15)
Actual basis
Basis period 1 November 2014 to 5 April 2015
5/9 × £18,000   £10,000

Second tax year (2015/16)
Period of account ending in second tax year less than 12 months
Basis period 1 November 2014 to 31 October 2015
9 months to 31 July 2015   £18,000
1 August 2015 to 31 October 2015: 3/12 × £48,000   £12,000
                                                                        £30,000

Answer to Interactive question 2

First tax year (2013/14)
Actual basis
Basis period 1 January 2014 to 5 April 2014
3/6 × £28,500   £14,250

Second tax year (2014/15)
Period of account in second tax year less than 12 months
Basis period 1 January 2014 to 31 December 2014
6 months to 30 June 2014   £28,500
1 July 2014 to 31 December 2014: 6/12 × £48,000   £24,000
                                                                        £52,500

Third tax year (2015/16)
12-month period of account ending in third tax year
Basis period 1 July 2014 to 30 June 2015
y/e 30 June 2015   £48,000

Overlap profits
Period of overlap 1 January 2014 to 5 April 2014 and 1 July 2014 to 31 December 2014
Overlap profits
3/6 × £28,500   £14,250
6/12 × £48,000   £24,000
                                                                        £38,250

Answer to Interactive question 3

First tax year (2011/12)
Actual basis
Basis period 1 August 2011 to 5 April 2012
8/10 × £24,000 .... **£19,200**

Second tax year (2012/13)
Period of account in second tax year less than 12 months
Basis period 1 August 2011 to 31 July 2012

10 months to 31 May 2012	£24,000	
1 June 2012 to 31 July 2012: 2/12 × £31,000	£5,167	
		£29,167

Third tax year (2013/14)
CYB
Basis period 1 June 2012 to 31 May 2013
y/e 31 May 2013 .... **£31,000**

Overlap profits
Period of overlap 1 August 2011 to 5 April 2012 and 1 June 2012 to 31 July 2012
Overlap profits

8/10 × £24,000	£19,200	
2/12 × £31,000	£5,167	
		£24,367

Penultimate tax year (2014/15)
CYB
Basis period 1 June 2013 to 31 May 2014
y/e 31 May 2014 .... **£44,000**

Final tax year (2015/16)
End of previous basis period to cessation

Basis period 1 June 2014 to 30 April 2015	£38,000	
Less overlap profits	£(24,367)	
		£13,633

Answer to Interactive question 4

	Total £	Calder £	Scott £	Tim £
First PSR period				
1 June 2014 to 30 September 2014				
PSR (1:1:1)				
£136,000 × 4/12	45,333	15,111	15,111	15,111
Second PSR period				
1 October 2014 to 31 May 2015				
Salaries (× 8/12)	80,000	33,333	26,667	20,000
PSR (25%: 35%: 40%)	10,667	2,667	3,733	4,267
Total	136,000	51,111	45,511	39,378

1 B – £14,000

Current year basis applies to a continuing business. The taxable trading profit taxed in 2015/16 is that of the year ended 31 May 2015.

2 C – £7,000

The basis of assessment in the first tax year is the actual basis between commencement and the following 5 April.

7/8 × £8,000

Basis period 1 September 2015 to 5 April 2016	£7,000

3 D – £4,860

First tax year (2014/15)
Actual basis
Basis period 1 January 2015 to 5 April 2015

Second tax year (2015/16)
Period of account in second tax year less than 12 months
Basis period 1 January 2015 to 31 December 2015

Third tax year (2016/17)
Current year basis
Basis period 1 November 2015 to 31 October 2016

Overlap profits
Period of overlap 1 January 2015 to 5 April 2015 and 1 November 2015 to 31 December 2015

Overlap profits		
3/10 × £3,000	£900	
2/12 × £23,760	£3,960	
		£4,860

4 B – £7,800

Final tax year (2015/16)

Basis period 1 January 2015 to 31 March 2016		
y/e 31 December 2015	£5,600	
p/e 31 March 2016	£4,500	
	£10,100	
Less: overlap profits	£(2,300)	
		£7,800

5 B – Anne £73,425, Jane £74,325

	Total £	Anne £	Jane £
Salary	22,800	10,500	12,300
Interest (5% × £52,500/£34,500)	4,350	2,625	1,725
PSR 1:1	120,600	60,300	60,300
Totals	147,750	73,425	74,325

As the partnership is not new this will be taxed on each partner on a CYB in 2015/16.

6 B – Add back £10,000; deduct capital allowances of £1,800

No adjustment is required in respect of the payment for the machine as the payment is deductible when made. The £10,000 payment for the car must be added back to the profit per the accounts. Andrew can claim capital allowances on the car at 18%.

CHAPTER 8

National insurance contributions

Introduction
Examination context
Topic List
Summary and Self-test
Technical reference
Answers to Interactive questions
Answers to Self-test

Learning objectives

- Identify the key features of the PAYE and national insurance system

- Calculate the total national insurance contributions payable by employees, employers and self-employed individuals

Specific syllabus references for this chapter are: 2b, 3k.

Syllabus links

It is important that you understand the calculations in this chapter as they are a vital element in considering the overall tax position of an individual and should not be overlooked.

When you tackle the Tax Compliance paper later on in the Professional Level, you will learn more about national insurance contributions, for example those paid by directors.

Examination context

In the examination, in the objective test questions, candidates may be required to:

- Calculate national insurance contributions payable by employees and their employers
- Calculate national insurance contributions payable by sole traders and partners

For extra question practice on these topics go to the section of the Question Bank covering this chapter.

1 Classes and payment of national insurance contributions

Section overview

- National insurance contributions (NICs) are used to fund state benefits.
- Class 1 contributions are paid by employees and employers.
- Class 1A contributions are paid by employers.
- Class 2 contributions and Class 4 contributions are paid by self-employed individuals.
- NICs are administered by HMRC's National Insurance Contributions Office.

1.1 What are national insurance contributions?

National insurance contributions (NICs) are paid by self-employed individuals, employees and their employers. The contributions are used to bear part of the liability of the government to pay state benefits such as jobseekers allowance and state pensions.

Some benefits are only available to individuals who have paid sufficient NICs (based on their 'contributions record').

Anyone over 16 wishing to work in the UK needs a national insurance number. UK citizens are issued with a national insurance number by the age of 16.

1.2 Classes of national insurance contributions

The classes of national insurance contributions with which you are concerned are:

Class 1   Paid by employees and their employers
Class 1A   Paid by employers
Class 2   Paid by self-employed individuals
Class 4   Paid by self-employed individuals

Note that when calculating NICs you should round mathematically at each step of your computation.

1.3 Payment of national insurance contributions

National insurance contributions are administered by the National Insurance Contributions Office (NICO) which is part of HM Revenue & Customs.

You have already seen that Class 1 contributions are collected under the PAYE system on a monthly basis.

Class 1A contributions are payable by 19 July (22 July if paid electronically) following the end of the tax year to which they relate.

Class 2 contributions come within the self-assessment system (discussed later in this Text) from 2015/16 onwards.

Class 4 contributions are collected together with income tax under the self-assessment system.

2 Class 1 NICs

Section overview

- Class 1 primary contributions are paid by employees.
- Class 1 secondary contributions are paid by employers.
- Contributions are based on the employee's earnings period (usually weekly or monthly).
- No contributions are due on earnings below the earnings threshold.
- For primary contributions only, there is an upper earnings limit above which contributions are due at a lower rate.

2.1 Introduction

An employed individual is liable to Class 1 primary NICs. The employer is liable to Class 1 secondary NICs.

The amount of Class 1 NICs payable depends on the age of the employee, the level of the employee's earnings in the 'earnings period' and whether he is 'contracted out' of the Additional State Pension (previously known as the State Second Pension or S2P).

All employees aged between 16 and state pension age are liable to pay Class 1 primary NICs. Payments start on the employee's 16th birthday and cease when the employee reaches state pension age.

State pension age is currently 65 for men, and around 62 for women, varying slightly depending on date of birth, and rising to 65 by November 2018. From December 2018 the state pension age for both men and women will start to increase to reach 66 in October 2020, with further increases after that. For the purposes of your exam, you should note that any taxpayer aged 65 or over has reached state pension age.

Part of Class 1 NICs are used to fund the Additional State Pension. If the employee has contracted out of the Additional State Pension via membership of his employer's occupational pension scheme, Class 1 NICs are payable at a reduced rate. Contracting out is only available for salary-related schemes. Individuals cannot contract out of the Additional State Pension if they are members of a personal pension scheme. However, for the purposes of this exam, you should assume that employees are not contracted out of the Additional State Pension.

Employers must pay Class 1 secondary NICs for all employees aged over 16, although the limits are different depending on whether employees are aged 16 to 20, or 21 and above. There is no upper age limit for Class 1 secondary NICs.

2.2 Earnings for Class 1 NICs

An employee's earnings for Class 1 NIC purposes include all earnings received in monetary form: salary, commission, bonus plus vouchers exchangeable for cash, goods or services. Earnings do not usually include any taxable benefits.

Most employees are paid at regular intervals (weekly or monthly). This period is the **earnings period**.

2.3 Primary Class 1 contributions

The primary Class 1 NICs for 2015/16 for employees aged 16 or over and not contracted out of the Additional State Pension are as follows:

Employee's earnings	Primary contributions payable
Not above primary threshold (PT) (£155 per week or £672 per month)	Nil
Between PT and upper earnings limit (UEL) (£815 per week or £3,532 per month)	Earnings less PT × 12%
In excess of UEL	UEL less PT × 12% plus Earnings less UEL × 2%

Worked example: Class 1 primary contributions

Meg is employed by Green Ltd and is paid £424 weekly.

Munroe is also employed by Green Ltd and is paid £4,080 monthly.

Requirement

What are the weekly and monthly Class 1 primary contributions of Meg and Munroe respectively?

Solution

Meg

(£424 – £155) = £269 × 12%	£32

Munroe

	£
(£3,532– £672) = £2,860 × 12% =	343
(£4,080 – £3,532) = £548 × 2% =	11
Total	354

In the examination, you might be asked to work out the annual NICs payable by an employee. In this case, it is acceptable to use the annualised limits of £8,060 (PT) and £42,385 (UEL) if the employee is paid evenly throughout the tax year. If the employee receives an additional payment such as a bonus in one earnings period, it will be necessary to calculate the NICs in relation to weekly or monthly earnings periods instead.

Worked example: Annual Class 1 primary contributions

Raj and Debbie are employed by Magenta Ltd. They are each paid £2,300 a month. In addition, Raj is paid a bonus in January 2016 of £2,000.

Requirement

What are the Class 1 primary contributions payable by Raj and Debbie for 2015/16?

Solution

Raj
11 months

	£
(£2,300 – £672) = £1,628 × 12% = £195 × 11 months	2,145

1 month

(£3,532 – £672) = £2,860 × 12% =	343
(£4,300 – £3,532) = £768 × 2%	15
	2,503
Debbie	
£2,300 × 12 = £27,600 – £8,060 = £19,540 × 12%	2,345

Note the rounding at each stage of the calculation

2.4 Secondary Class 1 contributions

The secondary Class 1 NICs for 2015/16 for employees aged 21 or over and not contracted out of the Additional State Pension are as follows:

Employee's earnings	Secondary contributions payable
Not above secondary threshold (ST) (£156 per week or £676 per month)	Nil
Above ST	Earnings less ST × 13.8%

C H A P T E R

8

Most employers may then deduct an employment allowance – see 2.5 below.

The secondary Class 1 NICs for 2015/16 for employees aged under 21 years old and not contracted out of the Additional State Pension are as follows:

Employee's earnings	Secondary contributions payable
Not above upper secondary threshold (UST) (£815 per week or £3,532 per month)	Nil
Above UST	Earnings less UST × 13.8%

You should assume that the taxpayer is aged 21 or over, unless told otherwise.

Worked example: Class 1 secondary contributions

Meg is employed by Green Ltd and paid is £424 weekly.

Munroe is also employed by Green Ltd and paid is £4,080 monthly.

Requirement

Calculate the weekly and monthly secondary Class 1 contributions payable by Green Ltd in respect of Meg and Munroe respectively. Ignore Green Ltd's employment allowance.

Solution

Meg
(£424 – £156) = £268 × 13.8%   £37

Munroe
(£4,080 – £676) = £3,404 × 13.8%   £470

Again, if you are required to compute the annual secondary NICs payable by an employer, you can use the annualised ST of £8,112. In this case, the payment of additional amounts, such as bonuses, will not affect the calculation since there is no upper earnings limit for secondary contributions.

Worked example: Class 1 secondary contributions – under aged 21

Nora, aged 18, is employed by Blue Ltd and paid is £424 weekly.

Oliver, aged 19, is also employed by Blue Ltd and paid is £4,080 monthly.

Requirement

Calculate the weekly and monthly secondary Class 1 contributions payable by Blue Ltd in respect of Nora and Oliver respectively. Ignore Blue Ltd's employment allowance.

Solution

Nora
Nora's weekly wage is below the upper secondary threshold of £815 per week   £0

Oliver
(£4,080 – £3,532) = £548 × 13.8%   £76

Interactive question 1: Class 1 contributions   [Difficulty level: Exam standard]

Chloe is an employee of Cyan Ltd. She earns a salary of £26,196 which is paid monthly. In November 2015, she receives a bonus of £4,415.

Requirement

Using the standard format below, compute the Class 1 contributions payable in respect of Chloe's employment for 2015/16. Ignore the employment allowance.

Class 1 Primary contributions
11 months

£

£ (............ – ....) = £............ × ....% = ... × 11 months

1 month
£ (............ – ....) = £............ × ....% =
£ (............ – ....) = £............ × ....% =

_____

Class 1 Secondary contributions
11 months

£

£ (............ – ....) = £............ × ....% = ... × 11 months

1 month
£ (............ – ....) = £............ × ....% =

_____

See **Answer** at the end of this chapter.

2.5 Employment allowance

The total secondary Class 1 NICs of most employers is reduced by £2,000 per year. This is an allowance per employer, not per employee. If the employer's total secondary Class 1 NIC liability for all employees is less than £2,000 for 2015/16, the employer pays no secondary Class 1 NIC for the year.

In the exam you should include the employment allowance in calculations of secondary Class 1 NIC unless you are told otherwise.

3 Class 1A NICs

Section overview

• Class 1A contributions are payable by employers on taxable benefits provided to employees.

3.1 Class 1A contributions

Employers are also liable to pay Class 1A contributions on taxable benefits provided to employees at the rate of 13.8%.

The value of the taxable benefits for NICs is generally the same as the taxable value for income tax. However, any benefits taxed as earnings under Class 1 are not also subject to Class 1A charge.

Worked example: Class 1A contributions

Beryl is employed by Z plc. During 2015/16, she received the following benefits:

	£
Medical insurance	810
Car benefit	3,500
Vouchers exchangeable for goods	750
Pension advice (available to all employees)	100

Beryl is a higher rate taxpayer.

Requirement

Calculate the Class 1A contributions payable by Z plc.

Solution

Class 1A

(£810 + £3,500) = £4,310 × 13.8% — £595

The vouchers exchangeable for goods are earnings and so will be subject to Class 1 NICs. Pension advice up to £150 is an exempt benefit.

4 Class 2 and Class 4 NICs

Section overview

- Class 2 contributions are paid by the self-employed calculated at a fixed weekly rate.

- Class 2 is not payable where profits are below the small profits threshold.

- Class 4 contributions are paid by the self-employed based on tax adjusted earnings.

- Class 4 contributions are due on earnings above the annual lower profits limit.

- From 2015/16, Class 2 as well as Class 4 NICs will be dealt with mainly via self assessment.

4.1 Introduction

Self-employed taxpayers are liable to both Class 2 and Class 4 NICs. Previously these were administered separately, but Class 2 is currently being brought within the self-assessment regime.

Class 2 payments count towards an individual's contributions record, while Class 4 payments do not.

4.2 Class 2 NICs

A self-employed individual aged between 16 and state pension age is required to pay Class 2 contributions (equivalent of £2.80 per week of self-employment for 2015/16).

Payments start on the individual's 16th birthday and cease when the individual reaches state pension age.

No Class 2 contributions are required if the individual's profits are below the small profits threshold (£5,965 for 2015/16). Taxpayers with profits below the threshold are not liable for Class 2 NICs but are given the option to pay these voluntarily to protect their entitlement to contributory benefits.

4.3 Class 4 NICs

In addition to the flat rate Class 2 liability, self-employed individuals may also be liable to pay Class 4 NICs based on their taxable trading profit.

An individual is liable to pay Class 4 contributions if aged 16 or over at the start of the tax year and ceases to be liable if his state pension age has been reached by the start of the tax year.

In a partnership, each partner is responsible for paying his own Class 2 and Class 4 contributions based on his own share of the profits.

Class 4 NICs for 2015/16 are as follows:

Earnings	Class 4 contributions payable
Not above lower profits limit (£8,060)	Nil
Between lower profits limit and upper profits limit (£42,385)	Earnings less lower profits limit × 9%
In excess of upper profits limit	Upper profits limit less lower profits limit × 9% plus Earnings less upper profits limit × 2%

Worked example: Class 2 and 4 contributions

Andreas has been self-employed for many years. His accounts to 5 April 2016 showed a taxable profit of £8,150.

Requirement

What are the Class 2 and Class 4 NICs payable by Andreas for 2015/16?

Solution

	£
Class 2 contributions	
Above small earnings exception 52 × £2.80	146
Class 4 contributions	
(£8,150 – £8,060) = £90 × 9%	8

Interactive question 2: Class 2 and 4 contributions   [Difficulty level: Exam standard]

Nisar is self employed. He makes up accounts to 31 December each year. His taxable trading profit for the year ended 31 December 2015 is £45,000 and he estimates his taxable trading profit for the year to 31 December 2016 will exceed this figure.

Requirement

Using the standard format below, compute the Class 2 and Class 4 NICs payable by Nisar for 2015/16.

	£
Class 2 contributions	
.... × £	
Class 4 contributions	
(£............. – £.............) = £............. × ....%	
(£............. – £.............) = £............. × ....%	

See **Answer** at the end of this chapter.

4.4 Registering to pay self-employed NICs

A newly self-employed individual should register with HMRC. Registration is made jointly for income tax and NIC purposes (Class 2 and Class 4). To avoid penalties, registration must be made in time for a return to be issued for completion, submission and payment of any liability due by 31 January following the tax year during which self employment commenced.

Summary and Self-test

Summary

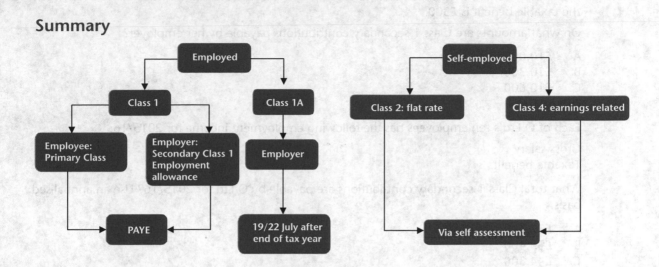

Self-test

Answer the following questions.

1   Caroline receives a £10,000 annual salary, paid monthly, in 2015/16. In addition, she receives a bonus of £600 in December 2015 and her employer provides her with a video camera for which the taxable benefit is £300.

On what amounts are Class 1 secondary contributions payable by her employer?

A   £10,000
B   £10,300
C   £10,600
D   £10,900

2   Each of Q Ltd's ten employees has the following employment income for 2015/16:

Gross salary   £35,210
Taxable benefits   £5,000

What total Class 1 secondary contributions are payable by Q Ltd for 2015/16? Use an annualised basis.

A   £37,400
B   £35,400
C   £44,300
D   £42,300

3   Maureen is employed by Treen Ltd. In 2015/16, she was paid a monthly salary of £2,518. In September 2015 she was paid a bonus of £5,000.

What are the Class 1 primary contributions payable by Maureen for 2015/16?

A   £3,259
B   £2,865
C   £4,226
D   £3,748

4   James has been self-employed for many years. His taxable trading profits are as follows:

y/e 31 October 2015   £14,210
y/e 31 October 2016   £20,000

What are his Class 4 NICs for 2015/16?

A   £554
B   £814
C   £738
D   £1,279

5   Len is self-employed. He makes up his accounts to 31 March each year and for the year ended 31 March 2016, his taxable trading profit is £55,000.

What are the total NICs payable by Len for 2015/16?

A   £3,341
B   £3,487
C   £4,052
D   £4,517

6   Julie works for D Ltd earning £15,000 per year. She benefits from childcare vouchers provided by D Ltd of £55 per week for 50 weeks in the tax year. Julie has a company car on which there is a taxable benefit of £4,500 per year.

What Class 1A National Insurance contributions are D Ltd required to make?

Class 1A contributions £ [   ]

Your answer to this question must be to the nearest whole number.

Now go back to the Learning objectives in the Introduction. If you are satisfied you have achieved these objectives, please tick them off.

Technical reference

Legislation

References relate to Social Security Contributions and Benefits Act 1992 (*SSCBA 1992*)

Class 1 contributions   ss.5 – 9

Class 1A contributions   s.10

Class 2 contributions   s.11

Class 4 contributions   ss.15 – 16

HMRC manual

National insurance manual (Found at http://www.hmrc.gov.uk/manuals/nimmanual/index.htm)

Class 1 Structural Overview: General   NIM01001

Class 1A Liability: Liability for Class 1A NICs   NIM13001

Class 2 Liability: Introduction   NIM20001

Class 4 NIC Liability: General   NIM24001

This technical reference section is designed to assist you. It should help you to know where to look for
further information on the topics covered in this chapter. **You will not be examined on the
contents of this section in your examination**.

Answer to Interactive question 1

Class 1 Primary contributions

11 months

	£
(£2,183 – £672) = £1,511 × 12% = £181 (rounded) × 11 months	1,991

1 month

(£3,532 – £672) = £2,860 × 12%	343
(£6,598 – £3,532) = £3,066 × 2%	61
	2,395

Class 1 Secondary contributions

11 months

	£
(£2,183 – £676) = £1,507 × 13.8% = £208 × 11 months	2,288

1 month

(£6,598 – £676) = £5,922 × 13.8%	817
	3,105

You could also have used the annualised method which would give:

(£30,611 – £8,112) = £22,499 × 13.8%	£3,105

Answer to Interactive question 2

Class 2 contributions

Clearly above small profits threshold

	£
52 × £2.80	146

Class 4 contributions

y/e 31 December 2015

(£42,385 – £8,060) = £34,325 × 9%	3,089
(£45,000 – £42,385) = £2,615 × 2%	52
	3,141

1   C – Class 1 secondary contributions on £10,600.

2   B – £35,400

     Class 1 Secondary contributions
     (£35,210 – £8,112) = £27,098 × 13.8% = £3,740 x 10 = £37,400 - £2,000 =   <u>35,400</u>

3   B – £2,865

     Class 1 Primary contributions
     11 months

                                                                 £

     (£2,518 – £672) = £1,846 × 12% = £222 × 11 months   2,442

     1 month
     (£3,532 – £672) = £2,860 × 12%   343
     (£7,518 – £3,532) = £3,986 × 2%   <u>80</u>
                                                                 <u>2,865</u>

4   A – £554

     Class 4 contributions
     y/e 31 October 2015
     (£14,210 – £8,060) = £6,150 × 9%   <u>554</u>

5   B – £3,487 (£3,341 + £146)

     Class 2 contributions
     52 × £2.80   146

     Class 4 contributions

     y/e 31 March 2016

                                                        £
     (£42,385 – £8,060) = £34,325 × 9%   3,089
     (£55,000 – £42,385) = £12,615 × 2%   <u>252</u>
                                                                 <u>3,341</u>

6   The correct answer is £ | 621 |

     Class 1A is payable by D Ltd at 13.8% on the value of the car benefit of £4,500.

     D Ltd would pay Class 1 secondary contributions on Julie's earnings. Childcare vouchers up to £55 per week are exempt as she is a basic-rate taxpayer.

CHAPTER 8

CHAPTER 9

Capital gains tax – individuals

Introduction

Examination context

Topic List

Learning objectives

- Classify persons, assets and disposals as either chargeable or exempt for capital gains purposes

- Calculate the chargeable gains and losses on the disposal of assets

- Calculate total taxable gains for both individuals and companies and for individuals calculate the capital gains tax payable

Specific syllabus references for this chapter are: 4a, b, c.

Syllabus links

The topics in this chapter are basic knowledge that you will be expected to know very well when you study for the Tax Compliance paper and the Business Planning: Taxation paper.

In the Tax Compliance paper, you will learn more about capital gains, including the rules for more complicated disposals such as shares and leases, how to use capital losses and capital gains tax reliefs.

Examination context

In the examination, in the objective test questions, candidates may be required to:

- Determine when a gain or loss arises
- Compute a gain or loss on disposal of a capital asset
- Calculate the capital gains tax payable for the tax year
- Calculate any gain or loss on disposal of a chattel

For extra question practice on these topics go to the section of the Question Bank covering this chapter.

1 Chargeable and exempt persons, assets and disposals

> **Section overview**
>
> - Chargeable persons include individuals, partners and companies.
> - Individuals pay capital gains tax (CGT) on their taxable gains, companies pay corporation tax on their chargeable gains.
> - Chargeable disposals include sales and gifts.
> - Death is not an occasion of charge for CGT, but there is a tax-free uplift of the value of assets passed on death.
> - Chargeable assets include tangible and intangible assets
> - Exempt assets include cars, some chattels and investments held in NISAs.

1.1 Introduction

A capital gain may arise on the disposal of a capital asset such as land, shares or a work of art. Usually, if the asset has increased in value since it was acquired, there will be a chargeable gain on its disposal. If the asset has fallen in value, there will be an allowable loss on its disposal.

In this chapter we will deal primarily with the rules on capital gains for individuals. Individuals pay capital gains tax (CGT) on their taxable gains. CGT applies to taxable gains in a tax year. For example, an individual will be liable to CGT in 2015/16 on gains arising between 6 April 2015 and 5 April 2016.

Similar rules apply to capital gains realised by companies and we will deal with the differences between the two sets of rules when you study corporation tax later in this text.

The first step in deciding whether there is a chargeable gain or allowable loss is to ascertain whether a **chargeable person** has made a **chargeable disposal** of a **chargeable asset**. We will deal with this question in the remainder of this section.

1.2 Chargeable persons

Chargeable persons include:

- Individuals
- Business partners, who are each treated as owning a share of partnership assets and taxed individually on the disposal of that share (details not in your syllabus)
- Companies, which normally pay corporation tax, not CGT, on their chargeable gains, and which do not receive an annual exempt amount (see later in this Chapter)

Some persons are specifically exempt from capital gains. These include registered charities and friendly societies, local authorities, registered pension schemes, investment trusts and approved scientific research associations.

1.3 Chargeable disposals

Chargeable disposals include:

- The sale of the whole or part of an asset
- The gift of the whole or part of an asset
- The loss or destruction of the whole or part of an asset

Exempt disposals include gifts to charities, art galleries, museums and similar institutions, provided that the asset is used for the purposes of the institution.

Death is not a disposal for capital gains tax purposes and so no CGT applies on death. However, the people entitled to receive the assets from the estate of the deceased person will acquire those assets at probate value (market value at the date of death). This is sometimes called the **tax-free uplift** on death.

The date of disposal is the date when the contract for sale is made. If the contract is conditional, the date of disposal is the date when all conditions are satisfied. The date legal title passes, or physical possession is obtained, or payment is made, is irrelevant.

1.4 Chargeable and exempt assets

Chargeable assets are defined as all capital assets except those which are specifically exempt from CGT.

Chargeable assets include both tangible assets (such as land, furniture, works of art) and intangible assets (such as the goodwill of a business, shares, leases).

Exempt assets include:

- Legal tender (ie cash)

- Motor cars (including vintage and classic cars)

- Most wasting chattels

- Chattels which are not wasting chattels, if acquisition cost and gross disposal consideration do not exceed £6,000

- Gilt-edged securities (such as Exchequer Stock or Treasury Stock)

- National Savings Certificates and premium bonds

- Shares and investments held in a New Individual Savings Account (NISA)

2 Computing a gain or loss

Section overview

- A gain or loss is calculated by deducting allowable costs from disposal consideration.

- Disposal consideration is sale proceeds or market value.

- Allowable costs include costs of acquiring the asset and cost of enhancing its value.

Overview of computation of a chargeable gain or allowable loss:

	£
Disposal consideration	X
Less incidental costs of disposal	(X)
Net disposal consideration	X
Less allowable costs	(X)
Chargeable gain/Allowable loss	X/(X)

2.1 Disposal consideration

If the asset is sold in a commercial transaction, ie sold at arm's length, the disposal consideration is the gross sale proceeds.

If the asset is not sold at arm's length, for example the asset is gifted, the disposal consideration is the market value of the asset.

From the disposal value, incidental costs of disposal can be deducted to give the net disposal consideration.

Incidental costs of disposal include legal fees, estate agents' and auctioneers' fees and advertising costs.

2.2 Allowable costs for CGT purposes

In order to calculate a gain or loss, you need to deduct allowable costs from the net disposal consideration.

Allowable costs are:

- Acquisition cost of the asset: purchase price if bought, market value of asset if gifted, probate value if acquired on death

- Incidental costs of acquisition such as legal fees, surveyor's or valuer's fees, stamp duty land tax, stamp duty

- Enhancement expenditure: capital costs of additions and improvements to the asset reflected in the value of the asset at the date of disposal, such as extensions, planning permission and architects' fees for extensions

Worked example: Allowable costs

Paul bought a holiday cottage in June 2001. The cottage cost £120,000 and he paid surveyor's fees of £1,500 and legal fees of £1,000 in connection with the acquisition.

In August 2002, Paul spent the following on improvements to the cottage:

£2,000 installing central heating

£500 on repairs to the roof

£1,200 redecoration

£5,000 on a sun room extension

In December 2006, during a storm, the sun room was destroyed and not replaced.

Paul sold the cottage at auction in July 2015. The gross sale proceeds were £180,000. Auctioneers' fees were £4,500 and he also paid legal fees of £1,200 on the sale.

Requirement

What is Paul's chargeable gain on sale?

Solution

	£	£
Gross sale proceeds	180,000	
Less: auctioneers' fees	(4,500)	
legal fees	(1,200)	
Net disposal consideration		174,300
Less: acquisition cost	120,000	
surveyor's fees	1,500	
legal fees	1,000	
enhancement expenditure (central heating)	2,000	(124,500)
Chargeable gain		49,800

Note that the repairs to the roof and the redecoration are not capital expenditure and so cannot qualify as enhancement expenditure. The cost of the sun room is not deductible as enhancement expenditure because it is not reflected in the value of the cottage at the time of disposal.

Interactive question 1: Allowable costs

[Difficulty level: Exam standard]

Mark bought a plot of land in May 1998 for £70,000. He incurred legal costs of £2,000 on the purchase and surveyor's fees of £1,400.

Mark sold the land in July 2015 for £76,000. He incurred advertising costs of £1,800 and legal costs of £2,600 on the sale.

Requirement

Using the standard format below, calculate Mark's chargeable gain/allowable loss on sale.

	£	£
Gross sale proceeds		
Less incidental costs of sale		
Net disposal consideration		
Less allowable costs		
		( )
Chargeable gain/Allowable loss		

See **Answer** at the end of this chapter.

3 Capital gains tax payable by individuals

Section overview

- Each individual is entitled to an annual exempt amount each tax year.
- CGT is chargeable separately from income tax, at 18% or 28%, depending on the individual's taxable income.

3.1 Annual exempt amount

Each individual is entitled to an annual exempt amount each tax year. For 2015/16 the annual exempt amount is £11,100.

The annual exempt amount is deducted from chargeable gains to produce gains liable to CGT, called **taxable gains.**

If the annual exempt amount is unused in a year it is wasted, and cannot be used in any other tax year.

3.2 Computing capital gains tax

Individuals are taxed on their taxable gains separately from their taxable income.

Taxable gains are taxed at the rate of 18% or 28% depending on the level of the individual's taxable income. Remember that an individual's taxable income is net of the personal allowance.

The rate of CGT is 28% if the individual is a higher or additional rate taxpayer. If the individual is a basic rate taxpayer then CGT is payable at 18% on an amount of taxable gains up to the amount of the individual's unused basic rate band and at 28% on the excess.

Worked example: CGT liability

Olly has taxable income in 2015/16 of £26,060. He makes taxable gains of £20,000 in the year. Olly's sister Alice has taxable income of £5,000 in 2015/16. She makes taxable gains of £17,000 in the year.

Requirement

Calculate Olly's and Alice's CGT liability for 2015/16.

Solution

	£
Olly	
(£31,785 – £26,060) = £5,725 × 18%	1,031
(£20,000 – £5,725) = £14,275 × 28%	3,997
CGT liability	5,028

Taxable gains are already net of the annual exempt amount.

Taxable income is net of the personal allowance. Olly has £5,725 of unused basic rate band remaining and this amount of his taxable gains is taxed at 18%. The remaining gain of £14,275 is taxed at 28%.

	£
Alice	
£17,000 × 18%	3,060

Alice has £26,785 unused basic rate band so her taxable gains are all taxed at 18%

Interactive question 2: CGT liability [Difficulty level: Exam standard]

Philippa made the following disposals during 2015/16:

- Vintage car (sold for £2,000, cost £9,500)
- Antique vase (sold for £45,000, cost £12,500)
- Cash (gift to her brother) £8,000
- Treasury stock (sold for £12,300, cost £8,250)

Philippa is a higher rate taxpayer.

Requirement

Using the standard format below, compute Philippa's taxable gains and capital gains tax liability for 2015/16.

	£
Net chargeable gains	
Less annual exempt amount	( )
Taxable gains	
CGT liability:	

See **Answer** at the end of this chapter.

4 Chattels

Section overview

- Chattels are tangible moveable property.
- Wasting chattels are usually exempt from CGT.
- Non-wasting chattels are usually chargeable to CGT.
- Non-wasting chattels bought and sold for £6,000 or less are exempt.
- Marginal relief applies to gains on non-wasting chattels sold for more than £6,000.
- Losses are restricted on non-wasting chattels sold for less than £6,000.

4.1 What are chattels?

A chattel is an item of tangible moveable property, and specifically does not include goodwill, shares or leases.

A chattel is a **wasting chattel** if it has a predictable life at the date of disposal not exceeding 50 years. Examples include caravans, boats, and computers and animals. Plant and machinery are always treated as having a useful life of less than 50 years.

A **non-wasting chattel** is one with a predictable life at the date of disposal of more than 50 years. Examples include antiques, jewellery and works of art.

4.2 Wasting chattels

Wasting chattels are usually exempt from CGT so there will be no chargeable gain or allowable loss on disposal.

However, if the asset has been used solely in a business and the owner has, or could have, claimed capital allowances on the asset, it will be treated as a non-wasting chattel.

4.3 Non-wasting chattels

Non-wasting chattels are generally chargeable to CGT, subject to some special rules.

- If the asset is disposed of for gross disposal proceeds of £6,000 or less and acquired for £6,000 or less it is exempt.

- If the asset is disposed for gross disposal proceeds of more than £6,000 and the acquisition cost is £6,000 or less, there is marginal relief for the gain. The gain cannot exceed:

  5/3 × (Gross proceeds less £6,000)

Worked example: Chattels – gain

Martin bought a vase for £4,000 in July 2005. He sold it at auction for £7,000 in December 2015. The costs of sale amounted to £350.

Requirement

What is Martin's chargeable gain on sale?

Solution

	£	£
Gross proceeds	7,000	
Less costs of sale	(350)	
Net disposal proceeds		6,650
Less cost		(4,000)
Gain		2,650
Gain cannot exceed 5/3 × £(7,000 – 6,000)		1,667
Therefore chargeable gain on sale		1,667

If the chattel is sold for less than £6,000 and the disposal would result in a loss, the loss is restricted by assuming that the gross disposal proceeds were £6,000. This rule cannot turn a loss into a gain, only reduce the amount of the loss to nil.

Worked example: Chattels – loss

Lucinda bought an antique necklace in May 2005 for £8,000 and sold it at auction in July 2015 for £5,400. The costs of sale were £270.

Requirement

What is Lucinda's allowable loss?

Solution

	£	£
Gross proceeds (deemed)	6,000	
Less costs of sale	(270)	
Net disposal proceeds		5,730
Less cost		(8,000)
Allowable loss		(2,270)

CHAPTER

9

Summary

Capital gains tax:
Disposal of capital asset resulting in gain or loss

Chargeable person:
Individual, partner
Companies pay
corporation tax on gains

Chargeable disposal:
Sale, gift, loss or destruction.
Death is not chargeable
disposal

Chargeable asset:
Most assets but not eg cars,
most wasting chattels, non-
wasting chattels brought and
sold for less than £6,000.
shares in NISAs

Computing gain or loss:
Disposal consideration less allowable costs (eg acquisition
costs, enhancement expenditure).

Annual exempt amount

CGT payable: tax @ 18%
and 28%

Self-test

Answer the following questions.

1   Michael bought an asset in July 2002 for £10,000 and sold it for £26,000 in August 2015.
    Incidental costs of disposal amounted to £1,250. Michael made no other disposals in 2015/16.
    Michael had taxable income after deducting the personal allowance of £30,415 for 2015/16.

    What is Michael's capital gains tax liability for 2015/16?

    A   £885
    B   £1,235
    C   £3,993
    D   £1,022

2   Which **TWO** of the following are exempt assets for CGT?

    A   A vintage Bentley car
    B   A shop used by a sole trader in his business
    C   Painting worth £4,500 (cost £1,500)
    D   Shares in an unquoted trading company

3   George sold a holiday flat in October 2015. He had bought the flat in May 2001.

    Select **TWO** of the following costs which will be deductible in computing George's chargeable gain
    on sale.

    A   Cost of advertising on sale
    B   Minor repairs to guttering
    C   Installing completely new heating system
    D   Repainting walls

4   Norman inherited a painting from his aunt in July 2006. His aunt had bought the painting in 1997
    for £9,000. The market value of the painting at the date of her death was £15,000.

    Norman sold the painting for £40,000 in November 2015. He incurred auctioneers' costs of
    £2,000 on the sale.

    What is Norman's chargeable gain on the sale?

    A   £23,000
    B   £25,000
    C   £29,000
    D   £31,000

5   Which of the following statements is true?

    A   The gift of any asset is always an exempt disposal
    B   Goodwill is an exempt asset for individuals
    C   Shares are always exempt assets for individuals
    D   The gift of a painting to a charity is an exempt disposal

Now, go back to the Learning objectives in the Introduction. If you are satisfied you have achieved these
objectives, please tick them off.

Technical reference

Legislation

References relate to Taxation of Chargeable Gains Act 1992 (*TCGA 1992*)

Chargeable persons	s.2
Assets and disposals	s.21
Computation of gains and losses	ss.15 – 17
Allowable deductions	ss.37 – 39
Annual exempt amount	s.3
Rates of tax	s.4
Chattels	s. 262

HMRC manual

Capital gains manual (Found at http://www.hmrc.gov.uk/manuals/cgmanual/index.htm)

Persons chargeable: general	CG10700
Chargeable assets: exemptions from capital gains charge	CG12600
Computation: introduction	CG14200
Chattels and wasting assets: introduction	CG76550

> This technical reference section is designed to assist you. It should help you to know where to look for further information on the topics covered in this chapter. **You will not be examined on the contents of this section in your examination**.

Answer to Interactive question 1

	£	£
Gross sale proceeds		76,000
Less incidental costs of sale:		
Advertising costs		(1,800)
Legal costs		(2,600)
		71,600
Net disposal consideration		
Less allowable costs:		
Acquisition cost	70,000	
Legal costs	2,000	
Surveyor's fees	1,400	
		(73,400)
Chargeable gain/Allowable loss		(1,800)

Answer to Interactive question 2

	£
Net chargeable gains (£45,000 – £12,500)	32,500
Less: annual exempt amount	(11,100)
Taxable gains	21,400
CGT liability: £21,400 × 28%	5,992

The vintage car, cash and Treasury stock are all exempt assets.

Philippa is a higher rate taxpayer therefore all her taxable gains are taxed at 28%.

C
H
A
P
T
E
R

9

1   A – £885

	£	£
Gross proceeds	26,000	
Less costs of sale	(1,250)	
Net disposal proceeds		24,750
Less cost		(10,000)
Chargeable gain		14,750
Less annual exempt amount		(11,100)
Taxable gain		3,650
(£31,785 – £30,415) £1,370 @ 18%		247
(£3,650 – £1,370) £2,280 @ 28%		638
CGT liability		885

2   A and C.

A vintage Bentley car – all cars are exempt assets.

Painting worth £4,500 (cost £1,500) – non-wasting chattel acquisition cost and disposal proceeds of £6,000 or less.

3   A and C.

Cost of advertising on sale.

Installing completely new heating system.

Repairs and redecoration are not capital in nature and are not enhancement expenditure.

4   A – £23,000

	£	£
Gross proceeds	40,000	
Less auctioneers' fees	(2,000)	
Net disposal consideration		38,000
Less acquisition cost (MV at date of death)		(15,000)
Chargeable gain		23,000

5   D – Gift of a painting to a charity is an exempt disposal.

The gift of an asset is a chargeable disposal unless the gift is to a charity, art gallery, museum or similar institution or the gift is made on the death of an individual.

Goodwill is a chargeable asset for individuals.

Shares are only exempt assets if held in a NISA.

CHAPTER 10

Corporation tax

Introduction
Examination context
Topic List

Introduction

Learning objectives

- Calculate total taxable gains for companies

- Identify accounting periods for a company

- Recognise the interaction of having one or more related 51% group company and corporation tax payment dates

- Allocate given items of business expenditure as allowable or disallowable for tax purposes and calculate the adjusted trading profits after capital allowances on plant and machinery

- Calculate the taxable total profits and the corporation tax payable for a company resident in the UK which has a period of account of 12 months or less

Specific syllabus references for this chapter are: 4c, 5a, b, c, d.

Syllabus links

The topics in this chapter form the basis of the charge to tax on companies. You will learn more details about how companies are taxed in the Tax Compliance paper and in the Business Planning: Taxation paper, for example the use of trading losses and groups of companies.

Examination context

In the examination, in the objective test questions, candidates may be required to:

- Identify the correct accounting periods of a company

- Calculate the corporation tax payable by a company

In the examination, in the scenario-based question for corporation tax, candidates may be required to:

- Calculate the taxable total profits for a company

- Demonstrate understanding of the impact of related 51% group companies on corporation tax payment dates

For extra question practice on these topics go to the section of the Question Bank covering this chapter and to the section of the Question Bank containing scenario-based questions for corporation tax.

1 Charge to corporation tax

Section overview

- Companies are chargeable to corporation tax.

- A UK resident company is chargeable on its worldwide profits.

- A company is charged to tax for an accounting period which cannot exceed 12 months.

1.1 Who is chargeable to corporation tax?

Corporation tax is charged on the income and gains of a company. These are known as taxable total profits.

A UK company is formed by incorporation under the Companies Acts. A company is a legal person. It has a separate legal entity from its owners (shareholders) and its managers (directors).

1.2 Residence

A company is liable to corporation tax on its worldwide profits if it is resident in the United Kingdom.

A company is resident in the UK if either:

- It is incorporated in the UK; or
- It is incorporated outside the UK, but its central management and control are exercised in the UK

1.3 Accounting periods

A company is charged to corporation tax in respect of an **accounting period**.

The accounting period will usually be the same as the company's period of account (the period for which the company prepares its accounts).

An accounting period starts:

- When the company begins to trade or acquires a source of chargeable income

- When the previous accounting period ends and the company is still within the charge to corporation tax

An accounting period ends on the earliest of:

- The end of 12 months from the start of the accounting period; or
- The date the company begins or ceases to trade; or
- The date the period of account ends.

If a company has a period of account exceeding 12 months, there will be two accounting periods, each giving rise to a separate corporation tax computation.

The first accounting period of such a long period of account will be the first 12 months of the period. The second accounting period will be the remainder of the period of account.

Worked example: Long period of account

M Ltd has made up accounts to 31 December each year. For commercial reasons, it decides to prepare its next set of accounts for the period 1 January 2015 to 30 April 2016.

Requirement

What are the accounting periods for this long period of account?

Solution

First accounting period: 1 January 2015 to 31 December 2015

Second accounting period: 1 January 2016 to 30 April 2016

2 Taxable total profits

Section overview

- Trading profits after capital allowances are dealt with as trading income.

- Income from renting out property is dealt with as property income.

- Loan relationships include interest income and interest expense. Loan relationships may include trading credits and debits and non-trading credits and debits.

- Gains made by companies are chargeable to corporation tax, with indexation allowance available.

- Qualifying donations are deducted to arrive at taxable total profits.

2.1 Overview of corporation tax computation

Per accounting period

	£
Trading income	X
Property income	X
Non trading loan relationships (non trading interest)	X
Miscellaneous income	
Income not otherwise charged	X
Chargeable gains	X
Qualifying donations	(X)
Taxable total profits	X

2.2 Trading income

A company's trading profits are calculated in a similar way to the taxable trading profits of a sole trader or partnership.

The company will produce accounts for a period of account and these must be adjusted for tax purposes. Capital allowances are then deducted to produce a figure for trading income.

In general, the adjustment to profits calculation will follow the same rules as for a sole trader or partnership, including WDAs, the AIA and FYAs, but there are some differences.

- As a company is a legal entity separate from its shareholders and directors, there is no adjustment to profits needed for private expenses met by the company.

- For the same reason, there will be no adjustment for appropriation of profits (eg salary paid to a director).

- Interest paid by a company in respect of a trading loan relationship will be an allowable expense in the calculation of its trading income (see later in this section for more detail on loan relationships).

- Dividends paid by a company are not allowable as a trading expense in the calculation of its trading income.

- If the company has a long period of account, the tax-adjusted profits should be time apportioned into the relevant accounting periods at this stage.

- Capital allowances for companies are computed for accounting periods, not periods of account. This means that capital allowances for companies can never be computed for a period longer than 12 months.

- Capital allowance computations for companies never include private use adjustments.

- A 100% FYA is available for expenditure incurred by a company between 1 April 2012 and 31 March 2020 on new (not second-hand) plant and machinery for use in a designated enterprise zone.

Worked example: Capital allowances and long period of account

D Ltd makes up accounts for the 15-month period to 30 June 2015.

Its tax-adjusted profits for the period were £300,000.

The tax written down value of the main pool at 1 April 2014 was £24,000. D Ltd sold some plant in May 2015 for £3,000 (less than cost).

Requirement

What is the trading income for each accounting period?

Solution

Capital allowances

	Main pool £	Allowances £
Accounting period		
1 April 14 to 31 March 15		
TWDV b/f	24,000	
WDA @ 18%	(4,320)	4,320
TWDV c/f	19,680	
Accounting period		
1 April 15 to 30 June 15		
Disposal	(3,000)	
	16,680	
WDA @ 18% × $^3/_{12}$	(751)	751
TWDV c/f	15,929	

	1.4.14 to 31.3.15 £	1.4.15 to 30.6.15 £
Tax-adjusted profits (12:3)	240,000	60,000
Less capital allowances	(4,320)	(751)
Trading income	235,680	59,249

2.3 Property income

A company's rental income from property situated in the UK is taxed as property income. Rent received is dealt with on an accruals basis. This means that only rent relating to the accounting period is taken into account. The date of receipt is not relevant.

Worked example: Property income

H Ltd makes up its accounts to 31 July each year.

On 1 January 2015, H Ltd bought and immediately rented out a shop. The annual rental of £24,000 was payable on that date.

Requirement

What is the amount taxable as property income on H Ltd for the year ended 31 July 2015?

Solution

Rent accrued 1 January 2015 to 31 July 2015
£24,000 × 7/12   **£14,000**

Interest payable on a loan taken out by a company for the purpose of buying or improving let property is not an allowable expense for property income. Instead it is dealt with under the loan relationship rules (see later in this section). No further knowledge of the property income calculation is required at this level.

CHAPTER

10

2.4 Dividends received

A company rarely pays tax on dividends received from other companies. They are therefore ignored in computing taxable total profits. For the purposes of the exam, assume all dividends received by a company are exempt.

However, grossed-up dividends received from other companies are taken into account in determining when a company has to pay its corporation tax liability. This is dealt with in the next section of this chapter.

2.5 Loan relationships – interest

Interest payable and receivable, such as investment interest, is allowable and taxable respectively as a loss or profit on non-trading loan relationships (see later in this section).

This income is received gross.

2.6 Chargeable gains

Chargeable gains are included in the computation of taxable total profits.

Overview of computation of a chargeable gain for a company

	£
Disposal consideration	X
Less incidental costs of disposal	(X)
Net disposal consideration	X
Less allowable costs	(X)
Unindexed gain	X
Less indexation allowance	(X)
Chargeable gain	X

Gains are initially computed in the same way as for individuals (see earlier in this text), however, for companies, 'indexation allowance' is also available in arriving at the chargeable gain. Indexation allowance is designed to ensure that the inflationary element of gains is not subject to tax.

Each item of acquisition cost is indexed from the date when the expenditure was incurred to the date of the disposal. Costs incurred in the same month can be added together.

The indexation factor is calculated as follows:

$$\frac{RD - RI}{RI}$$

where RD is the Retail Prices Index (RPI) for the month of disposal and RI is the RPI for the month in which the expenditure was incurred. In this examination relevant RPIs will be provided. If RD is less than RI (ie the RPI falls) then the indexation factor is nil.

The indexation factor is rounded to three decimal places. It is then applied to the item of allowable cost as appropriate to produce the indexation allowance for that item.

Worked example: Indexed gain

Lilliput Ltd bought an asset on 3 March 1991 (RPI 131.4) for £19,560. In addition, there were legal expenses of £150 on the purchase.

The company sold the asset on 15 September 2015 (RPI 258.6) for £42,300, and paid legal costs of £450 on sale.

Requirement

What is Lilliput Ltd's chargeable gain on sale?

Solution

	£	£
Gross proceeds	42,300	
Less legal fees	(450)	
Net disposal consideration		41,850
Less: acquisition cost	19,560	
legal fees	150	(19,710)
Unindexed gain		22,140
Less indexation allowance		

$$\frac{258.6 - 131.4}{131.4} = 0.968 \times £19,710$$

		(19,079)
Chargeable gain		3,061

Interactive question 1: Company chargeable gain   [Difficulty level: Exam standard]

Swift Ltd bought a warehouse in July 2001 (RPI 173.3) for £120,000, including incidental costs of acquisition. It added an extension in August 2002 (RPI 176.4) at a cost of £45,000.

Swift Ltd sold the warehouse in November 2015 (RPI 259.0) for net disposal proceeds of £265,000.

Requirement

Using the standard format below, compute the chargeable gain of Swift Ltd.

	£	£
Net disposal consideration		
Less:　　　acquisition cost		
enhancement expenditure	....	(............)
Unindexed gain		
Less:　　　indexation allowance		
on acquisition cost		

$$\frac{............ - ....}{............} = ... \times £............$$

		(............)
on enhancement expenditure		

$$\frac{............ - ....}{............} = ... \times £............$$

		(............)
Chargeable gain		

See **Answer** at the end of this chapter.

The indexation allowance cannot create or increase an unindexed loss.

Worked example: Restriction of indexation allowance

Munodi plc bought a plot of land in May 1998 (RPI 163.5) for £70,000, incurring legal costs of £2,000 on the purchase and surveyors' fees of £1,400.

Munodi plc sold the land in July 2015 (RPI 258.2) for £80,000. The company incurred advertising costs of £1,800 and legal costs of £2,600 on the sale.

Requirements

(a) What is Munodi plc's chargeable gain or allowable loss on the sale?
(b) What would the chargeable gain or allowable loss be if the gross sale proceeds were £76,000?

Solution

	(a)		(b)	
	£	£	£	£
Gross proceeds	80,000		76,000	
Less incidental cost of disposal (£1,800 + £2,600)	(4,400)		(4,400)	
Net disposal consideration		75,600		71,600
Less acquisition cost	70,000		70,000	
Cost of acquisition (£2,000 + £1,400)	3,400		3,400	
		(73,400)		(73,400)
Unindexed gain/Allowable loss		2,200		(1,800)
Less indexation allowance				
$\frac{258.2-163.5}{163.5} = 0.579 \times £73,400 = £42,499$		(2,200)		–
(restricted)				
Chargeable gain/allowable loss		0		(1,800)

(a) There is no chargeable gain nor allowable loss on the disposal as indexation cannot create a loss.
(b) The allowable loss is £1,800. Indexation cannot increase an allowable loss.

Companies are not entitled to an annual exempt amount.

Exempt assets for companies are as for individuals (see earlier in this text), with the addition of goodwill created or acquired on or after 1 April 2002 and the exclusion of gilt-edged securities. The examination will not require knowledge of the treatment of goodwill created or acquired by companies before 1 April 2002.

2.7 Miscellaneous income – income not otherwise charged

Miscellaneous income received by a company is taxable as income not otherwise charged. Such income is received gross.

2.8 Qualifying charitable donations

A company may make a charitable donation. The conditions for a donation to qualify for tax relief are the same as for individuals.

The method of tax relief for a company differs from that used for individuals.

A company makes qualifying donations gross. The amount **paid** in the accounting period is deducted from the company's total income and gains. This is called a qualifying donation.

2.9 Taxable total profits

A company's total income and gains less qualifying donations is its taxable total profits.

Worked example: Taxable total profits

X Ltd makes up its accounts for the 12 month period to 31 December 2015.

It has the following results:

Tax-adjusted trading profits before capital allowances	£120,000
Capital allowances	£10,000
Rental income after expenses	£5,000
Interest received from bank	£1,000
Chargeable gain	£2,000
Qualifying donation paid	£3,000

Requirement

What are the taxable total profits of X Ltd?

ICAEW

Solution

	£
Tax-adjusted trading profits before capital allowances	120,000
Less capital allowances	(10,000)
Trading income	110,000
Property income	5,000
Non-trading loan relationship (bank interest is received gross by companies)	1,000
Chargeable gains	2,000
	118,000
Less qualifying donations	(3,000)
Taxable total profits	115,000

2.10 Loan relationships

A company has a **loan relationship** if it loans money as a creditor or is loaned money as a debtor.

In practical terms, a loan relationship includes bank and building society accounts, bank overdrafts, government gilt-edged securities and loans to and from other companies which are often in the form of debentures. It does not include trade debts.

All profits and losses on loans (whether the company is a lender or borrower) are treated as income. Interest payments are taxed or relieved on an accruals basis.

If the company has been lent money for trade purposes there is a trading loan relationship.

Trading loan relationships

	Gross interest payable	Gross interest receivable
Treatment for corporation tax	Allowable trading expense to set against trading income	Trading receipt treated as trading income
Basis of assessment	Accruals basis	Accruals basis
Main examples	Bank overdraft interest Interest on loans to buy plant and machinery Interest on loans to buy premises for use in the trade	Rare – a company will not usually lend money for trade purposes

If the company has been lent money or lends money for a non-trade purpose, there is a non-trading loan relationship.

Non-trading loan relationships (NTLR)

	Gross interest payable	Gross interest receivable
Treatment for corporation tax	Non-trading loan relationship 'debit'	Non-trading loan relationship 'credit'
Basis of assessment	Accruals basis	Accruals basis
Main examples	Interest on loans to: • Purchase/improve a let property • Acquire shares in another company • Interest on overdue corporation tax • Write off of a non-trading loan such as a loan to a former employee	Interest on • Bank and building society accounts • Gilt-edged securities • Debentures and other loan stock • Repayments of overpaid corporation tax (repayment interest)

The **credits** (income) and **debits** (expenses) on loan relationships are combined. If there is a net profit, this amount is taxable as a non-trading loan relationship.

If there is a net deficit, there will be no amount taxable under loan relationships. The deficit can be relieved in a number of ways, but these are beyond the syllabus of this exam.

Worked example: Non-trading loan relationships

K Ltd makes up its accounts to 31 December each year.

In the year to 31 December 2015, K Ltd had the following accrued income received and interest paid:

Building society interest receivable	£5,000
Bank interest receivable	£2,000
Repayment interest on overpaid corporation tax	£50
Payable on loan taken out to acquire let property	£3,250

Requirement

What is the amount taxable as a non-trading loan relationship?

Solution

	£
Building society interest	5,000
Bank interest	2,000
Repayment interest on overpaid tax	50
	7,050
Less interest on loan taken out to acquire let property	(3,250)
Non-trading loan relationship	3,800

3 Computation and payment of corporation tax

Section overview

- Corporation tax is charged on the taxable total profits of a company.

- The date(s) for payment of corporation tax will depend on the company's level of augmented profits, compared with a limit of £1,500,000.

- The limit is scaled down where there are one or more related 51% group companies.

- A company with augmented profits exceeding the limit (a large company) pays corporation tax in instalments.

- Other companies have a single payment date.

3.1 Computation of corporation tax

A company's corporation tax liability is computed by applying the corporation tax rate to the company's taxable total profits.

Rates of corporation tax are fixed for Financial Years (FYs). FY 2015 runs from 1 April 2015 to 31 March 2016. The rate for FY 2015 is 20%. In previous Financial Years, there were varying rates of corporation tax for companies with different levels of profit but these are not examinable. Therefore, you will not be required to calculate the corporation tax for a company with an accounting period which begins before 1 April 2015.

Worked example: Computation of corporation tax

T Ltd makes up its accounts to 31 March each year. In the year to 31 March 2016, the company has taxable total profits of £1,300,000.

Requirement

What is the corporation tax liability of T Ltd?

Solution

	£
Taxable total profits	1,300,000
£1,300,000 × 20%	260,000

3.2 Augmented profits

As seen above, a company's taxable total profits are used to calculate the corporation tax liability of a company.

To determine the payment date(s) for corporation tax, you also need to calculate the augmented profits of a company.

Definitions

Augmented profits: taxable total profits plus franked investment income.

Franked investment income (FII): exempt dividends and tax credits received from UK and overseas companies, other than those received from companies which are 51% subsidiaries of the receiving company. The net dividend received needs to be grossed up by 100/90 to arrive at FII.

Worked example: Augmented profits

Z Ltd makes up its accounts to 31 March each year. In the year to 31 March 2016, the company has taxable total profits of £500,000 and receives exempt dividends from unrelated UK companies of £9,000, and exempt dividends of £7,200 from its wholly-owned subsidiary.

Requirement

What are Z Ltd's augmented profits?

Solution

	£
Taxable total profits	500,000
Add £9,000 × 100/90	10,000
Augmented profits	510,000

A company's augmented profits are then compared with the limit of £1,500,000 to determine the payment date(s) (see later in this Chapter).

The limit of £1,500,000 (FY 2015) applies for a 12-month accounting period, for a company with no related 51% group companies. The limit is scaled down for shorter accounting periods so the limit for, say, a nine month period is £1,125,000 (£1,500,000 × 9/12).

The limit is also scaled down if the company has related 51% group companies at the end of the previous accounting period.

3.3 Related 51% group companies

Companies A and B are related 51% group companies if A is a 51% subsidiary of B, or B is a 51% subsidiary of A, or both A and B are 51% subsidiaries of the same company. B is a 51% subsidiary of A if more than 50% of B's ordinary share capital is owned directly or indirectly by A.

Therefore, sub-subsidiaries, where one company owns shares in another, which in turn owns shares in another, may also be included as related 51% group companies if the indirect holding exceeds 50%.

Non-UK resident companies may be included.

Companies count as related 51% group companies even if they meet this definition for only part of the accounting period. However, a related 51% group company is ignored if it does not carry on a trade, or is passive (dormant).

Worked example: Related 51% group companies

X Ltd owns 80% of Y Ltd which in turn owns 80% of Z Ltd.

Requirement

How many related 51% group companies are there?

Solution

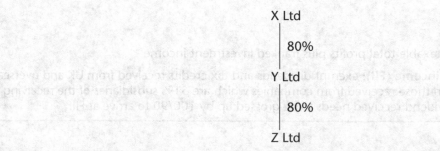

X Ltd

80%

Y Ltd

80%

Z Ltd

Y Ltd is a 51% subsidiary of X Ltd as X Ltd owns more than 50%. X Ltd also indirectly owns more than 50% of Z Ltd ie 64% (80% x 80%) through its shareholding in Y Ltd and so Z Ltd is also a 51% subsidiary of X Ltd.

Therefore, there are three related 51% group companies in total, X Ltd, Y Ltd and Z Ltd.

The number of related 51% group companies is important as the limit for determining a company's corporation tax payment date(s) is divided by the number of related 51% group companies, including the company itself. However, the number that is relevant is the number of related 51% group companies at the end of the previous accounting period.

Worked example: Effect of related 51% group companies on £1,500,000 limit

L plc owns 100% of M Ltd and 100% of N Ltd, and has done for a number of years.

Requirement

What is the limit to be used when determining the payment date(s) for L plc's corporation tax for the year ended 31 March 2016?

Solution

At 31 March 2015 (the end of the previous accounting period), L plc has two 51% subsidiaries (M Ltd and N Ltd) so there are three related 51% group companies.

Limit for 3 related 51% group companies:
Limit £1,500,000 ÷ 3 = £500,000

3.4 Payment – large companies

Augmented profits are compared to the limit as adjusted for the number of related 51% group companies at the end of the previous accounting period. A **large company** is one with augmented profits exceeding the limit.

However, a company is not treated as large if:

- It has a tax liability of less than £10,000; or

- It was not a large company in the preceding 12 months and it has augmented profits of £10 million or less in this accounting period

If the company has related 51% group companies, the £10 million limit is divided between the company and its related 51% group companies. As for the adjustments to the £1,500,000 limit, related companies are only taken into account if they were related 51% group companies at the **end** of the previous accounting period.

A large company must pay corporation tax in four equal instalments based on the company's estimated liability for the accounting period. The instalments are due on the 14th day of the 7th, 10th, 13th and 16th months after the start of a 12-month accounting period. In this examination, you will not have to determine the payment dates for a large company with a shorter accounting period, but you may be required to determine the limit for such a period.

In practice, since the total liability cannot be known until the end of the accounting period, the company will make revised estimates of how much each instalment should be as the accounting period progresses.

Worked example: Payment by instalments

T Ltd has augmented profits exceeding the limit and makes up accounts to 31 December each year.

Requirement

When will T Ltd be required to pay instalments of corporation tax for the year ended 31 December 2015?

Solution

Accounting period starts 1 January 2015.

Instalments due 14 July 2015, 14 October 2015, 14 January 2016 and 14 April 2016

3.5 Payment – other companies

The due date for corporation tax payable by companies not treated as large is nine months and one day after the end of the accounting period.

Worked example: Payment of corporation tax

Q Ltd has augmented profits below the limit. The company has an accounting period ending on 30 April 2015.

Requirement

What is the due date for payment of Q Ltd's corporation tax for the year ended 30 April 2015?

Solution

1 February 2016

Summary

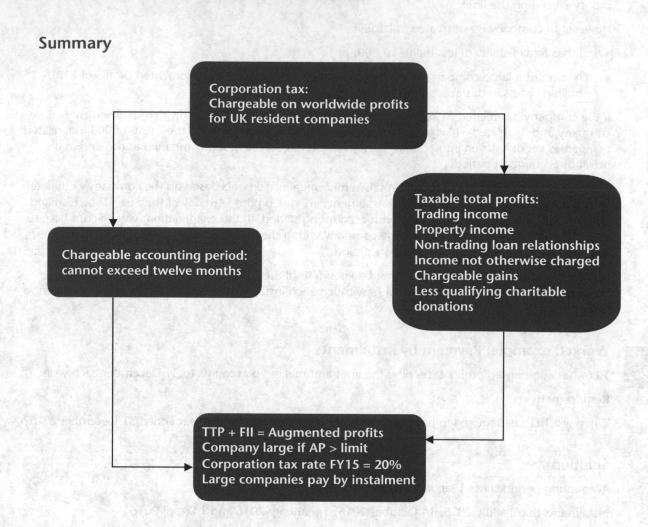

Corporation tax:
Chargeable on worldwide profits
for UK resident companies

Chargeable accounting period:
cannot exceed twelve months

Taxable total profits:
Trading income
Property income
Non-trading loan relationships
Income not otherwise charged
Chargeable gains
Less qualifying charitable
donations

TTP + FII = Augmented profits
Company large if AP > limit
Corporation tax rate FY15 = 20%
Large companies pay by instalment

Self-test

Answer the following questions.

1   G Ltd has a ten-month period of account from 1 April 2015 to 31 January 2016. The company bought a car (with CO_2 emissions of 123g/km) on 4 August 2015 for £20,000. The car is used 30% privately by one of the directors.

What are the maximum capital allowances that G Ltd can claim?

A   £2,100
B   £2,520
C   £3,000
D   £3,600

2   P Ltd started trading on 1 December 2014 and made up its first set of accounts to 31 March 2016.

P Ltd's accounting periods will be:

A   4 months to 31 March 2015, 12 months to 31 March 2016
B   4 months to 5 April 2015, 12 months to 31 March 2016
C   12 months to 30 November 2015, 4 months to 31 March 2016
D   16 months to 31 March 2016

3   Which **TWO** of the following are non-trading loan relationship debits of a company under the loan relationship rules?

A   Interest payable on loan to purchase property to let
B   Bank overdraft interest
C   Interest on loan to purchase machinery
D   Interest on overdue corporation tax

4   R Ltd has produced the following results for the year ended 31 March 2016.

Trading income	£490,000
Chargeable gains	£60,000
Interest accrued on gilts	£90,000
Qualifying donation paid	£50,000

What is the amount of corporation tax payable by R Ltd?

A   £106,000
B   £122,500
C   £118,000
D   £128,000

5   R Ltd had the following shareholdings:

S Ltd 40%
T Ltd 60%
U Ltd 75% (company is a passive company with no trade)
V Ltd 90%

Which companies are related 51% group companies for the purposes of determining the limit for R Ltd's corporation tax payment dates?

A   R Ltd, S Ltd, T Ltd and V Ltd
B   R Ltd, T Ltd, U Ltd and V Ltd
C   R Ltd, T Ltd and V Ltd
D   All of them

6   W Ltd sold a building in June 2015 (RPI 258.0) for £200,000, which had cost £145,000 in February 1995 (RPI 146.9).

The indexation allowance relating to the building is £............................

7   J Ltd makes up its accounts to 31 March each year. In the year to 31 March 2016, the company has taxable total profits of £1,310,000 and receives exempt dividend income from unrelated companies of £270,000. These results are similar to previous years.

What is the amount of corporation tax payable by J Ltd for the year ended 31 March 2016, and what is (are) the payment date(s)?

8   Aquarius plc allowed the following amounts in arriving at its draft trade profits of £53,000.

Select how each item should be treated in the adjustment-to-profits working in order to determine Aquarius plc's final trade profits.

Aquarius plc included £1,090 relating to the profit on disposal of an item of machinery

A   Add back £1,090
B   Deduct £1,090
C   Do not adjust

Aquarius plc included an expense of £21,400 relating to director bonuses and salaries (the directors are also the majority shareholders)

D   Add back £21,400
E   Deduct £21,400
F   Do not adjust

9   Capricorn plc has calculated the following amounts which have yet to be included in its final trade profits.

Select how each item should be treated in the adjustment to profits working in order to determine Capricorn plc's final trade profits.

Capricorn plc has calculated a balancing charge of £500 arising as a result of the disposal of plant

A   Increase trade profits by £500
B   Reduce trade profits by £500
C   Do not include in trade profits

Capricorn plc made a £100 donation to the local children's hospital after one of its employee's children was treated there

D   Increase trade profits by £100
E   Reduce trade profits by £100
F   Do not include in trade profits

10 Sagittarius plc deducted the following amounts in arriving at its draft trade profits of £654,544 for the year ended 31 January 2016.

Select whether an adjustment to profits should be made for each of the following items in order to determine Sagittarius plc's final trade profits for tax purposes.

£599 of legal costs relating to the renewal of a 25-year lease

A   Adjust
B   Do not adjust

Irrecoverable VAT of £3,500 on a company car purchased for an employee's use

C   Adjust
D   Do not adjust

11 Virgo Ltd, a manufacturing company, included £35,000 relating to pension costs in arriving at its draft trade profits for the year ended 31 December 2015. This included a closing accrual of £12,000 with only the balance actually being paid into a registered pension scheme during the year.

How much should be added back in order to determine Virgo Ltd's final trade profits?

A   £0
B   £12,000
C   £23,000
D   £35,000

12 Pisces Ltd included £26,500 relating to interest costs in arriving at its draft trade profits. £20,000 related to interest payable on a loan used to build a new factory, including a closing accrual of £4,000. The remaining £6,500 related to interest payable on a loan used to purchase shares in a subsidiary.

How much interest is allowable against trade profits?

A £0
B £16,000
C £20,000
D £26,500

13 Scorpio plc charged the following items in arriving at its net profit for the year to 31 March 2016:

	£
Amount written off stock to reduce it to net realisable value	4,600
Interest on late payment of corporation tax	16,456

How much should be disallowed when calculating Scorpio plc's trade profits for the year?

A £0
B £4,600
C £16,456
D £21,056

14 Rome plc charged the following items in arriving at its net profit for the year to 31 March 2016:

	£
Gifts of industrial trade samples to UK customers	950
Gifts to UK customers (one calendar each) – wall calendars bearing company logo costing £46.50 each	4,650

How much should be allowed when calculating Rome plc's trade profits for the year?

A £0
B £950
C £4,650
D £5,600

15 Paris plc prepared its first set of accounts for the twelve months ended 31 March 2016. On 1 January 2016 it purchased a new car for £14,400 (CO_2 emissions 120g/km).

What is the maximum amount of capital allowances Paris plc may claim for the twelve months ended 31 March 2016?

A £648
B £2,592
C £3,600
D £14,400

16 Copenhagen Ltd prepares accounts to 31 March each year. The tax written down value of the main pool at 1 April 2015 was £13,400. During the year ended 31 March 2016, the following transaction took place:

	£
2 January 2016 Sold car (cost £10,000 in May 2010, CO_2 emissions 150 g/km)	3,500

Calculate the maximum amount of capital allowances Copenhagen Ltd may claim for the year ended 31 March 2016.

17 Cashew Ltd drew up accounts for the six-month period to 30 June 2016. Cashew Ltd pays interest on its £20,000 9% debenture stock annually on 31 March.

How much interest is allowable for tax purposes for the six months ended 30 June 2016?

A £720
B £900
C £1,440
D £1,800

18 Gorilla Ltd commenced trading on 1 April 2015 and purchased a motor car for £8,500 (a low emissions car) for the use of an employee (75% business use, 25% private).

What is the maximum amount of capital allowances Gorilla Ltd may claim on the car for the six months ended 30 September 2015?

A £3,188
B £4,250
C £6,375
D £8,500

19 In the year ended 31 July 2016, Cat Ltd has bank interest receivable of £103,000 and interest payable as set out below.

	£
On loan to acquire investment property	14,000
On loan to acquire factory premises	42,000
On loan to acquire shares in a subsidiary company	6,000

What is Cat Ltd's assessable non-trading loan relationship credit for the year ended 31 July 2016 and what amount of interest is deductible in arriving at the company's trade profits?

	Non-trading Loan relationships	Trading deduction
A	£41,000	£0
B	£61,000	£20,000
C	£83,000	£42,000
D	£97,000	£56,000

20 Labrador Ltd has incurred the following legal expenses in its first accounting period.

	£
Preparation of directors' employment contracts (the directors are also the shareholders)	4,600
Issue of share capital	2,000
Acquiring a 30-year lease	3,000

How much legal expense is disallowed for tax purposes?

A £2,000
B £3,000
C £5,000
D £9,600

21 Collie plc commenced trading on 1 August 2015 and purchased a motor car (CO_2 emissions 123g/km) for £16,800 for the use of a director (25% private use). Collie plc prepared its first accounts for the eight months to 31 March 2016.

Calculate Collie plc's maximum capital allowance available for the car for the eight months ended 31 March 2016.

22 Alsatian Ltd has plant and machinery with a tax written down value of £20,000 on 1 June 2015. During the seven-month accounting period to 31 December 2015, it purchased a machine for £7,000.

What is the maximum amount of capital allowances available to Alsatian Ltd for the seven months ended 31 December 2015?

A £4,860
B £2,835
C £9,100
D £10,600

23 Hovawart plc included the following amounts in arriving at its draft trading income of £666,888 for the year ended 31 May 2016.

Select whether an adjustment to profits should be made for each of the following items in order to determine Hovawart plc's final trading income.

Depreciation of £156,742

A Adjust
B Do not adjust

Interest of £1,500 received on a loan to an employee

C Adjust
D Do not adjust

24 Russell plc allowed the following amounts in arriving at its draft trading income of £1,555,000.

Select how each item should be treated in the adjustment to profits working in order to determine Russell plc's final trading income.

Russell plc included £4,000 relating to the loss on disposal of an item of machinery

A Add back £4,000
B Deduct £4,000
C Do not adjust

Russell plc included £144,400 relating to redundancy costs (employees received an amount equal to their annual salary)

D Add back £144,400
E Deduct £144,400
F Do not adjust

25 Spitz plc has calculated the following amounts which have yet to be included in its final trading income.

Select how each item should be treated in the adjustment to profits working in order to determine Spitz plc's final trading income.

Spitz plc has calculated a balancing charge of £2,500 arising as a result of a disposal from the main pool

A Increase trading income by £2,500
B Reduce trading income by £2,500
C Do not include in trading income

Spitz plc sponsored three employees for £100 each for taking part in a marathon on behalf of Oxfam (an internationally registered charity)

D Increase trading income by £300
E Reduce trading income by £300
F Do not include in trading income

26 Newfoundland Ltd, a trading company, included £47,300 relating to pension costs in arriving at its draft trading income. In addition, £17,000 being an opening accrual was paid. No closing accrual was required.

What adjustment is required in order to determine Newfoundland Ltd's final trading income?

A £17,000
B £0
C £64,300
D £47,300

27 Pug Ltd included £33,400 relating to interest costs in arriving at its draft trading income. £13,000 related to interest payable on a loan used to purchase new machinery. The remaining £20,400 related to interest payable on a loan used to buy an investment.

How much interest is allowable against trading income?

A £0
B £13,000
C £33,400
D £20,400

28 Rottweiler Ltd acquired £1,540,000 of 10% debentures for investment purposes on 1 January 2016. Interest is payable half yearly on 31 December and 30 June each year. Accordingly, Rottweiler Ltd did not actually receive any interest during the year to 29 February 2016.

How much interest is taxable in the year ended 29 February 2016?

A £154,000 as trading income
B £25,667 as a non-trading loan relationship credit
C £0
D £154,000 as a non-trading loan relationship credit
E £25,667 as trading income

29 Arabesque Ltd prepared its first set of accounts for the eight months ended 31 October 2015. On 1 May 2015 it purchased a new car for £18,000 (CO_2 emissions of 129g/km).

What is the maximum amount of capital allowances Arabesque plc may claim for the eight months ended 31 October 2015?

A £2,160
B £3,240
C £12,000
D £18,000

30 Pirouette Ltd prepares accounts to 31 December each year. The tax written down value of the main pool at 1 January 2015 was £890. During the period of account, the following transaction took place:

		£
31 June 2015	Purchased new delivery van	10,000

Calculate the maximum amount of capital allowances Pirouette Ltd may claim for the year ended 31 December 2015.

31 Precipice plc has produced the following results for the year ended 31 March 2016:

	£
Trading income	4,000,000
Chargeable gains	25,000
Interest receivable	95,000
Qualifying donations (of which £35,000 accrued at the year end)	50,000

What is Precipice plc's corporation tax liability for its year ended 31 March 2016?

A £825,750
B £818,750
C £821,000
D £814,000

32 Puy Ltd drew up accounts for the nine-month period to 30 June 2015. The company pays interest on its £600,000 5% debenture stock annually on 31 December.

How much interest is allowable for tax purposes for the nine months ended 30 June 2015?

A £24,000
B £22,500
C £30,000
D £0

33 Esquilino plc has recently begun to rent out the top floor of its office building; the other two floors are used in its trade. Building running costs of £3,000 have been incurred for the year ended 31 December 2015. In addition interest on the loan to purchase the building was £3,900 for the year.

In relation to the building, what amount will be an allowable deduction against trading income for the year ended 31 December 2015?

A £2,300
B £3,000
C £4,600
D £6,900

34 Turner Ltd has included the following items in its profit before tax for the year ended 31 December 2015. For each item, select the adjustment that must be made to arrive at the trading income for the year ended 31 December 2015.

Depreciation of the office building

A Add back
B Deduct
C No adjustment

Entertaining staff at a party, which cost £85 per head

D Add back
E Deduct
F No adjustment

35 Which **TWO** of the following items are deductible in arriving at the trading income of a UK company which manufactures furniture?

A Employer's national insurance contributions
B Gift of a £15 bottle of wine to a customer
C Interest on a loan taken out to purchase shares in a subsidiary
D Interest on overdue corporation tax
E Replacement of roof tiles on the company's head office building

36 Worrall Ltd purchased the following items during the year ended 31 December 2015.

Car used 20% for business purposes by the managing director	£16,000
Computer	£6,900
Low emission car	£13,500

The balance on the main pool on 1 January 2015 was £54,000.

The managing director's car has CO_2 emissions of 120g/km.

Calculate the maximum capital allowances available to Worrall Ltd on the low emission car for the year ended 31 December 2015.

37 Worrall Ltd purchased the following items during the year ended 31 December 2015.

Car used 20% for business purposes by the managing director £16,000
Computer £6,900
Low emission car £13,500

The balance on the main pool on 1 January 2015 was £54,000.

The managing director's car has CO_2 emissions of 120g/km.

Calculate the maximum capital allowances available to Worrall Ltd on the computer for the year ended 31 December 2015.

38 Worrall Ltd purchased the following items during the year ended 31 December 2015.

Car used 20% for business purposes by the managing director £16,000
Computer £6,900
Low emission car £13,500

The balance on the main pool on 1 January 2015 was £54,000.

The managing director's car has CO_2 emissions of 120g/km.

Calculate the maximum capital allowances available to Worrall Ltd on the main pool for the year ended 31 December 2015.

39 Which **TWO** of the following items are treated as a profit or loss on non-trading loan relationships for Bright Ltd?

A   Bank overdraft interest

B   Finance lease interest payable on the purchase of a company car for one of Bright Ltd's employees

C   Interest payable on a loan to purchase a factory which is used to manufacture Bright Ltd's goods

D   Interest payable on a loan to purchase an investment property

E   Interest payable on a loan to purchase shares in Dim Ltd, another trading company

40 Walters Ltd has taxable total profits of £230,000 for the year ended 31 March 2016. However, this figure is before the effect of the following items, which were omitted from the financial statements.

Select the effect of each item on Walters Ltd's taxable total profits.

Qualifying donations to charity

A   Increase
B   Decrease
C   No effect

Recovery of previously written off trade debts

D   Increase
E   Decrease
F   No effect

41 Guava Ltd, a small trading company, incurred the following expenditure in the year to 30 September 2015.

	£
Incidental costs of long-term finance used for trade purposes	23,500
Gifts of trading stock to a local charity	2,780

How much should be disallowed when calculating Guava Ltd's trading income for the year?

A   £0
B   £2,780
C   £23,500
D   £26,280

42 Ivy Ltd has the following results for its year ended 31 December 2015.

	£
Qualifying donation paid to UNICEF (a registered charity)	(4,000)
Trading income	256,000
Chargeable gain	18,350
Dividends received from unrelated company	29,700
Rental income accrued	7,900

What are Ivy Ltd's augmented profits for the purpose of determining when the corporation tax is payable?

A £311,250
B £278,250
C £307,950
D £315,250

43 Wubzy plc deducted the following amounts in arriving at its draft trading income of £468,295 for the year ended 31 August 2015.

Select whether an adjustment to profits should be made for each of the following items in order to determine Wubzy plc's final trading income.

£12,962 loss on disposal of fixed assets

A Adjust
B Do not adjust

Interest of £3,542 paid on a loan to finance the purchase of an investment property

C Adjust
D Do not adjust

44 Flowertot plc has deducted the following amounts in arriving at its draft trading income.

Select how each item should be treated in the adjustments to profits working in order to determine Flowertot plc's final trading income.

Flowertot plc has paid a dividend to its shareholders of £4,600

A Adjust trading income by adding back £4,600
B Do not adjust

Flowertot plc is expanding and has taken out a new 20-year lease on office premises. The legal fees relating to this were £1,900

C Adjust trading income by adding back £1,900
D Do not adjust

45 Cinders plc has produced the following results for the year ended 31 August 2015:

	£
Trading income	890,000
Dividends received from a 5% holding in a UK company	45,000
Interest receivable	95,000
Interest payable on a non-trading loan	25,000
Qualifying donation paid	40,000

What are Cinders plc's augmented profits for the purposes of determining when Cinders plc should pay its corporation tax?

A £920,000
B £965,000
C £970,000
D £995,000

46　In the year ended 31 March 2016, Gladstone Ltd has interest receivable of £53,000 and interest payable as set out below.

	£
On loan to acquire rental property	13,000
On loan to acquire factory premises	39,000
On loan to acquire subsidiary company	11,000

How much of Gladstone Ltd's income is assessable as a non-trading loan relationship for the year ended 31 March 2016 and how much interest is deductible in arriving at the company's trading income?

	Non-trading loan relationship income	Trading deduction
A	£42,000	£52,000
B	£42,000	£39,000
C	£29,000	£39,000
D	£53,000	£50,000

47　Oak Ltd has incurred the following legal expenses in its first accounting period.

	£
Preparation of memorandum and articles of association	3,500
Issue of share capital	1,000
Obtaining an injunction against a trading competitor	2,000

How much legal expense is allowable for tax purposes?

A　£2,000
B　£3,000
C　£5,500
D　£6,500

48　Banana plc, a small company, commenced trading on 1 August 2015 and purchased a motor car (a low emission car) for £7,200 for the use of a director (20% private use). Banana plc prepared its first accounts to the 31 March 2016.

Calculate Banana plc's maximum capital allowance available for the car for the eight months ended 31 March 2016.

49　Cucumber Ltd has the following results for its year ended 31 March 2016.

	£
Trading income	200,000
UK dividends received net from unrelated company	9,900
Rental income accrued	5,600
Chargeable gain	6,000
Qualifying donation paid to Oxfam (a registered charity)	(800)

What are Cucumber Ltd's augmented profits?

A　£210,800
B　£220,700
C　£221,800
D　£222,600

50 Potato Ltd, a trading company, received the following sundry income during the year ended 31 March 2016.

	£
Franked investment income	14,900
Recovery of bad debt written off in previous accounting period	17,360
Interest received on overpaid corporation tax	4,560

How much sundry income will be taxed as part of trading income in the year ended 31 March 2016?

A   £0
B   £17,360
C   £21,920
D   £36,820

51 Which **TWO** of the following statements about corporation tax are true?

A   Dividends paid by a company are allowable against trading income

B   Interest paid on a loan to purchase a new factory for use by the business is a non-trading loan relationship debit

C   Companies may deduct qualifying donations paid when calculating taxable total profits

D   Charitable donations made to small, local charities are allowable against trading income

E   Dividends received from UK companies are taxable income to be included in calculating taxable total profits

52 Universe plc deducted the following amounts in arriving at its draft trading income of £717,199 for the year ended 31 July 2015.

Select whether an adjustment to profits should be made for each of the following items in order to determine Universe plc's final trading income.

£48,656 depreciation

A   Adjust
B   Do not adjust

Interest of £1,500 paid on a loan to finance a new item of machinery

C   Adjust
D   Do not adjust

53 Taurus Ltd acquired £315,000 of 9% debentures for investment purposes on 1 May 2015. Interest is payable half yearly on 31 August and 28 February each year. Accordingly, Taurus Ltd did not actually receive any interest during the year to 31 July 2015.

How much interest is taxable in the year ended 31 July 2015?

A   £0
B   £7,088 as trading income
C   £7,088 as a non-trading loan relationship
D   £28,350 as trading income
E   £28,350 as a non-trading loan relationship

54 Feijoa Ltd, prepares accounts to the 31 December each year. The tax written down value of the main pool at 1 January 2015 was £50,000. During the period of account, the following transactions took place.

		£
2 July 2015	Purchased new car (CO_2 emissions of 127g/km)	14,500
31 December 2015	Purchased new office equipment	22,000

Calculate the maximum amount of capital allowances Feijoa Ltd may claim for the year ended 31 December 2015, for the car and for the office equipment.

55 Which **TWO** of the following statements about corporation tax are true?

    A   A company with augmented profits of £1.5m in both the current year and the prior year will pay corporation tax by instalments.

    B   A company with a short accounting period must have profits of at least £1,500,000 before it will pay corporation tax by instalments.

    C   A company with two related 51% group companies and a 12 month accounting period, will have a higher limit for the purposes of corporation tax payment dates compared to the limit for a company with a four month accounting period and no related 51% group companies.

    D   A company pays corporation tax at a flat rate on its taxable total profits.

56 Giraffe Ltd received exempt cash dividends of £36,000 from its wholly owned UK subsidiary in the year ended 31 May 2016. During the year it also received exempt dividends of £4,500 from a 10% holding in Lion Ltd.

What is Giraffe Ltd's franked investment income for the year ended 31 May 2016?

    A   £4,500
    B   £5,000
    C   £40,500
    D   £45,000

57 Setter Ltd has forecast the following results for its year ended 31 December 2015.

	£
Trading income	50,000
UK dividends received in cash from 15% holding in Boxer Ltd	18,000
Chargeable gain	7,500
Qualifying donation paid to UNICEF (a registered charity)	(8,000)

What are Setter Ltd's augmented profits?

    A   £67,500
    B   £49,500
    C   £77,500
    D   £69,500

58 Which **TWO** of the following statements about corporation tax are true?

    A   Exempt gross dividends received from unrelated UK companies are used to determine when a company pays its corporation tax.

    B   Companies may deduct qualifying donations paid and accrued when calculating taxable total profits.

    C   Dividends paid by a company are a valid business expense.

    D   Interest paid on a loan to purchase a new factory is a trading expense.

    E   Charitable donations made to national charities are allowable against trading income.

59 Fouette plc owns 50.2% of the shares in Tutu Ltd which in turn owns 50.1% of the shares in Plie Ltd. Fouette plc also owns 100% of the shares in Pointe SA, a company incorporated and managed and controlled in France. Fouette plc also has a 75% shareholding in a company called Brise plc which is not active. All companies, excluding Brise plc, are trading companies.

How many companies are in a related 51% group company relationship with Fouette plc?

    A   Four
    B   Three
    C   Two
    D   One

60   Mountain Ltd's parent company has two other wholly owned subsidiaries, which it has owned for several years. Mountain Ltd prepared its first set of accounts for the six months to 31 January 2016.

      What is the limit for Mountain Ltd for the purpose of determining its corporation tax payment date for the six months ended 31 January 2016?

      A   £375,000
      B   £250,000
      C   £750,000
      D   £187,500

61   Campo Ltd has taxable total profits of £225,677 for the year ended 31 December 2015. During November 2015 it received exempt dividends from UK companies of £85,000 of which £12,000 were received from an 80% subsidiary.

      What are Campo Ltd's augmented profits for the year ended 31 December 2015?

      A   £225,677
      B   £306,788
      C   £310,677
      D   £320,121

62   Which of the following statements about corporation tax is true?

      A   A company will pay corporation tax on exempt dividends received from unrelated companies

      B   A company with augmented profits of £200,000 and no related 51% group companies will pay corporation tax on a single payment date

      C   A company with no related 51% group companies and a nine-month accounting period will pay corporation tax by instalments only if its augmented profits exceed £1.5 million

      D   A company with augmented profits of less than £1.5 million will never pay corporation tax in instalments

63   Shirt plc owns 80% of the shares in Jumper Ltd and Vest Ltd. Jumper Ltd also owns 35% of the shares in Shorts Ltd and 70% of the shares in Kilt Ltd. All companies are trading companies.

      How many of the companies are related 51% group companies?

64   Select whether the following statements are true or false.

      The corporation tax rate is multiplied by augmented profits to calculate the corporation tax liability

      A   True
      B   False

      Companies with augmented profits below the limit pay corporation tax by instalments

      C   True
      D   False

      Franked investment income is the gross amount of exempt dividends received from companies which are not 51% subsidiaries in the accounting period

      E   True
      F   False

65   Venus plc owns 100% of the shares in Saturn Ltd and Jupiter Ltd. Venus plc also owns 25% of the shares in Mars Ltd and 51% of the shares in Milky Way Ltd.

      What is the total number of related 51% group companies?

      A   Two
      B   Three
      C   Four
      D   Five

66 Hake plc owns 75% of the shares in Bass Ltd which in turn owns 75% of the shares in Salmon Ltd. Hake plc also owns 100% of the shares in Prawn Inc, a company incorporated and managed and controlled in the USA. Hake plc also has a 65% shareholding in a dormant company called Cod plc. All companies, excluding Cod plc are trading companies.

What is the total number of related 51% group companies?

A   Two
B   Three
C   Four
D   Five

67 Peach Ltd has owned two wholly owned UK subsidiaries for a number of years. In the nine months ended 31 March 2016, Peach Ltd had taxable total profits of £250,000 and no franked investment income.

What is the limit for Peach Ltd for the nine months ended 31 March 2016?

A   £375,000
B   £562,500
C   £750,000
D   £1,125,000

68 L Ltd makes up a 12-month set of accounts to 30 June 2015. It pays corporation tax by instalments.

When must L Ltd make its second instalment payment on account of corporation tax?

A   14 October 2015
B   14 July 2015
C   14 April 2015
D   14 January 2015

69 S Ltd makes up its accounts to 30 November each year. It has no related 51% group companies.

It has had the following taxable total profits in its first three years of trading:

y/e 30.11.14   £800,000
y/e 30.11.15   £1,650,000
y/e 30.11.16   £2,100,000

How will S Ltd pay its corporation tax for the years to 30 November 2015 and 30 November 2016?

	y/e 30.11.15	y/e 30.11.16
A	One payment by 1 September 2016	One payment by 1 September 2017
B	One payment by 1 September 2016	By instalments
C	One payment by 30 November 2016	By instalments
D	By instalments	By instalments

70 Stone plc has no related 51% group companies and taxable total profits of £1,000,000 for its first year of trade, which ended on 31 March 2016. It has no dividend income for the year.

When should Stone plc pay its corporation tax liability for the year ended 31 March 2016?

A   By instalments
B   31 December 2016
C   1 January 2017
D   31 March 2017

71 Bone Ltd started to trade on 1 October 2013 and has no related 51% group companies. Bone Ltd had taxable total profits of £1,600,000 for its first year ended 30 September 2014 and £1,800,000 for its second year ended 30 September 2015. The company received no franked investment income during either period.

State the due date for payment of the corporation tax for each accounting period.

Payment date for year ended 30 September 2014

A   By 1 July 2015
B   By 30 Sep 2015
C   By instalments

Payment date for year ended 30 September 2015

D   By 1 July 2016
E   By 30 Sep 2016
F   By instalments

72 Ivory plc has no related 51% group companies and taxable total profits of £600,000 for the six months ended 31 December 2015. It received gross dividend income of £500,000 during this six-month period. Ivory plc's profits and dividend income have been at a similar level for a number of years and are earned evenly throughout the year.

When should Ivory plc pay its corporation tax liability for the period ended 31 December 2015?

A   By instalments
B   30 September 2016
C   1 October 2016
D   31 December 2016

Now go back to the Learning objectives in the Introduction. If you are satisfied you have achieved these objectives, please tick them off.

Technical reference

Legislation

References relate to Corporation Tax Act (*CTA 2009*) unless otherwise stated

Charge to corporation tax	ss.2-3
General scheme of corporation tax	s.5 and s.8
Accounting periods	ss.9-10
Computation of income	s.19
Loan relationships	ss.295-301
Payment of tax	FA 1998 s.30

HMRC manual

Company Taxation manual (Found at http://www.hmrc.gov.uk/manuals/ctmanual/index.htm)

> This technical reference section is designed to assist you. It should help you to know where to look for further information on the topics covered in this chapter. **You will not be examined on the contents of this section in your examination.**

Answer to Interactive question 1

	£	£
Net disposal consideration (November 2015)		265,000
Less: acquisition cost (July 2001)	120,000	
enhancement expenditure (August 2002)	45,000	(165,000)
Unindexed gain		100,000
Less: indexation allowance		
on acquisition cost		

$$\frac{259.0 - 173.3}{173.3} = 0.495 \times £120,000 \qquad (59,400)$$

on enhancement expenditure

$$\frac{259.0 - 176.4}{176.4} = 0.468 \times £45,000 \qquad (21,060)$$

Chargeable gain	19,540

1   C – £3,000

£20,000 × 18% × 10/12 = £3,000

There is no private use reduction for companies. A taxable benefit will arise for the director.

2   C – 12 months to 30 November 2014, 4 months to 31 March 2015

An accounting period cannot be more than 12 months long. A long period of account is always split into a first accounting period of 12 months and then a second accounting period of the remainder of the period of account.

3   A and D – interest payable on loan to purchase property to let and interest on overdue corporation tax.

Bank overdraft interest and interest on a loan to purchase machinery are dealt with as trading loan relationships and deductible from trading income.

4   C – £118,000

	£
Trading income	490,000
Chargeable gains	60,000
Loan relationships	90,000
	640,000
Less: Qualifying donation	(50,000)
Taxable total profits	590,000
Corporation tax payable £590,000 × 20%	118,000

5   C – R Ltd, T Ltd and V Ltd

S Ltd is not a related 51% group company because R Ltd does not control over 50% of the shares.

U Ltd is not a related 51% group company because it does not trade and is passive.

6   £109,620

$$\frac{258.0 - 146.9}{146.9} = 0.756 \text{ (to 3 dp)} \times £145,000 = £109,620$$

7

Corporation tax liability: £1,310,000 × 20%   262,000

The company's augmented profits = £1,310,000 + £300,000 = £1,610,000 > £1,500,000 and so instalments are due on 14 October 2015, 14 January 2016, 14 April 2016 and 14 July 2016. Note that because the results were similar last year, this is not the first year of the company being large, so there is no exception from quarterly instalment payments.

8   B   Machinery disposal – deduct £1,090

F   Directors – do not adjust

The profit on disposal is capital related and therefore not treated as part of trading income. As it would originally have been an income item in arriving at the draft trade profits figure, it needs to be deducted to eliminate it.

Directors' emoluments are a valid trading expense even where the directors are also the shareholders. There is no concept of drawings for a company. No adjustment is therefore required.

9   A   Balancing charge – increase trade profits

    E   Donation – reduce trade profits

    A balancing charge may arise on the main pool where disposal proceeds of an asset sold exceed the tax written down value brought forward on the pool. Excess capital allowances previously given are reclaimed by adding the balancing charge to trade profits. Trade profits therefore need to be increased by £500.

    Charitable donations are normally disallowed in calculating taxable profits. However, where the donation is to a small local charity, it is an allowable trading expense. Trade profits therefore need to be reduced by £100.

10 B   Legal costs – do not adjust

    C   Irrecoverable VAT – adjust

    Legal costs relating to the renewal of a short lease (<50 years) is a specifically allowable expense. No adjustment is therefore required.

    Irrecoverable VAT is allowable if the item of expenditure to which it relates is also allowable. In this case the car should have been included in the capital allowances computation at its gross value and therefore relief for the irrecoverable VAT will be given over the life of the car. The £3,500 should therefore be added back in calculating the final trade profits figure.

11 B   £12,000

    Only the amount actually paid to a registered pension scheme during the accounting period is allowable against trade profits. The £12,000 accrual therefore needs to be added back in order to calculate the final trade profits figure.

12 C   £20,000

    Interest is calculated on an accruals basis. Only interest relating to trade is allowable in computing trade profits. Interest on a loan to acquire shares in a subsidiary is not trade related and should be included in loan relationships. Only the interest on the loan to build a factory, including the accrual, is allowed for trade profits.

13 C   £16,456

    The stock write-down is specific and is allowable against trade profits. The interest on overdue corporation tax is loss from a non trading loan relationship, not an allowable trading expense.

14 D   £5,600

    The trade samples are a business expense and are therefore allowable. As the calendars cost less than £50 each, are not food, alcohol or tobacco, and bear the company logo, they are also allowable.

15 B   £2,592

    The maximum capital allowance for a car with CO_2 emissions of between 76g/km and 130g/km for a 12 month accounting period is 18%. The WDA here is £14,400 × 18% = £2,592.

16 The balance of the main pool after the disposal of the car is £13,400 – £3,500 = £9,900. The WDA is £9,900 × 18% = £1,782.

17 B   £900

    The gross amount charged on the accruals basis is allowable under the loan relationship rules. As the accounting period is 6 months in length, the gross accrued interest is £900 (£20,000 × 9% × 6/12). Remember that it is the gross amount of debenture interest which is included not the net.

18 D   £8,500

    First year allowances at 100% are available to any size of business which purchases a low emission car. First year allowances are never prorated where the accounting period is not 12 months, or where there is private use by an employee.

19 C *Non-trading Loan relationships*   *Trading deduction*
     £83,000   £42,000

Non-trading loan relationship = £103,000 – £14,000 – £6,000 = £83,000

Trading expenses = £42,000

For companies the interest on the loans to acquire an investment property and a subsidiary company are non-trade related and are therefore included as non-trading loan relationships. Unless a company's trade is financial, all interest receivable is also included in non-trading loan relationships. Allowable interest for trade profits only includes the loan used to purchase a factory.

20 C £5,000

£4,600 for the employment contracts is an allowable trading expense. The other two items relate to capital expenditure and are therefore disallowed. Legal costs associated with the acquisition of a short lease (<50 years) are disallowed, although they are allowed for the renewal of a short lease.

21   Maximum WDA is £16,800 × 18% × 8/12 = £2,016

Note that private use of an asset does not affect capital allowances for a company.

22 C £9,100

AIA covers new machine	£7,000
WDA £20,000 @ 18% × $^7/_{12}$ =	£2,100
	£9,100

23 A Depreciation – adjust

   C Interest – adjust

As depreciation is a capital item it must be added back to arrive at trading income. Capital allowances will be deducted instead of depreciation.

The interest is not for trading purposes and should be deducted from trading income and included as a non-trading loan relationship credit.

24 A Machinery disposal – add back £4,000

   F Redundancy – do not adjust

The loss on disposal is capital related and therefore not allowed as a trading expense. As it would originally have been an expense item in arriving at the draft trading income figure, it needs to be added back to eliminate it.

Redundancy costs are a valid trading expense. No adjustment is therefore required.

25 A Balancing charge – increase trading income by £2,500

   F Donation – do not include

A balancing charge may arise on the main pool where disposal proceeds of an asset sold exceed the tax written down value brought forward on the pool. Excess allowances given are reclaimed by adding the balancing charge to trading income. Trading income therefore needs to be increased by £2,500.

Charitable donations are normally included in taxable total profits as a qualifying donation. Only where the donation is to a small local charity, is it an allowable trading expense. In this case it is a donation to an international charity, so it should be excluded from trading income.

26　A　£17,000

Only the amount actually paid to a registered pension scheme during the accounting period is allowable against trading income. In the previous year the closing accrual of £17,000 would have been disallowed as it had yet to be paid. As it was paid in the current year it is allowed in the current year. As there is no closing accrual, the full amount of £47,300 has been paid in the current year. Thus the additional £17,000 paid this year which relates to last year needs to be deducted in arriving at trading income.

27　B　£13,000

Interest is calculated on an accruals basis. Only interest relating to the trade is allowable in computing trading income. Interest on a loan to acquire an investment is not trade related and should be included in non-trading loan relationships. Only the interest on the loan to purchase new machinery is allowed for trading income.

28　B　£25,667 as a non-trading loan relationship

Debenture interest receivable is assessed on the accruals basis. As the debentures were only owned for two months of the year, the amount assessable is £25,667 (£1,540,000 × 10% × 2/12). The fact that no interest was actually received during the accounting period is not relevant. As the debentures are non-trade related (for investment), the interest will be assessed to tax as a non-trading loan relationship credit.

29　A　£2,160

The maximum capital allowance for the car for an eight month accounting period is:

£18,000 × 18% × 8/12 = £2,160

30　The van is covered by the AIA. The main pool does not exceed £1,000, so may be written off.

Total capital allowances = £10,000 + £890 = £10,890

31　C　£821,000

Precipice plc has taxable total profits of £4,105,000 ie £4,000,000 + £25,000 + £95,000 − £15,000. Only the qualifying donation actually paid in the year is deducted as a qualifying charitable donation.

32　B　£22,500

The gross amount charged on the accruals basis is allowable as a loan relationship debit. As the accounting period is 9 months in length, the gross accrued interest is £22,500 (£600,000 × 5% × 9/12). Remember that it is the gross amount of debenture interest which is included, not the net.

33　C　£4,600

The costs associated with renting out the top floor are not business related and are therefore not allowed for trading income purposes. As two floors of the office building are used in the company's trade, two thirds of the loan interest is allowed as a trading expense.
The remaining interest is a loss on loan relationships as it is not trade related. The allowable expense is £3,000 × 2/3 + £3,900 × 2/3 = £4,600.

34　A　Depreciation of the office building – add back

　　F　Entertaining staff at a party which costs £85 per head – no adjustment

35　A　Employer's national insurance contributions

　　E　Replacement of roof tiles

Gifts of food, drink or tobacco are disallowed. Interest on a loan to purchase shares in a subsidiary and interest on overdue corporation tax are expenses in arriving at profits on non-trading loan relationships.

36　FYA @ 100% × £13,500 = £13,500

37 AIA is available to cover the purchase of the computer.

38

	£
TWDV b/f	54,000
Additions (AIA)	6,900
AIA	(6,900)
Additions – car	16,000
	70,000
WDA @ 18%	(12,600)
TWDV c/f	57,400

There is no private use restriction in respect of a *company's* capital allowances.

The total allowances due are AIA of £6,900 + FYA of £13,500 + WDA of £12,600 = £33,000

39 D Interest payable on a loan to purchase an investment property

E Interest payable on a loan to purchase shares in Dim Ltd, another trading company

40 B A qualifying donation to charity – Decrease

D Recovery of previously written off trade debts – Increase

41 The correct answer is A

Incidental costs of long-term loan finance are allowed as a business expense if the loan is used for trade purposes. Gifts of trading stock to charities are specifically allowable.

42 The correct answer is A

	£
Trading income	256,000
Property income	7,900
Chargeable gain	18,350
	282,250
Less: Qualifying donation paid	(4,000)
Taxable total profits	278,250
FII £29,700 × 100/90	33,000
Augmented profits	311,250

43 The correct answer is A, C

A loss on disposal of fixed assets is a capital item it must be added back to arrive at trading income. This will be dealt with by capital allowances.

The interest is for non trading purposes and is therefore not a valid trading expense. It is added back and included as a non-trading loan relationship expense.

44 The correct answer is A, C

Dividends paid to shareholders are an appropriation of profits and not an allowable deduction for trade purposes. As a result the dividend paid must be added back.

Legal fees on the taking out of a new short lease relate to the capital increase in the company and are therefore a disallowable expense in calculating trading income. The fees must be added back. If the legal fees had related to the renewal of a short lease they would have been an allowable deduction and no adjustment would have been required.

45 The correct answer is C

	£	£
Trading income		890,000
Interest receivable	95,000	
Interest payable on a non trading loan	(25,000)	70,000
Qualifying donation paid		(40,000)
Taxable total profits		920,000
FII (45,000 × 100/90)		50,000
Augmented profits		970,000

46 The correct answer is C

Non-trading loan relationship income   *Trading deduction*

£29,000   £39,000

Non-trading loan relationships = £53,000 – £13,000 – £11,000 = £29,000

Trading expenses = £39,000

For companies, all non-trading interest is included as non-trading loan relationships. Thus the interest on the loans to acquire a rental property and a subsidiary company are non-trading loan relationships. Unless a company's trade is financial, all interest receivable is taxable as a non-trading loan relationship. Allowable interest for trading purposes is the loan used to purchase a factory.

47 The correct answer is A

£2,000 for the injunction is an allowable trading expense. The other two items relate to capital expenditure and are therefore disallowed.

48 8-month accounting period.

FYA @ 100% available. FYAs are not pro-rated.

Note that private use of an asset by the director of a company does not restrict capital allowances.

49 The correct answer is C

	£
Trading income	200,000
Property income	5,600
Chargeable gain	6,000
	211,600
Less Qualifying donation paid	(800)
Taxable total profits	210,800
FII £9,900 × 100/90	11,000
Augmented profits	221,800

50 The correct answer is B

Franked investment income is ignored when calculating taxable total profits although it is of relevance in determining the payment date for corporation tax. The bad debt expense will have been allowed against trading income in the previous accounting period so must be taxed as income when recovered. Interest received is always taxable as a non-trading loan relationship credit for a trading company.

51 The correct answer is C, D

Companies may deduct qualifying donations paid when calculating taxable total profits.

Charitable donations made to small, local charities are allowable against trading income.

Dividends paid are ignored in calculating taxable total profits as they are merely an appropriation of profit, not a business expense.

Dividends received from UK companies are not taxable income but if received from companies which are not 51% subsidiaries they will be franked investment income and are used to determine the payment date of corporation tax.

Interest paid on a loan to purchase a new factory is trade related and therefore is a trading income expense not a non-trading loan relationship debit.

52 The correct answer is A, D

Depreciation – adjust, Interest – do not adjust.

As depreciation is a capital item it must be added back to arrive at trading income. Capital allowances will be deducted instead of depreciation.

The interest is for trading purposes and is therefore a valid trade expense. Had it been non-trade related it would have been added back and included as a non-trading loan relationship debit.

53 The correct answer is C

Debenture interest receivable is assessed on an accruals basis. As the debentures were only owned for three months of the year, the amount assessable is £7,088 (£315,000 × 9% × 3/12). The fact that no interest was actually received during the accounting period is not relevant. As the debentures are non-trade related, the interest will be assessed to tax as a non-trading loan relationship.

54 The car receives a WDA of 18%. £14,500 @ 18% = £2,610

The office equipment will be fully covered by the AIA as it cost less than £500,000.

55 A A company with augmented profits of £1.5m in both the current year and the prior year will pay corporation tax by instalments.

D A company pays corporation tax at a flat rate on its taxable total profits.

A company with a short accounting period (AP) must have profits of at least £1,500,000 *prorated for the number of months in its AP* before it will pay corporation tax by instalments.

A company with two related 51% group companies will have *the same* limit for the purposes of corporation tax payment dates compared to the limit for a company with a four month accounting period.

56 B £5,000

Franked investment income (FII) is gross exempt dividends received from companies which are not 51% subsidiaries. As Giraffe Ltd has a 100% holding in its UK subsidiary the dividends can be ignored. The dividends received from Lion Ltd, however are relevant giving gross FII of £4,500 × 100/90 = £5,000.

57 D £69,500

	£
Trading income	50,000
Chargeable gain	7,500
	57,500
Less qualifying donations	(8,000)
Taxable total profits	49,500
FII £18,000 × 100/90	20,000
Augmented profits	69,500

58 A Exempt gross dividends received from unrelated UK companies are used to determine when a company pays its corporation tax.

D Interest paid on a loan to purchase a new factory is a trading expense.

Companies may *only* deduct qualifying donations *paid* when calculating taxable total profits.

Dividends paid by a company *are an appropriation of profit not a* valid business expense.

Small charitable donations made to *local* charities are allowable against trading income.

59 C Two

Fouette plc's related 51% group companies are all the active companies resident anywhere in the world which are its 51% subsidiaries. As it has a 50.2% holding in Tutu Ltd, Tutu Ltd is a related 51% group company. Fouette plc does not have an indirect holding of more than 50% over Plie Ltd (50.2 x 50.1%) which is therefore not a related 51% group company for Fouette plc. Pointe SA is a 51% subsidiary of Fouette plc so is also a related 51% group company regardless of the fact it is resident in France. Brise plc is ignored as it is a 'passive' company. Thus Fouette plc has two related 51% group companies (Tutu Ltd and Pointe SA).

60   D   £187,500

As Mountain Ltd's parent company has two other wholly owned subsidiaries, there are four related 51% group companies: Parent + Mountain Ltd + two other subsidiaries. The revised limit becomes £375,000

As Mountain Ltd has also prepared its accounts for a six month period, the limit needs to be further prorated to account for the short accounting period:

£375,000 × 6/12 = £187,500

61   B   £306,788 (£225,677 + (100/90 × £73,000))

62   The correct answer is B

A company will not pay corporation tax on exempt dividends received from unrelated companies. The dividends represent Franked Investment Income which might affect the corporation tax payment date, but corporation tax is only paid on taxable total profits which excludes exempt dividends received.

A company with no related 51% group companies and a nine-month accounting period will pay corporation tax by instalments only if its augmented profits exceed £1,125,000. The nine-month accounting period means that the limit is pro rated.

A company with augmented profits of less than £1.5 million will not pay corporation tax in instalments as long as it has no related 51% group companies, and does not have a short accounting period.

63   The correct answer is 4

Jumper Ltd and Vest Ltd are 51% subsidiaries of Shirt plc. Kilt Ltd is also a 51% subsidiary of Shirt plc because Shirt plc has an indirect holding of 56% (80% x 70%). Including Shirt plc there are four related 51% group companies.

64   The correct answer is B, D, E

The corporation tax liability is calculated as the CT rate × taxable total profits (not augmented profits)

Where a company has augmented profits below the limit of £1,500,000, the tax is paid on a single payment date nine months and one day after the accounting period end

Franked investment income is gross not net dividends. It does not include those from 51% subsidiaries.

65   The correct answer is C

A company is a related 51% group company if it is a 51% subsidiary. Venus plc has three 51% subsidiaries Saturn Ltd, Jupiter Ltd and Milky Way Ltd. Therefore, including Venus plc there are four related 51% group companies.

66   The correct answer is C

Hake plc is in a related 51% group with all the active companies resident anywhere in the world which are its 51% subsidiaries. Bass Ltd, Salmon Ltd and Prawn Inc (despite being resident in the USA) are all 51% subsidiaries of Hake plc. Cod plc is ignored as it is a dormant company. There are therefore four related 51% group companies.

67   The correct answer is A

£375,000

As Peach Ltd has two wholly owned subsidiaries, there are three related 51% group companies. The revised limit becomes £500,000. As Peach Ltd has also prepared its accounts for a nine-month period, the limit needs to be further pro rated to account for the short accounting period, ie £500,000 × 9/12 = £375,000.

68   C – 14 April 2015

The second instalment is due in the 10th month of the accounting period.

69 B – for y/e 30 November 2015 by 1 September 2016, for y/e 30 November 2016 by instalments.

S Ltd is a large company for the first time in the year ended 30 November 2015 and so does not have to pay tax by instalments in that year. It is also a large company in the year ended 30 November 2016 and so does have to pay tax in instalments in that year.

70 C 1 January 2017

A company with augmented profits (here £1,000,000) below the limit is required to pay its corporation tax liability within nine months and one day of its accounting period end.

71 A Y/e 30 September 2014 – By 1 July 2015

F Y/e 30 September 2015– By instalments

A company does not have to pay tax by instalments in the first accounting period that its augmented profits exceed the limit provided its augmented profits ≤ £10,000,000

72 The correct answer is A

A company which has augmented profits above the limit is required to pay its corporation tax liability by instalments. As this is a short accounting period the limit of £1.5 million needs to be pro rated, ie £1.5m × 6/12 = £750,000

The dividend income is stated gross and as Ivory plc has no subsidiaries, it must be franked investment income. The augmented profits for the six months are therefore £1,100,000 (£600,000 + £500,000).

Ivory plc had similar profits in the previous year and therefore this is not the first accounting period in which its augmented profits exceeded the limit. It is therefore required to pay its corporation tax liability by instalments.

CHAPTER 11

Value added tax

Introduction
Examination context
Topic List
1   The principles of value added tax (VAT)
2   Classification of supplies
3   Registration and deregistration
4   Output VAT
5   Input VAT
Summary and Self-test
Technical reference
Answer to Interactive question
Answers to Self-test

Introduction

Learning objectives

- Classify supplies in straightforward situations as exempt, zero rated, standard rated, subject to a reduced rate of 5% or outside the scope of VAT ☐

- Recognise the implications of supplies being classified as standard rated, zero rated or exempt ☐

- Identify when a business could or should register or deregister for VAT and state the time limits ☐

- Determine the tax point for a supply of goods or services ☐

- State the principles of VAT payable or repayable on the supply of goods or services by a taxable person ☐

Specific syllabus references for this chapter are: 6a, b, c, d, e.

Syllabus links

The topics in this chapter and the following chapter form the basis of your understanding of value added tax.

In the Tax Compliance paper you will deal with further aspects of VAT such as overseas transactions.

Examination context

In the examination, in the objective test questions, candidates may be required to:

- Determine when a transaction is within the scope of VAT, and the impact of it being a taxable or exempt supply

- Identify when VAT registration/deregistration are required/desirable

- Calculate the VAT applying to a supply, starting at either the VAT-inclusive or exclusive figure

- Determine the tax point of a supply

- Deal with additional aspects of input tax and output tax such as bad debts, discounts etc

For extra question practice on these topics go to the section of the Question Bank covering this chapter.

Candidates have historically been weak at VAT questions. This is probably because there are a large number of small issues to learn rather than one main pro forma to contend with. It is essential that candidates take time to understand and become competent at VAT at an early stage.

1 The principles of value added tax (VAT)

Section overview

- VAT is payable by the final consumer of goods and services.

- VAT is collected at each stage of the distribution chain.

- VAT is charged on a taxable supply by a taxable person in the course of a business carried on by him.

1.1 How VAT works

Value added tax (VAT) is a tax payable on the consumption of goods and services by the final consumer.

However, instead of all the tax being collected at the final point of consumption, VAT is collected as value is added to the goods or services.

As the goods or services go through the production and distribution process, each VAT-registered business charges VAT on the value of the goods or services it supplies. This is called **output VAT**.

Each VAT-registered business receives credit for any VAT that it has paid. This is called **input VAT**.

The business sets off input VAT against output VAT. Usually this results in a net excess of output VAT which the business pays over to HMRC.

The total tax is ultimately borne by the final consumer of the goods or services at the end of the distribution chain.

Worked example: Operation of VAT

Gerald makes car components which attract VAT of 20%. He sells them to William, a car component wholesaler, for £80 plus VAT of £16 (20% of £80).

William holds the car components in stock until he sells them to Fiona, who runs a car dealership, for £120 plus VAT of £24 (20% of £120).

Fiona sells the components to Richard, a private customer, for £160 plus VAT of £32 (20% of £160).

Requirement

How does VAT operate in this distribution chain?

Solution

	Gerald £	William £	Fiona £
Output tax	16	24	32
Less input tax	(nil)	(16)	(24)
Net excess	16	8	8

The total amount payable to HMRC is (£16 + £8 + £8) = £32

Richard is unable to reclaim any VAT as he is a private customer and not VAT registered and therefore suffers the total VAT charge of £32. Gerald, William and Fiona do no suffer any net VAT; they merely collect and pay the VAT to HMRC.

We will look at the administration of VAT later in this text.

1.2 Scope of VAT

VAT is charged on the **taxable supply** of goods and services in the United Kingdom (UK) by a **taxable person** in the course of a business carried on by him.

Definition

Taxable supply: any supply of goods or services made in the UK other than an exempt supply or a supply outside the scope of VAT.

We will look at this definition in more detail when we consider the classification of supplies later in this chapter.

Definition

Taxable person: a person making taxable supplies who is, or who is required to be, registered for VAT. Person includes a sole trader, a partnership (not the individual partners) and a company.

A taxable person is required to charge output VAT on any taxable supplies made, and may also recover input VAT on supplies paid for. A person who is not a taxable person cannot charge output VAT on supplies or recover input VAT.

We look at the conditions to register for VAT later in this chapter.

2 Classification of supplies

Section overview

- Supplies may be outside the scope of VAT, exempt or taxable.

- A supply of goods arises when ownership of goods passes from one person to another.

- A supply of services arises when there is a supply for consideration which is not a supply of goods.

- Exempt supplies do not have output VAT charged on them.

- Taxable supplies may be at zero rate, reduced rate or standard rate.

- Taxable supplies have output VAT charged on them.

2.1 Supplies of goods and services

A supply of goods or services may fall into one of three categories:

- Outside the scope of VAT
- Exempt supplies
- Taxable supplies

We will look at each type of supply in turn in the rest of this section.

First, however, we need to consider the meaning of a **supply** upon which VAT should be accounted for.

A supply of goods takes place when ownership of the goods passes from one person to another.

Examples of supplies of goods include:

- Sales of goods for consideration

- Gifts of business assets except samples or where total gifts made to the same person do not exceed £50 in any 12-month period. Unlimited samples can be given to the same person without the need to account for output tax

- Goods permanently taken out of a business for private use by the owner or an employee

- Sales of goods on hire purchase

A supply of services is any supply for a consideration which is not a supply of goods. Consideration is any form of payment in money or in kind. Therefore a gift of services is not a taxable supply. Examples of supplies include:

- Sales of services for consideration

- Hiring of goods to a customer

- Goods owned by a business temporarily taken for private use by the owner or an employee

- Private use, by the owner or an employee, of business services supplied to the business

- Private use of fuel for motoring by the owner or an employee (but not the private use of a business motor car itself)

2.2 Supplies outside the scope of VAT

Supplies outside the scope of VAT do not have any effect for VAT.

Examples include the payment of wages and dividends.

An awareness that these supplies are outside the scope of VAT will be required in the examination.

2.3 Exempt supplies

An exempt supply is one on which output VAT cannot be charged. In general, input VAT cannot be recovered by a trader making exempt supplies.

Examples include some supplies of land, insurance and postal services.

If a person only makes exempt supplies, VAT registration is not allowed. The person cannot be a taxable person, but is treated as the final consumer of the goods or services.

In the examination you will not be expected to identify that a specific supply is exempt.

2.4 Taxable supplies

Taxable supplies fall into one of three categories:

- Zero rated (0%)
- Reduced rate (5%)
- Standard rated (20%)

A taxable supply is one on which output VAT is chargeable and input VAT can be recovered. Note the difference between exempt supplies (no input VAT recoverable) and zero-rated supplies (input VAT can be recovered).

Examples of zero-rated supplies include human and animal food, books and newspapers and drugs and medicines on prescription or provided by private hospitals.

Examples of reduced rate supplies include domestic fuel and children's car seats.

Any taxable supply not classified as zero rated or reduced rate is a standard-rated supply.

In the examination you will not be expected to classify specific taxable supplies into each category.

3 Registration and deregistration

Section overview

- Compulsory registration is required if a person's taxable turnover exceeds the registration threshold.

- Voluntary registration may be applied for if a person is making taxable supplies below the registration threshold.

- There is an exemption from registration if a person is making only or mostly zero-rated supplies.

- Deregistration applies if taxable supplies cease or fall below the deregistration threshold.

3.1 Compulsory registration

A person making taxable supplies is required to register for VAT if the total value of taxable supplies (**taxable turnover**) exceeds the statutory threshold. Taxable supplies include zero-rated, reduced-rate and standard-rated supplies. It does not include supplies of capital assets of the business.

A person's registration covers all of his business activities as it is the person who is registered, not his business. VAT registration can be completed online.

The statutory threshold from 1 April 2015 is £82,000.

There are two situations where compulsory registration is required: the **future prospects test** and the **historic test**. A taxable person must register once he exceeds the threshold under either of the tests.

3.1.1 Future prospects test

Under the future prospects test, the person must register for VAT if, at any time, there are reasonable grounds for believing that the taxable turnover in the next 30 days alone will exceed the threshold.

If a person is liable to register under the future prospects test, he must notify HMRC by the end of the 30-day period in which the threshold is expected to be exceeded. This 30-day period includes the date the trader becomes aware that the threshold is likely to be exceeded.

Registration takes effect from the beginning of the same 30-day period.

3.1.2 Historic test

Under the historic test, a person must register for VAT if, at the end of any month, the taxable turnover in the prior period exceeds the threshold. The prior period is the previous 12 months or the period from the commencement of the business, whichever is the shorter.

If a person is liable to register under the historic test, he must notify HMRC within thirty days of the end of the month in which the threshold was exceeded (the **relevant month**).

Registration takes effect from the first day after the end of the month following the relevant month.

Worked example: Tests for VAT registration

Caroline started trading on 1 July 2015. Her monthly turnover (excluding VAT) is:

	£
Standard-rated supplies	7,350
Zero-rated supplies	950
Exempt supplies	500
	8,800

On 1 February 2016, Caroline sold a machine used in her business for £2,500 (excluding VAT).

Requirement

On what date is the VAT registration threshold first exceeded by Caroline, by what date will she need to notify HMRC and what is the date from which she will be registered?

Solution

Exempt supplies and supply of a capital asset of the business are not taken into account.

At no point is it likely that the taxable turnover in the next 30 days alone will exceed the threshold. The future prospects test therefore does not apply.

The taxable monthly supplies are therefore:

	£
Standard-rated supplies	7,350
Zero-rated supplies	950
	8,300

Under the historic test, the threshold will therefore be exceeded after 10 months (£8,300 × 10 = £83,000) which is 30 April 2016.

Caroline must notify HMRC by 30 May 2016.

She will be registered from 1 June 2016.

Registration is not required if the taxable turnover during the next twelve months will not exceed the deregistration threshold (see later in this section).

For both the historic and the future prospects tests, a person failing to apply for registration is still liable to account for output VAT on taxable turnover from the compulsory registration date, as if registration had taken place at the correct time. This taxable turnover is treated as being the VAT-inclusive amount (see later in this chapter).

If a taxpayer fails to notify HMRC of the liability to register on time, a penalty is payable (see Chapter 13).

3.2 Voluntary registration

A person making taxable supplies below the registration threshold may apply for voluntary registration. HMRC will register that person for VAT from a mutually agreed date.

The main advantage of voluntary registration is the ability to recover input VAT.

3.3 Exemption from registration

Where a person is making only zero-rated supplies, he may request exemption from registration.

HMRC may also allow exemption from registration if only a small proportion of supplies are standard rated and the person would normally have a net recovery of input VAT.

3.4 Deregistration

Deregistration may be compulsory or voluntary.

Deregistration is **compulsory** if a person ceases to make taxable supplies and has no intention of making taxable supplies. The person must notify HMRC within 30 days. Deregistration will take effect on the date taxable supplies ceased.

A person is eligible for **voluntary** deregistration if his estimated taxable turnover for the next twelve months will not exceed the statutory deregistration threshold.

From 1 April 2015, the deregistration threshold is £80,000.

Voluntary deregistration takes effect from the date on which the request is made or from an agreed later date.

VAT deregistration can be completed online.

On deregistration, a VAT charge is made on a deemed supply of trading stock and capital assets on which input VAT has been recovered. Output tax is then paid on the deemed supply. If the amount of output VAT is £1,000 or less, it does not have to be paid.

4 Output VAT

Section overview

- VAT is charged on the value of the taxable supply.
- The time of supply is called the tax point.
- The basic tax point is when goods are removed or made available or when services are completed.
- The actual tax point may be before or after the basic tax point.
- A prompt payment discount, if taken up, is taken into account when valuing the supply.
- Fuel for private motoring by the owner or an employee is charged at a scale rate.
- Bad debt relief is given for debts more than six months old.

4.1 Charge to VAT

VAT charged on taxable supplies is based on the VAT-exclusive value of the supply. For standard rated items, the rate of VAT is 20%. If the VAT-inclusive price is given, the VAT component of the consideration is:

$$\frac{20}{120} \text{ or } \frac{1}{6}$$

This is called the **VAT fraction**.

Worked example: Charge to VAT – standard-rated supplies

J Ltd makes standard-rated supplies. It makes the following supplies:

VAT-exclusive supplies	£395
VAT-inclusive supplies	£3,450

Requirement

What is the VAT charged?

Solution

VAT on VAT-exclusive supplies	
£395 × 20%	£79
VAT on VAT-inclusive supplies	
£3,450 × 1/6	£575

For reduced rate supplies VAT is charged at 5% on the VAT-exclusive value of the supply.

If the VAT-inclusive price is given for reduced rate supplies, the VAT component of the consideration is 5/105.

Worked example: Charge to VAT – reduced-rate supplies

H Ltd makes reduced-rate supplies. It makes the following supplies:

VAT-exclusive supplies	£500
VAT-inclusive supplies	£1,260

Requirement

What is the VAT charged?

Solution

VAT on VAT-exclusive supplies
£500 × 5%   £25

VAT on VAT-inclusive supplies
£1,260 × 5/105   £60

If VAT is not charged on a taxable supply in error then it is the responsibility of the trader who made the supply to pay the outstanding VAT over to HMRC. The amount received by the trader on the sale is treated as being inclusive of VAT.

4.2 Time of supply (tax point)

VAT becomes due on a supply of goods or services at the time of supply. This is called the **tax point**. Normally VAT must be accounted for on the VAT return for the period in which the tax point occurs.

The **basic tax point** is the date on which goods are removed or made available to the customer or the date on which services are completed.

However, the **actual tax point** may occur before or after the basic tax point as follows:

- Payment received before the basic tax point: actual tax point is the date of payment

- Invoice issued before the basic tax point: actual tax point is the date of invoice

- Invoice issued within 14 days after basic tax point: actual tax point is the date of invoice (can be extended by agreement with HMRC, eg for month-end invoicing)

The actual tax point cannot be later than the date on which payment is actually received.

If a deposit is paid, this creates its own tax point and there will be separate tax points for the deposit and the balancing payment.

Goods supplied on a sale or return basis (ie if the customer does not sell the goods, they may be returned to the supplier) are treated as having a basic tax point which is the earlier of the adoption of the goods by the customer or twelve months after the date of dispatch.

The basic tax point may be overridden by an actual tax point as described above.

Interactive question 1: Tax point   [Difficulty level: Exam standard]

What is the tax point for each of these supplies of goods? Give brief reasons for your answer.

Question	Fill in your answer
Goods removed 10 May, invoice issued 26 May, payment received 1 June	
Goods removed 28 May, invoice issued 26 May, payment received 1 June	
Goods removed 16 May, invoice issued 26 May, payment received 1 June	
Goods removed 20 May, invoice issued 26 May, payment received 18 May	
Goods removed 8 May, invoice issued 26 May, deposit received 1 May, balance received 1 June	

See **Answer** at end of this chapter.

4.3 Value of supply

Usually the value of the supply is the amount charged by the supplier, exclusive of any VAT.

Where the supply is a gift of business assets, the value of the supply is the VAT-exclusive amount that would be payable by the person making the supply at that time to purchase goods identical to the goods concerned (ie replacement cost).

Non-business use of business assets is valued at the full cost of provision to the taxable person.

4.3.1 Value of discounted supplies

Supplies offered at a discount (eg for prompt payment, or a trade discount) are generally valued **net of the maximum discount.**

From 1 April 2015, this rule only applies to prompt payment discounts (sometimes referred to as settlement discounts) if the prompt payment discount is taken up ie if the customer pays within the prompt payment terms. It is often not known at the time of issuing an invoice whether prompt payment will be made. The supplier can therefore choose one of two approaches:

1. The supplier can charge the full amount of VAT on the undiscounted amount, and then later issue a credit note if the prompt payment discount is taken up; or alternatively,

2. If the supplier does not wish to issue a credit note, the invoice must contain the terms of the discount and a statement that the customer can only recover as input tax the VAT actually paid to the supplier. In the case of no credit note, invoices may also show the discounted price, VAT on this and the total amount due if the discount is taken up.

Worked example: Sale with discount

B Ltd makes a standard-rated taxable supply of goods. It issues an invoice for £1,000 (exclusive of VAT) to V Ltd on 30 June 2015.

A 3% discount is offered for payment within 30 days of the invoice date.

Requirement

What is the value of the supply and how much output VAT is charged overall, assuming that V Ltd pays the invoice within 30 days?

Solution

	£
Value before discount	1,000
Less discount (3% × £1,000)	(30)
Value of supply	970
VAT charged (£970 × 20%)	£194

Note that if the payment had not been made within the prompt payment period, the full VAT of £200 would have been payable.

4.3.2 Fuel

Fuel provided for private motoring by the owner or an employee is charged at a scale rate. The **fuel scale charge** is based solely on the CO_2 rating of a car. There are no adjustments for fuel type. Fuel scale charges will be provided in the exam when fuel for private motoring is tested.

Worked example: Fuel scale charge

Jethro is employed by A Ltd. He is provided with a car with CO_2 emissions of 175g/km and petrol for business and private use.

The VAT-inclusive quarterly scale rate for a car with CO_2 emissions between 175g/km and 179g/km is £334.

Requirement

What is the output VAT due for the quarter to 31 March 2016?

Solution

£334 × 1/6   £56

4.4 Bad debts

Output VAT is accounted for according to the tax point and therefore output VAT may be payable before payment of an invoice has been received from the customer.

Where an invoice has not been paid for more than six months after the due date of payment and the debt has been written off in the supplier's accounts, bad debt relief is available.

Bad debt claims must be made within four years of the time the debt became eligible for relief. The supplier must have a copy of the VAT invoice and records to show that the output VAT has been paid. The VAT is reclaimed in the supplier's VAT return together with input tax on purchases.

5 Input VAT

Section overview

- Most input VAT can be recovered by a taxable person who is VAT registered.

- VAT is not recoverable on motor cars (unless used exclusively for business purposes) or business entertaining.

- Pre-registration input VAT may be recoverable.

5.1 Recoverable VAT

Normally, a taxable person making wholly taxable supplies (zero rated, reduced rate or standard rated) can recover input VAT on purchases and expenses relating to the taxable supply of goods.

The goods or services must actually be supplied for a taxable person to be able to recover the input tax.

The input VAT recoverable must be supported by a VAT invoice.

The goods or services must be used for a business purpose. Where goods are bought partly for business use, the taxable person may either:

- Deduct all the input tax and account for the output tax in respect of private use; or
- Deduct only the business proportion of input tax

Where services are bought partly for private use, only the second method can be used.

Input VAT is also recoverable on fuel supplied for private use where the VAT scale charge for output tax applies.

Input tax on assets purchased for the use of employees (as opposed to directors or sole traders or partners) which have an element of private use is allowable in full. Such benefits are a legitimate business expense and are provided for the purposes of the business – mainly to reward or motivate staff. The VAT incurred on their provision is consequently all input tax and no apportionment is necessary to reflect the private use. Examples include the cost of purchasing a mobile telephone (but not the cost of usage), or a computer but not cars which have special rules regarding private usage (see below).

5.2 Irrecoverable VAT

Input VAT is not usually recoverable in respect of:

- Motor cars (including optional extras acquired with the car) unless the car is used exclusively for business purposes

- Goods or services used for the purposes of business entertaining which is not allowable when computing taxable trading profits. Input VAT **is** however usually recoverable in respect of staff entertainment as well as entertainment of foreign customers (but not other foreign business contacts)

- Non-business items

- Items for which no VAT receipt is held

5.3 Pre-registration VAT

Input VAT can be recovered on goods supplied in the four years before registration. The goods must have been supplied to the taxable person for business purposes and must still be on hand at the time of registration. They must not have been supplied onwards or consumed.

Input VAT can be recovered on services supplied in the six months before registration. The services must have been supplied to the taxable person for business purposes.

Summary and Self-test

Summary

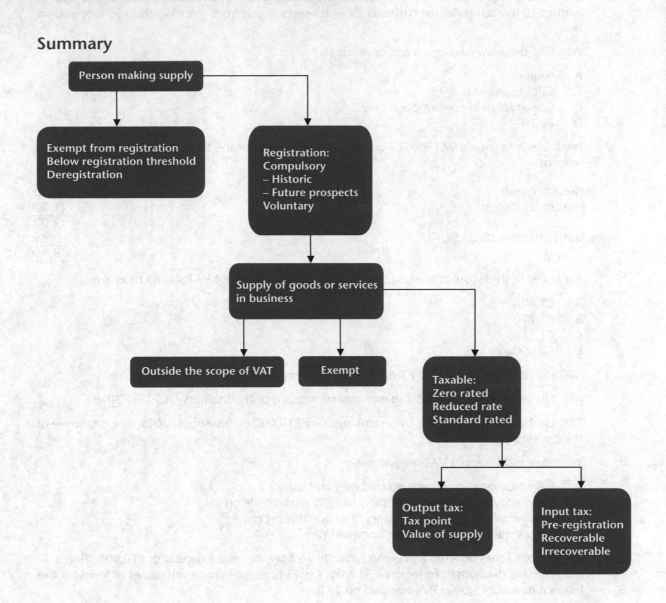

Person making supply

Exempt from registration
Below registration threshold
Deregistration

Registration:
Compulsory
– Historic
– Future prospects
Voluntary

Supply of goods or services
in business

Outside the scope of VAT

Exempt

Taxable:
Zero rated
Reduced rate
Standard rated

Output tax:
Tax point
Value of supply

Input tax:
Pre-registration
Recoverable
Irrecoverable

Self-test

Answer the following questions.

1   Gita, who is registered for VAT, runs a business selling beauty products. She gives one sample worth £10 to each potential customer. She also takes goods from stock worth £150 for her own use.

    Which of these transactions is a taxable supply?

    A   Neither
    B   Gift of sample only
    C   Goods for own consumption only
    D   Both

2   Joel intends to issue a VAT invoice on 30 November 2015 for the sale of standard-rated goods as follows:

	£
Value of goods	10,000
Less trade discount	(1,000)
	9,000
Less settlement discount	(450)
	8,550

    Assuming both discounts are taken up, how much overall output VAT should be charged?

    A   £1,800
    B   £1,710
    C   £1,910
    D   £2,000

3   ABC Ltd registered for VAT on 1 August 2015. It only makes standard-rated supplies.

    ABC Ltd incurred VAT on accountancy services relating to the business on 1 May 2015.

    ABC Ltd bought a car for use by an employee for £10,000 on 15 August 2015. The employee uses the car 40% privately.

    To what extent is input VAT recoverable?

    A   Fully recoverable on both accountancy and car
    B   Fully recoverable on accountancy, partially recoverable on car
    C   Fully recoverable on accountancy, irrecoverable on car
    D   Irrecoverable on both accountancy and car

4   On 30 April, Jones ordered a new machine. On 16 May, he paid a deposit of £10,000. The machine was dispatched to Jones on 31 May. On 13 June, an invoice was issued to Jones for the balance due of £45,000. This was paid on 20 June.

    What is the tax point for the £10,000 deposit?

    A   30 April
    B   16 May
    C   31 May
    D   13 June

5   Julie should have registered for VAT on 1 March 2016.

    On 5 March 2016, she supplied services to Wilma for £1,000 without charging VAT. Wilma is also registered for VAT and makes standard rate supplies.

    How much output VAT is payable on this supply and who should pay it?

    A   £167 payable by Julie
    B   £167 payable by Wilma
    C   £200 payable by Julie
    D   £200 payable by Wilma

Now go back to the Learning objectives in the Introduction. If you are satisfied you have achieved these objectives, please tick them off.

Technical reference

Legislation

References relate to Value Added Tax Act 1994 (*VATA 1994*) unless otherwise stated

Scope of VAT on taxable supplies	s.4
Taxable persons	s.3
Exempt supplies	s.31
Standard rate	s.2
Reduced rate	s.29A
Zero rate	s.30
Registration	Sch 1
Input and output tax	s.24
Time of supply	s.6
Value of supply	s.19
Fuel for private use	ss.56-57
Bad debts	s.36
Input tax disallowance on cars	SI 1992/3222 art 7
Pre-registration input tax	SI 1995/2518 reg 111

To find out more practical information about VAT, access the relevant section of the gov.uk website through the page https://www.gov.uk/government/organisations/hm-revenue-customs.

Information is available online at https://www.gov.uk/business-tax/vat. For example, the pages under the heading 'Introductory guidance' summarise some of the common VAT issues and are a good place to start finding out how VAT affects you and your business.

There is also a VAT telephone helpline: 0300 200 3700 (+44 2920 501 261 from abroad)

> This technical reference section is designed to assist you. It should help you to know where to look for further information on the topics covered in this chapter. **You will not be examined on the contents of this section in your examination**.

Answer to Interactive question 1

Question	Fill in your answer
Goods removed 10 May, invoice issued 26 May, payment received 1 June	10 May (basic tax point)
Goods removed 28 May, invoice issued 26 May, payment received 1 June	26 May (actual tax point, invoice before basic tax point)
Goods removed 16 May, invoice issued 26 May, payment received 1 June	26 May (actual tax point, invoice within 14 days after basic tax point)
Goods removed 20 May, invoice issued 26 May, payment received 18 May	18 May (actual tax point, payment before basic tax point)
Goods removed 8 May, invoice issued 26 May, deposit received 1 May, balance received 1 June	Deposit: 1 May (actual tax point, payment before basic tax point) Balance: 8 May (basic tax point)

Answers to Self-test

1   C – goods taken for own use are a taxable supply

Gifts of trade samples are not taxable supplies.

2   B – £1,710

Value of supply is after discounts actually taken up.

£8,550 × 20%   £1,710

3   C – fully recoverable on accountancy, irrecoverable on car

The VAT on accountancy services is pre-registration VAT incurred for business purposes within six months of registration.

VAT on motor cars is not recoverable unless the car is used exclusively for business purposes.

4   B – 16 May

There is a separate tax point for the deposit. The actual tax point is the date of payment since this is before the basic tax point (date of dispatch of goods).

5   A – £167 payable by Julie

VAT-inclusive supply

£1,000 × 1/6   £167

Although Julie failed to apply for registration on time, she is still liable to account to HMRC for output VAT on her taxable supplies from the compulsory registration date.

CHAPTER 12

Value added tax – further aspects

Introduction
Examination context
Topic List
   1   Accounting for VAT
   2   Small business reliefs
   3   VAT records and accounts
Summary and Self-test
Technical reference
Answer to Interactive question
Answers to Self-test

Introduction

Learning objectives

Tick off

- Identify the records which companies and individuals must retain for tax purposes ☐
- Determine, in straightforward cases, due dates for businesses' VAT returns and payments ☐
- Calculate the monthly, quarterly and annual VAT payable or repayable by a business ☐
- State the alternative schemes for payment of VAT by businesses ☐

Specific syllabus references for this chapter are: 2a, d, 6e, f.

Syllabus links

The topics in this chapter and the previous chapter form the basis of your understanding of value added tax.

Many of the administrative aspects of VAT are not tested in the Tax Compliance paper, so you may expect to find them in the Principles of Taxation paper. At Professional Level you will deal with further aspects of VAT such as groups and overseas transactions.

Examination context

In the examination, in the objective test questions, candidates may be required to:

- Calculate the VAT payable or reclaimable for a period
- Identify the schemes available to small businesses and apply the rules of the schemes

For extra question practice on these topics go to the section of the Question Bank covering this chapter.

1 Accounting for VAT

Section overview

- VAT is normally accounted for in quarterly VAT periods.
- The VAT return and VAT payable are due one month and seven days after the end of the VAT period.
- Substantial traders must make payments on account of VAT for each quarter.

1.1 VAT periods

The period covered by a VAT return is called a **VAT period** or tax period. Normally the VAT period is a quarter (a three-month period). The end date of the first VAT period is specified in the certificate of registration and dictates what the quarter dates will be going forward.

HMRC will allow taxable persons to have a one-month VAT period where input tax regularly exceeds output tax, ie where the taxable person is in a net VAT repayment position.

Small businesses may submit a single annual VAT return (see later in this chapter).

1.2 VAT return

All VAT-registered businesses must submit their VAT returns (Form VAT100) online and pay any VAT due in respect of those returns electronically.

The VAT return must show the amount of VAT payable or recoverable and be submitted to HMRC not later than seven calendar days after the last day of the month following the end of the return period. This is also usually the due date for any VAT payment. If payment is made by direct debit, it is automatically collected a further three working days after the due date.

Businesses that file annual returns or make payments on account have special due dates for their returns and payments (see later in this chapter).

Worked example: VAT due

F Ltd is a manufacturing company. For the quarter to 30 September 2015, the following information is given (all figures excluding VAT):

	£	£
Sales (standard rated)		134,285
Sales (zero rated)		12,500
		146,785
Purchases	37,750	
Wages	23,000	
Bad debt written off	1,500	
UK customer entertaining	750	
Staff entertaining	14,464	(77,464)
Profit		69,321

All purchases and entertaining expenses are standard rated. The bad debt, in respect of a standard rated supply, was written off in August 2015. The payment for the original sale was due on 31 January 2015.

Requirement

What is the VAT payable for the quarter and when is it due for payment?

Solution

Output tax

	£
Standard-rated supplies (£134,285 × 20%)	26,857

Input tax

	£	
Purchases	37,750	
Bad debt	1,500	
Staff entertaining	14,464	
	53,714 × 20%	(10,743)
VAT payable (due electronically by 7.11.15)		16,114

Bad debt relief is available because the debt is more than six months old from the due date of payment.

Wages are outside the scope of VAT.

Input tax on UK customer entertaining is irrecoverable.

Worked example: Tax point and accounting for VAT

Jason has the following standard-rated sales during the quarter ended 30 June 2015:

Order 1

Goods dispatched on 2 March 2015. Invoice issued on 25 March 2015 for £1,200 plus VAT. Payment was received on 12 June 2015.

Order 2

Goods dispatched on 28 March 2015. Invoice issued on 10 April 2015 for £680 plus VAT. Payment was received on 7 July 2015.

Requirement

What is the VAT payable for the quarter ended 30 June 2015 and when is it due for payment?

Solution

Tax point is the basic tax point for order 1, and the invoice date for order 2 (as it is within 14 days of basic tax point and before payment received).

The quarter ended 30 June 2015 only includes the VAT charged on order 2 as the quarter runs from 1 April 2015 to 30 June 2015. The VAT payable electronically on 7 August 2015 is £136.

Order 2

Tax point is 10 April 2015	
VAT @ 20% of £680	£136

Interactive question 1: VAT due   [Difficulty level: Exam standard]

Dev is registered for VAT. His VAT period ends on 31 March 2016.

During this period Dev made zero-rated supplies of £46,000 and standard-rated supplies of £59,070. These are VAT-exclusive figures.

Dev made standard-rated purchases of £59,489 (inclusive of VAT) during the period. Purchases included a new car for 90% business use by Dev, which he bought for £15,000 plus VAT.

Requirement

Using the standard format below, compute the VAT payable/repayable for the quarter.

Output tax

	£
	_____

Input tax   £

	_____
	_____ × (_____)

VAT payable/repayable

See **Answer** at the end of this chapter.

1.3 Payments on account

'Substantial' traders are taxable persons with an annual VAT liability in excess of £2.3m. A substantial trader must make **payments on account** of VAT for each quarter. This must be done electronically.

Payments are due at the end of the second and third months of the quarter. The amount of each payment is 1/24 of the total VAT liability for the previous year.

The balancing payment for the quarter is due with the VAT return at the end of the month following the end of the quarter.

2 Small business reliefs

Section overview

- The annual accounting scheme allows a business to submit one VAT return per year.

- The cash accounting scheme allows a business to account for VAT on a cash basis.

- Under the flat rate scheme, output VAT is based on a fixed percentage of VAT inclusive turnover but there is no recovery of input VAT.

2.1 Annual accounting scheme

The annual accounting scheme is helpful to small businesses as it cuts down on the administrative burden of VAT by allowing the business to submit one VAT return every 12 months. The VAT return is due within two months of the end of the year.

A business may join the annual accounting scheme if the value of taxable supplies (excluding VAT and supplies of capital items) in the following year is not expected to exceed £1.35m.

Businesses already in the scheme may continue to use it until the value of taxable supplies in the previous 12 months exceeds £1.6m.

The annual accounting scheme requires the trader to make payments on account either as:

- Nine interim payments at monthly intervals throughout the year, or
- Three quarterly interim payments throughout the year

The trader then must either pay any outstanding VAT or receive a refund if he has overpaid VAT, after the end of the year (see below). In total the trader will therefore either make ten payments or four.

If the trader has opted to make nine equal monthly payments, each payment must be electronic and will be 10% of the total VAT liability for the previous year, or 10% of the estimated VAT liability for the current year if the trader has been registered for VAT for less than 12 months. The first payment is due at the end of the fourth month, with no seven day extension, and then every month after that.

If the trader has opted to make three quarterly instalments, each payment must be electronic and will be 25% of the previous year's VAT liability, or 25% of the estimated VAT liability for the current year if the trader has been registered for VAT for less than 12 months. The payments are due by the end of months 4, 7 and 10 of the annual accounting year.

In the examination, you will always be given the VAT liability for the previous year or HMRC's estimate of the VAT liability for the current year where a trader has been registered for VAT for less than 12 months.

Any balancing payment is due when the VAT return is made, ie by the last day of the second month after the end of the year. If paid by direct debit, HMRC will collect it three working days after the due date for the return.

Worked example: Annual accounting scheme

W Ltd joined the annual accounting scheme two years ago. W Ltd's total VAT liability for the year to 31 May 2015 was £12,800.

The actual VAT liability for the year to 31 May 2016 was £16,250.

Requirement

For the year to 31 May 2016, what are the payments on account and balancing payment and when are they due?

Solution

Payments on account
$1/10 \times £12,800$ £1,280

Due by 30 September 2015 and then at the end of each month until 31 May 2016

Balancing payment
$(£16,250 - [£1,280 \times 9])$ £4,730

Due by 31 July 2016

The main advantages of the annual accounting scheme are therefore:

- The reduction in the number of VAT returns required
- Two months to complete the annual return and make the balancing payment

The annual accounting scheme can be used in conjunction with either the cash accounting scheme or the flat rate scheme.

2.2 Cash accounting scheme

The cash accounting scheme allows businesses to account for VAT on the basis of cash paid and received, rather than on invoices received and issued.

Small businesses may join the cash accounting scheme if the value of taxable supplies (excluding VAT and supplies of capital items) in the following year is not expected to exceed £1.35m. The business must have submitted all its VAT returns to date and paid all outstanding VAT. It must not have been convicted of a VAT offence or penalty in the previous twelve months.

Businesses already in the cash accounting scheme may continue to use it until the value of taxable supplies in the previous twelve months exceeds £1.6m.

The main advantages of the scheme are:

- Output VAT does not have to be accounted for until payment is received
- Automatic bad debt relief since no output VAT is payable if payment is not received

However, note that input VAT cannot be recovered until the business has actually paid the supplier for purchases.

2.3 Flat rate scheme

The flat rate scheme allows businesses to calculate net VAT due to HMRC by applying a flat rate percentage to their VAT-inclusive turnover rather than accounting for VAT on individual sales and purchases.

The flat rate percentage is set by the type of business carried on. It ranges from 4% (food retailers) to 14.5% (for example, building or construction services where labour only is supplied and accountancy services). There is a 1% reduction during the first year of VAT registration. For examination purposes, the percentage given in the question will include this 1% deduction where appropriate.

The business will issue tax invoices using the normal rules and applying the appropriate rate of VAT, eg standard rate, zero rate. It does not have to keep records of the input VAT on individual purchases.

The VAT payable to HMRC at the end of the VAT period is the flat rate percentage multiplied by the VAT-inclusive turnover for the period. There is no deduction for input VAT. The VAT-inclusive turnover includes taxable supplies, exempt supplies and supplies of capital assets.

Worked example: Flat rate scheme

Leon uses the flat rate scheme for his business. He has been registered for VAT for five years, making standard-rated supplies. The flat rate percentage is 9%.

In the quarter to 30 June 2015, Leon had the following transactions:

	£
Sales	25,200
Purchases	7,100
Expenses	2,500

All figures exclude VAT.

Requirement

What is the VAT due for the quarter?

Solution

VAT inclusive turnover

$£25,200 \times \dfrac{120}{100}$ (or $\dfrac{6}{5}$)   £30,240

VAT due £30,240 × 9%   £2,722

A business may join the flat rate scheme if the value of its annual taxable supplies (excluding VAT) does not exceed £150,000.

The main advantages of the scheme are:

- Reduction in the burden of administration of preparing the VAT return as no records of input VAT need be kept
- Frequently less VAT payable to HMRC than under the normal rules

If a business has total annual income (inclusive of VAT) in excess of £230,000 it must leave the flat rate scheme. This condition includes exempt income.

3   VAT records and accounts

Section overview

- VAT records must be kept to support output VAT charged and the claim for recoverable input VAT.

- Records must be kept for at least six years.

- A VAT invoice must contain details such as the tax point, VAT registration number and details of the supply.

3.1   Records

HMRC requires a taxable person to keep 'adequate' records and accounts of all transactions to support both output VAT charged and the claim for recoverable input VAT.

The main records to be kept should include:

- Sales invoices
- Order and delivery notes
- Purchase invoices, copy sales invoices and credit notes
- Purchase and sales day books
- Records of daily takings (eg till rolls)
- Cash book
- Bank statements and paying-in slips
- Annual accounts (P&L account and Balance Sheet)

3.2   VAT invoices

The VAT invoice is the key record to support a claim to recover input VAT and must therefore be issued when a taxable person makes a taxable supply to another taxable person.

A full VAT invoice must show the word 'invoice' and must contain a number of details:

- A unique identification number
- The business name, address and contact information
- The name and address of the customer
- A clear description of the goods or service
- The date of the invoice and the tax point if different
- The price, quantity and VAT rate for each item
- Any discount offered
- The amount charged excluding VAT
- The total VAT charged

In general, a trader must issue a full VAT invoice for every transaction. This rule is relaxed in some circumstances, such as sales for smaller amounts. A 'simplified' invoice can be issued for supplies under £250. A 'modified' invoice can be issued for retail supplies over £250.

It is not compulsory to issue VAT invoices to non-VAT registered customers unless requested.

Summary and Self-test

Summary

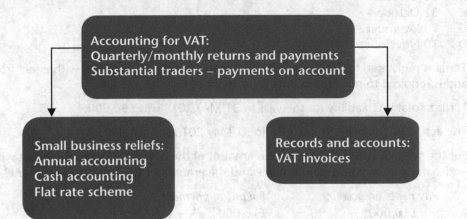

Accounting for VAT:
Quarterly/monthly returns and payments
Substantial traders – payments on account

Small business reliefs:
Annual accounting
Cash accounting
Flat rate scheme

Records and accounts:
VAT invoices

Self-test

Answer the following questions.

1   O Ltd's VAT accounting periods are in line with its accounting year which ends on 30 September.

    By what date must O Ltd submit its final VAT return for its accounting year?

    A   30 October
    B   31 October
    C   7 November
    D   10 November

2   Tertia is registered for VAT. She joins the annual accounting scheme with effect from 1 June 2015 and is required to make payments on account of her VAT liability.

    Tertia's total VAT liability for the year to 31 May 2015 was £90,000.

    The actual VAT liability for the year to 31 May 2016 is £108,000.

    For the year to 31 May 2016, what is amount of the payments on account that will be required under the annual accounting scheme and the amount of the balancing payment?

	Payments on account	*Balancing payment*
A	9 × £10,000	£18,000
B	9 × £9,000	£27,000
C	9 × £12,000	£0
D	9 × £10,800	£10,800

3   Which of the following statements about the cash accounting scheme is **NOT** true?

    A   VAT is accounted for on the basis of amounts received for supplies and amounts paid for purchases

    B   The scheme gives automatic bad debt relief

    C   The scheme allows deferral of payment for VAT where an extended time for payment is given to customers

    D   The scheme is compulsory for taxable persons who have taxable supplies not exceeding £1.35m in the following twelve months

4   Linda is registered for VAT and has opted to account for VAT under the flat rate scheme. The VAT rate applicable to her business is 5%.

    Which **TWO** of the following statements are true?

    A   Linda must calculate net VAT due by applying 5% to the value of her turnover (excluding VAT)

    B   Linda does not have to keep records of her input VAT

    C   Linda must calculate net VAT due by applying 5% to her VAT inclusive turnover

    D   Linda will issue tax invoices to her customers showing the value of the supply plus VAT at 5%

Now go back to the Learning objectives in the Introduction. If you are satisfied you have achieved these objectives, please tick them off.

Technical reference

Legislation

References relate to Statutory Instrument 1995/2518 (*SI 1995/2518*) unless otherwise stated

VAT returns	para 25
Payment of VAT	para 40
Substantial traders – payments on account	SI 1993/2001
Annual accounting scheme	paras 49-55
Cash accounting scheme	paras 56-65
Flat rate scheme	paras 55A-V
Records	para 31
Invoices	paras A13-16

To find out more practical information about VAT, access the relevant section of the gov.uk website through the page https://www.gov.uk/government/organisations/hm-revenue-customs.

A series of guides is available online at https://www.gov.uk/business-tax/vat which gives information about the range of special schemes and options to simplify VAT for small businesses is available under the heading 'Accounting for VAT'.

There is also a VAT telephone helpline: 0300 200 3700 (+44 2920 501 261 from abroad)

> This technical reference section is designed to assist you. It should help you to know where to look for further information on the topics covered in this chapter. **You will not be examined on the contents of this section in your examination.**

Answer to Interactive question 1

Output tax

	£
Standard rated supplies £59,070 × 20%	11,814

Input tax
The VAT on the car will not be recoverable

Purchases (59,489 – (15,000 x 120%)) = 41,489 × 1/6	(6,915)
VAT payable	4,899

1　C – 7 November

Businesses must file VAT returns (and pay their VAT liability) electronically. The deadline for both filing and payment is seven days after the end of the month following the return period. O Ltd must file its VAT return by 7 November.

2　B – Payments on account 9 × £9,000 and balancing payment of £27,000.

Payments on account are nine equal monthly payments which are 1/10 of the total VAT liability for the previous year.

3　D – the cash accounting scheme is not compulsory.

All the other statements are true. B and C are advantages of the cash accounting scheme that you should recognise.

4　B and C are true

Note that D is not true. Linda will issue tax invoices using the normal rules, eg standard rated, zero rated.

CHAPTER 13

Administration of tax

Introduction

Examination context

Topic List

Introduction

Learning objectives

- Identify the records which companies and individuals must retain for tax purposes and state the periods for which the records must be retained

- Identify the key features of the self assessment system for both companies and individuals

- Determine, in straightforward cases, due dates for:

  - Companies', sole traders', partnerships' and individuals' tax returns, tax payments and payments on account; and

  - Employers' PAYE and national insurance returns and payments

- Identify and calculate the interest and penalties due for:

  - Late submissions of and/or incorrect returns; and

  - Late and/or incorrect payments of tax

- Identify the periods within which HM Revenue & Customs can enquire into a taxpayer's returns or other information and tax liabilities and recognise the taxpayer's right of appeal and the process for dealing with disputes

Specific syllabus references for this chapter are: 2a, c, d, e, f.

Syllabus links

The topics in this chapter are important background knowledge which you will require for the Tax Compliance paper and the Business Planning: Taxation paper.

Examination context

In the examination candidates, in the objective test questions, may be required to:

- Determine due dates for employers' PAYE and national insurance returns and payments, including penalties for non compliance

- Determine when a tax return is required and its submission date, including the penalties for non compliance

- Identify the administrative issues affecting individuals and companies

- Determine the payment dates and amounts of payments to be made by both individuals and by companies of all sizes

- Identify and calculate the penalties and interest payable by individuals and companies for non compliance

- Recognise when penalties for VAT are due and determine the amount of the penalties

For extra question practice on these topics go to the section of the Question Bank covering this chapter.

1 Penalties for errors

Section overview

- A common penalty regime applies to the making of errors in tax returns.

- Penalties are based on the Potential Lost Revenue (PLR) arising as a result of the error.

- Maximum penalties range from 30% to 100% of the PLR dependent on whether the error is careless or deliberate.

- Penalties can be reduced if the taxpayer discloses the error to HMRC or if there is reasonable excuse. They can also be suspended in certain circumstances.

- Appeals can be made against the penalties levied.

1.1 Common penalty regime

A common penalty regime relates to situations where a taxpayer has made an error/inaccuracy in a tax return. The regime covers income tax, national insurance contributions, corporation tax and value added tax. Penalties are based on the Potential Lost Revenue (PLR) and range from 30% to 100% of the PLR. Penalties may be reduced or suspended.

The common penalty regime (for errors but also for late filing, failure to notify etc, as explained later in this chapter) is being phased in over time and is not yet fully in force for all penalties for all taxes. However, for the purposes of this examination, you are only required to know the 'new' rules that are detailed here.

1.2 Circumstances in which a penalty may be charged

A penalty is charged where a taxpayer makes an inaccurate return and the inaccuracy can be classified as:

- Careless – ie the taxpayer has not taken reasonable care in completing the return; or

- Deliberate but not concealed – ie the taxpayer has deliberately made an inaccurate return but has not positively done anything to conceal the inaccuracy; or

- Deliberate and concealed – ie the taxpayer has deliberately made an inaccurate return and has positively done something to conceal the inaccuracy such as produced false invoices or bank statements

In order for a penalty to be charged, the inaccurate return must result in:

- An understatement of the taxpayer's tax liability; or
- A false or increased loss for the taxpayer; or
- A false or increased repayment of tax to the taxpayer

If a return contains more than one error, a penalty can be charged for each error. Over and under statements can be offset and the penalty applied to the net error.

The rules also extend to errors in claims for allowances and reliefs, and in accounts submitted in relation to a tax liability.

Penalties for errors also apply where HMRC has issued an estimate of a person's liability where:

- A return has been issued to that person and it has not been returned, or
- The taxpayer was required to deliver a return to HMRC but has not delivered it.

The taxpayer will be charged a penalty where:

- The assessment understates the taxpayer's liability to income tax, capital gains tax, corporation tax or VAT, and

- The taxpayer fails to take reasonable steps within 30 days of the date of the assessment to tell HMRC that there is an under-assessment

Examples: categories of inaccuracy

Careless inaccuracy

- Keeping inaccurate books and records that are incomplete in some respects
- Omitting occasional items of income or gains
- Failing to check the return is consistent with the underlying records
- Making arithmetical errors that are too large or too many to be simply isolated mistakes

Deliberate inaccuracies

- Systematically paying wages without operating PAYE
- Not keeping books and records at all
- Including personal expenditure in business expenditure
- Omitting significant amounts of income in relation to overall liability from a return

Deliberate and concealed inaccuracies

- Creating false invoices
- Backdating or post-dating invoices
- Altering invoices or other documents
- Destroying books, records and documents in order that they are not available
- Creating fictitious minutes of meetings or minutes of fictitious meetings

1.3 Amount of the penalty

The amount of the penalty is based on the Potential Lost Revenue (PLR) to HMRC as a result of the error. For example, if there is an understatement of tax, this understatement is the PLR.

The maximum amount of the penalty depends on the type of error/inaccuracy.

There is no penalty if a person can demonstrate he took reasonable care to ensure his tax was right, but despite this, submits an incorrect return. Otherwise:

Type of error	Maximum penalty payable
Careless	30% of PLR
Deliberate but not concealed	70% of PLR
Deliberate and concealed	100% of PLR

Worked example: Penalties for errors

Ruth is a sole trader. She files her tax return for 2015/16 on 19 January 2017. The return shows her trading income to be £49,000, and that she has no other income. In fact, due to an arithmetical error this was incorrectly stated. Her trading income should have been £57,000.

Requirement

State the maximum penalty that HMRC could charge Ruth for her error.

Solution

The Potential Lost Revenue as a result of Ruth's error is:
£(57,000 – 49,000) = £8,000 × [40% (income tax) + 2% (NICs)]   £3,360

Ruth's error is careless so the maximum penalty is:
£3,360 × 30%   £1,008

1.4 Failure to send a return

The maximum penalty payable where tax has been under-assessed because the taxpayer has failed to send a return is 30% of Potential Lost Revenue.

1.5 Reduction of penalties for errors

A penalty may be reduced if the taxpayer tells HMRC about the error/ inaccuracy. The reduction depends on the circumstances of the disclosure and the help that the taxpayer gives to HMRC in relation to that disclosure.

An unprompted disclosure is one made at a time when there is no reason to believe that HMRC has discovered or is about to discover the error. Otherwise, the disclosure is a prompted disclosure.

The minimum penalties that can be imposed are as follows:

Type of error	Disclosure	
	Unprompted	Prompted
Careless	0% of PLR	15% of PLR
Deliberate but not concealed	20% of PLR	35% of PLR
Deliberate and concealed	30% of PLR	50% of PLR

Unprompted disclosure where a careless mistake has been made can reduce the penalty to nil.

1.6 Quality of disclosure of errors

The reductions that are given by HMRC depend on the quality of the disclosure. To calculate the reduction HMRC will consider three elements of disclosure and to what degree the taxpayer:

- Tells HMRC about the error, making full disclosure and explaining how the error was made
- Helps HMRC to work out what extra tax is due
- Allows access to business and other records and other relevant documents to check the figures

 Worked example: Reduction of a penalty

Graham is a sole trader. He files his tax return for 2015/16 on 31 January 2017. The return shows trading income of £65,000. HMRC initiates a compliance check into Graham's return and discovers interest received from a previously undisclosed bank account. He discloses that the account holds £12,000 of undisclosed property income relating to 2015/16.

Requirement

State the maximum and minimum penalties that Graham could be charged by HMRC for his error.

Solution

The Potential Lost Revenue as a result of Graham's error is:
£12,000 × 40%   £4,800

Graham's error is deliberate but not concealed so the maximum penalty for the error is:
£4,800 × 70%   £3,360

Graham has made a prompted disclosure so the minimum penalty for the error is:
£4,800 × 35%   £1,680

1.7 Reasonable care

Where a taxpayer has taken reasonable care in completing a return and has taken reasonable steps to disclose any errors, no penalty applies.

'Reasonable care' varies according to the person, their circumstances and their abilities.

HMRC expects taxpayers to make and keep sufficient records to provide a complete and accurate return and to check the position when they do not understand something.

If taxpayers do not promptly tell HMRC when they discover an error, HMRC will treat the errors as careless inaccuracies even where the taxpayer took reasonable care.

Where the taxpayer uses an agent such as an accountant to complete a return, it remains the taxpayer's responsibility to make sure that the return is correct.

1.8 Issue of penalty

If a person is liable to a penalty, HMRC sends him a penalty assessment. This states what he owes and that the penalty must be paid within 30 days.

The taxpayer must pay any:

- Tax that is due
- Penalties that are due
- Interest that is due on late tax and penalties

1.9 Suspension of penalties

A penalty may be suspended by HMRC to allow the taxpayer to take action to ensure that the error/ inaccuracy does not occur again (eg where the error has arisen from failure to keep proper records).

HMRC will impose conditions which the taxpayer has to satisfy eg establishing proper record keeping systems.

The penalty will be cancelled if the conditions imposed by HMRC are complied with by the taxpayer within a period of up to two years. Otherwise, if the conditions are not met, the penalty must be paid.

The penalty cannot be suspended if it results from a deliberate error/inaccuracy.

1.10 Appeals

Appeals can be made against:

- The imposition of a penalty
- The amount of a penalty
- A decision not to suspend a penalty
- The conditions set by HMRC in relation to the suspension of a penalty

Appeals are made to an independent tribunal, which will usually be the First-tier Tribunal of the Tax Chamber.

It is also possible to opt for an internal review by an independent HMRC officer. This is potentially a quick and inexpensive way to resolve a dispute.

2 Penalties for failure to notify

Section overview

- A common penalty regime applies to failures to notify chargeability.

- Maximum penalties are based upon Potential Lost Revenue but can be reduced under certain circumstances.

- Penalties may be mitigated if there is reasonable excuse.

2.1 Introduction

Where a duty to notify chargeability or liability to register occurs, a unified set of rules applies if the failure to fulfil the duty results in a loss of tax.

The rules apply to failure by either the taxpayer or his tax adviser, unless the taxpayer can show that he took all reasonable steps to avoid the failure.

Penalties can also be collected (in part or in full) from an officer (eg director) of a company if a 'deliberate action' is attributable to him.

The taxes affected are:

- Income tax
- National insurance contributions
- Income tax and NIC collected via PAYE
- Capital gains tax
- Corporation tax
- VAT

2.2 Amount of penalty

Penalties are behaviour related, increasing for more serious failures, and are based on the Potential Lost Revenue.

The 'Potential Lost Revenue' is the amount of tax outstanding as a result of the failure.

Reductions are available for disclosure, with higher reductions if the disclosure is unprompted.

The minimum and maximum penalties are as follows:

Behaviour	Maximum penalty	Minimum penalty with unprompted disclosure		Minimum penalty with prompted disclosure	
Deliberate and concealed	100%	30%		50%	
Deliberate but not concealed	70%	20%		35%	
		>12m	<12m	>12m	<12m
Any other case	30%	10%	Nil	20%	10%

The minimum penalties shown above presume that the maximum reductions for disclosure apply. In practice, however, the reductions given are up to the HMRC officer involved and could result in a higher penalty being payable.

Note that there is no zero penalty for reasonable care (unlike for penalties for errors on returns), although the penalty may be reduced to 0% if a non-deliberate failure is rectified within 12 months through unprompted disclosure.

The penalties may also be reduced at HMRC's discretion in 'special circumstances'. 'Special circumstances' are expected to be very rare.

2.3 Reasonable excuse

Where the taxpayer's failure is not classed as deliberate, there is no penalty if he can show he has a 'reasonable excuse'.

Reasonable excuse does **not** include having insufficient money to pay the penalty. In general, few circumstances have been accepted by HMRC as amounting to a reasonable excuse, however this is currently under review.

2.4 Appeals

Taxpayers have a right of appeal against penalty decisions to the First-tier Tribunal, which may confirm, substitute or cancel the penalty.

3 Record keeping

Section overview

- A common framework exists for record keeping.
- There are time limits for the retention of records and penalties may be levied for failure to do so.
- Large companies must appoint a senior accounting officer who is responsible for maintaining adequate tax accounting arrangements. Failure to do so can result in penalties.

3.1 Introduction

There is a common framework for record keeping for income tax, capital gains tax, corporation tax, VAT and PAYE.

One set of high level rules applies across the above taxes, but the detailed rules for each tax remain unchanged.

3.2 General provisions

Taxpayers must keep 'information' (rather than 'records') to show that they have prepared a complete and correct tax return. The information must also be able to be provided in a legible form on request. Records can be kept in electronic format.

HMRC can specify a shorter time limit for keeping records where the records are bulky and the information they contain can be provided in another way.

HMRC can inspect 'in-year' records, ie **before** a return is submitted, if it believes it is reasonably required to check a tax position.

3.3 Which records must be kept?

For income tax, capital gains tax, corporation tax and VAT the requirement is for taxable persons to keep 'adequate' business and accounting records.

'Adequate' means keeping records to be sure that the right profit, loss, tax declaration or claim is made.

For PAYE, employers are required to keep specified records.

3.4 Time limits for keeping records

The time limits for keeping records are:

(a) Corporation tax   – six years from end of accounting period

(b) Income and capital gains tax   – 5th anniversary of 31 January following end of tax year if the taxpayer is in business

      – 1st anniversary of 31 January following the end of the tax year if the taxpayer is not in business

(c) VAT   – six years

HMRC has the flexibility to shorten the periods for which records need to be retained.

3.5 Record keeping penalties

The maximum (mitigable) penalty for each failure to keep and retain records is £3,000 per tax year/accounting period.

3.6 Time limits for taxpayer claims

The general time limit for taxpayers making claims, which applies in the absence of any specific time limit, is four years from the end of the tax year or accounting period.

3.7 Duties of senior accounting officers

Senior accounting officers of 'qualifying' companies must take reasonable steps to establish and maintain appropriate tax accounting arrangements.

A qualifying company has, at the end of its previous financial year:

(a)   Turnover of more than £200 million, and/or
(b)   A balance sheet total of more than £2 billion

Qualifying companies must notify HMRC of the name of their senior accounting officer (SAO). The SAO must certify annually that the company's accounting systems are adequate for the purposes of accurate tax reporting or specify the nature of any inadequacies.

The SAO may be liable to a £5,000 penalty, in each of the following cases, for his failure to:

(a)   Establish and maintain appropriate tax accounting arrangements.

(b)   Provide an annual certificate to HMRC or provides a certificate that contains a careless or deliberate inaccuracy.

HMRC may impose a £5,000 penalty on the company for failure to notify the name of the SAO.

4 Penalties for late filing of returns

Section overview

- There is a common penalty regime for the late filing of tax returns.

- These penalties apply to returns for periods of at least six months and combine a mixture of fixed and tax geared penalties.

4.1 Introduction

There is a common penalty regime for the late filing of tax returns. Assume it applies to all the main taxes including income tax, capital gains tax and corporation tax. Remember that for your examination you only have to know these rules, even though they do not yet apply to all these taxes in practice.

4.2 Returns covered by the penalty regime

These late filing penalties apply to the following documents:

- Income tax – personal tax return, partnership tax return
- Capital gains tax – personal tax return
- Corporation tax – company tax return

These are all annual returns. There are separate penalty provisions for taxes where there are more frequent return obligations ie for periods of less than six months (see later in this chapter).

4.3 Amount of penalty

The penalties for late filing of a return are as follows:

- Immediate £100 fixed penalty, regardless of whether any tax is outstanding for payment (note that the £100 still applies even if the tax due is £0); and

- Daily fixed penalties of up to £10 per day if the return is more than three months late (for up to 90 days, so a maximum of £900); and

- Where the delay is greater than six months but less than twelve months, a tax-geared penalty of 5% of the tax due (for income tax purposes this means the tax payable for the year after the deduction of tax deducted at source), or £300 if greater; and

- Where the delay is greater than twelve months the following further tax-geared penalties apply:
  - 100% of tax due where withholding of information is deliberate and concealed
  - 70% of tax due where withholding of information is deliberate but not concealed
  - 5% of tax due in other cases

The tax-geared penalties above are again subject to a minimum of £300.

4.4 Reduction of penalties for late filing

Where the return is more than 12 months late and the withholding of information **was deliberate** the penalty can be reduced for disclosure, with higher reductions if the disclosure is unprompted, as follows:

Behaviour	Maximum penalty	Minimum penalty with prompted disclosure	Minimum penalty with unprompted disclosure
Deliberate and concealed	100%	50%	30%
Deliberate but not concealed	70%	35%	20%

5 Pay As You Earn (PAYE) – Real time information (RTI)

Section overview

- The reporting of PAYE is made in real time (Real Time Information or RTI). Each time an employee is paid, the details of his pay and deductions must be submitted to HMRC using a Full Payment Submission.

- There are a number of PAYE forms used to provide information to ensure that tax is deducted correctly, though these have been reduced in number as a result of the introduction of RTI.

- Non-compliance with PAYE requirements will lead to penalties.

5.1 Real time information (RTI)

Most employers have to report PAYE information in real time. Each time a payment is made to an employee, the details of the employee's pay and deductions must be submitted to HMRC using payroll software.

The payroll information must be submitted using a Full Payment Submission (FPS) and is due to HMRC on or before the day the employee is paid. The reports required will be generated by the payroll software and will include details of:

- The amount paid to each employee
- Deductions such as income tax and national insurance contributions
- Starter and leaver dates

It is necessary to include the details of all employees that are paid even if they earn below the national insurance lower earning s limit.

In addition, an Earlier Year Update (EYU) may be required where information supplied in a previous year needs to be updated.

5.2 PAYE forms

The PAYE system has many forms which are used to provide information to enable tax to be calculated correctly. The forms that are required are listed below:

Name	Function	Important dates
P9D	End of year form recording details of benefits provided to employees in excluded employment	Send to HMRC and copy to employee by 6 July following end of tax year
P11D	End of year form recording details of benefits provided to employees not in excluded employment	Send to HMRC and copy to employee by 6 July following end of tax year
P60	End of year form recording details of gross pay, tax deducted and NICs for both employer and employee	Supply to each employee by 31 May following end of tax year
P45	Particulars of employee leaving: records tax code, gross pay to date, tax and NICs deducted	Under RTI no parts of the form need to be submitted to HMRC. Starter and leaver details are included on the monthly FPS. Employees are provided with the form for their own records

Employers with at least 250 employees must pay income tax/Class 1 national insurance contributions electronically. They receive an extension of three days to make their payment, therefore payments are due by 22nd rather than 19th of a month. There is no change to the payment of PAYE under RTI.

5.3 PAYE forms: penalties

Penalties may be charged for both incorrect PAYE returns and for PAYE returns filed late.

The penalties for errors (Section 1) apply to incorrect FPS submissions under RTI.

There are penalties for the late filing of PAYE returns. A penalty will be charged for a late FPS. There are various relaxations to these penalties but these are not examinable, and so you should assume that the following penalties apply.

The penalty depends on how many employees the PAYE scheme has.

Number of employees	Monthly penalty
1 to 9	£100
10 to 49	£200
50 to 249	£300
250 or more	£400

If the form is more than three months late, an additional penalty is due of 5% of the tax and NIC that should have been reported.

Additionally, there is a £300 penalty per late P9D or P11D return, with an extra £60 per day charged if the delay continues.

5.4 PAYE payments: penalties

There is also a penalty for late payment of in-year deductions collected via PAYE (ie income tax and NIC apart from Class 1A and Class 1B. The penalty applies to all employers, irrespective of the number of employees.

The penalty depends on the number of defaults in a tax year.

Number of late payments	Percentage of tax unpaid
1st	Nil (as long as payment is less than 6 months late)
2nd to 4th	1%
5th to 7th	2%
8th to 10th	3%
11th and more	4%

The percentage penalty is applied to the total amount that is late in the relevant tax month, but ignoring the first late payment in the year. Where the tax remains unpaid at 6 months, a further penalty is 5% of tax unpaid, with a further 5% if tax remains unpaid at 12 months, even if there is only one late payment in the year.

Worked example: PAYE in-year late payment penalty

Genevieve is an employer with a regular monthly liability under PAYE of £12,000 but pays that amount one week late on eight occasions in the year.

Requirement

State the total penalty payable by Genevieve for the late payment of her PAYE liability in 2015/16.

Solution

As there are eight defaults in the year, the first is ignored, then three are charged at 1%, three at 2%, and the final default at 3%. Therefore the total penalty will be calculated as (3 × 1% × £12,000) + (3 × 2% × £12,000) + (3% × £12,000) = £1,440.

Late payment penalties can be suspended where the taxpayer agrees a time to pay arrangement, unless he abuses the arrangement.

6 Income tax and capital gains tax – returns and payment

Section overview

- Not all taxpayers have to submit a tax return.
- A taxpayer may be issued with a full tax return or a short tax return.
- Partnerships are required to submit a tax return.
- Income tax not deducted at source and Class 4 NICs are payable in a maximum of three instalments.
- Capital gains tax is payable in one lump sum.
- Some underpayments of tax may be collected through the PAYE system.

6.1 Issue of tax return

Under the self-assessment system, an individual may be required to submit a tax return giving details of his taxable income and gains for a tax year.

Some taxpayers do not have to submit a tax return, for example if tax has been deducted at source under PAYE and from savings income.

In April each tax year, HMRC issues tax returns and/or notices to file to taxpayers who are likely to need to file a return such as sole traders and higher/ additional rate taxpayers.

If a tax return or notice to file is not automatically issued, the individual must notify HMRC by 5 October following the end of the tax year unless the individual is certain that no return is required.

If HMRC has issued a tax return but subsequently withdraws it, the individual must notify HMRC by the later of 5 October following the tax year or 30 days from the day after the notice was withdrawn.

If notification of self employment has already been given to HMRC for NIC purposes (see Chapter 8) it is not necessary to make a separate request for the issue of a tax return.

If a taxpayer fails to notify HMRC, a penalty will be payable (see earlier in this chapter).

HMRC has the power to withdraw a notice to file a self assessment return on request by the taxpayer and cancel any late filing penalty issued in connection with that return.

In future, it is proposed that annual self assessment tax returns will be replaced with 'digital tax accounts'. Details are not required for the 2016 examinations.

6.2 Full tax return

A full tax return (SA100) consists of a summary form, additional and supplementary pages dealing with different types of income and gains, and a tax calculation section.

The individual must complete the summary form and such further pages as are relevant.

Completion of the tax calculation section is optional. If the taxpayer does complete the tax calculation, this is called a **self assessment**. Where tax returns are completed and submitted online, a calculation of the liability is carried out automatically.

Alternatively, the taxpayer may ask HMRC to calculate the tax liability. This is still treated as a self assessment by the taxpayer, not an official assessment by HMRC. As a result, the self assessment may be amended by the taxpayer (see later in this chapter).

The due date for submission of the tax return is determined according to whether a return is submitted online or on paper. The due date for submission of an electronic return online is the later of 31 January following the end of the tax year or three months after the return was issued. The due date for submission of a paper return is the later of 31 October following the end of the tax year or three months after the return was issued.

If the taxpayer wishes HMRC to calculate his tax liability for him, then the filing deadline for a paper return is slightly different and is the later of 31 October following the tax year end and two months after the notice to make a return is issued.

There are penalties for late submission (see earlier in this chapter).

Worked example: Submitting a tax return

Winifred was issued with a full tax return for 2015/16.

Requirement

By what date should Winifred submit her tax return to HMRC if:

(a) The return was issued on 10 April 2016 and Winifred wishes HMRC to compute her tax liability and submit a paper return

(b) The return was issued on 12 December 2016 and Winifred wishes to submit an electronic return online

(c) The return was issued on 14 October 2016, Winifred wishes to compute her own tax liability and submit a paper return

Solution

(a) Later of 31 October 2016 and 10 June 2016, ie 31 October 2016
(b) Later of 31 January 2017 and 12 March 2017, ie 12 March 2017
(c) Later of 31 October 2016 and 14 January 2017, ie 14 January 2017

If a taxpayer is sent a return by HMRC then unless it is agreed that the return is not required and will be withdrawn, it must be submitted to HMRC by the due date even if there is no income to declare.

6.3 Short tax return

Some taxpayers do not need to file a tax return at all. This applies to many employees and pensioners. Among those taxpayers who are required to file a return, some need only submit limited information. HMRC aims to send taxpayers a 'short', paper-only tax return if they are employees (not directors), pensioners, or sole traders with a turnover of less than £82,000 (the VAT registration limit).

The short tax return asks only for information likely to be relevant to these individuals and the form does not contain a tax calculation section. Therefore HMRC will automatically compute the tax liability.

The short tax return should be submitted by 31 October following the end of the tax year if possible, to enable HMRC to compute the tax liability. The latest submission date is 31 October or three months after the issue of the tax return. The short tax return is not available online.

It is the responsibility of the taxpayer to check whether his circumstances are still covered by the short tax return and to request a full tax return if necessary. Any taxpayer asked for a short tax return may choose instead to file a full return online if preferred.

6.4 Partnership tax returns

Although a partnership is not itself liable to tax on the income and gains of the partners, it is important for partnership income and gains to be reported to HMRC so that these can be checked against the partners' individual returns.

A partnership therefore submits a tax return to HMRC in the same way as individuals. The partnership tax return (SA800) must be submitted by the later of 31 January following the end of the tax year or three months after the return was issued where an electronic return is submitted online. If a paper return is submitted, the filing date is the later of 31 October following the end of the tax year or three months after the return was issued.

6.5 Right to amend tax returns

HMRC has the right to correct a taxpayer's tax return for obvious errors such as errors of principle and arithmetic errors. Such corrections must be made within nine months of the date the return is actually filed. HMRC's powers to correct a return extend to correct 'anything else in the return that the officer has reason to believe is incorrect in the light of information available to the officer'.

The taxpayer has the right to amend a tax return for any reason within 12 months of the normal due submission date (not the actual submission date). For amendment purposes, the due submission date is the later of 31 January following the end of the tax year or three months after the return was issued, regardless of whether it was submitted on paper or electronically.

In addition, a taxpayer may make a claim for 'overpayment relief' for errors in the tax return where tax would be overcharged as a result. Such a claim must be made within four years of the end of the tax year to which the tax return relates.

Interactive question 1: Important dates   [Difficulty level: Exam standard]

State the latest relevant date for the following questions.

Question	Fill in your answer
Normal due date for tax return for 2015/16 issued 20 November 2016, taxpayer to submit an electronic return online	
Notify HMRC of need to issue tax return for 2015/16	
Overpayment relief claim relating to 2015/16	
Keep business records for 2015/16	
Normal due date for tax return for 2015/16 issued 31 May 2016, HMRC to calculate tax and paper return to be submitted	
Keep personal records for 2015/16	
Amend tax return for 2015/16 submitted 30 November 2016	

See **Answer** at the end of this chapter.

6.6 Payment dates

Income tax (which has not been deducted at source) and Class 4 NICs are paid as follows:

- First payment on account by 31 January in the tax year
- Second payment on account by 31 July following the end of the tax year
- Balancing payment by 31 January following the end of the tax year

From 2015/16, Class 2 NIC is also being brought within the self-assessment system.

6.7 Payments on account

Each payment on account is half of the income tax and Class 4 NICs paid under self assessment for the previous year.

Worked example: Payment on account

Josiah is a sole trader who paid tax as follows in 2014/15:

Total income tax liability	£18,400
Tax deducted at source on savings income	£6,400
Class 4 NICs	£3,800

Requirement

What are his payments on account for 2015/16 and when are they due?

Solution

	£
Total income tax liability 2014/15	18,400
Less deducted at source	(6,400)
Income tax payable under self-assessment	12,000
Class 4 NICs	3,800
	15,800
Payments on account	
31 January 2016 £15,800 × ½	7,900
31 July 2016 £15,800 × ½	7,900

For the tax year 2015/16 payments on account are not required where the amount paid under self assessment in the previous year was less than:

- £1,000; or
- 20% of the total liability

6.8 Balancing payments

A balancing payment or repayment is due by 31 January following the end of the tax year. The balancing payment comprises any unpaid income tax and Class 4 NICs, together with capital gains tax payable for the year, and any Class 2 NIC liability for the year.

Worked example: Balancing payments

The following information relates to Irene for 2015/16:

Total income tax liability	£20,000
Tax deducted under PAYE and at source	£12,500
Payments on account:	
31 January 2016	£3,000
31 July 2016	£3,000
Capital gains tax liability 2015/16	£5,000

Requirement

What are the amounts payable by Irene by 31 January 2017?

Solution

Amounts payable on 31 January 2017:

	£
Total income tax liability	20,000
Less tax deducted under PAYE and at source	(12,500)
	7,500
Less payments on account 2 × £3,000	(6,000)
Balancing payment for 2015/16	1,500
CGT 2015/16	5,000
First payment on account for 2016/17 £7,500 × ½	3,750

6.9 Collection of unpaid tax via PAYE

6.9.1 Collection of tax due

If the tax payment due for the year is less than £3,000 and the taxpayer is an employee or receives a pension, it is possible for the tax due to be collected by adjusting his PAYE code for the following tax year.

For the tax due to be collected via PAYE the return must be filed on paper by 31 October following the tax year end or online by 30 December following the tax year end.

The taxpayer may instead choose to pay the tax due on the 31 January following the tax year end if he prefers.

If the tax return shows an underpayment, HMRC will assume that the same circumstances will apply in the following year leading to another underpayment. The taxpayer can choose to have this estimated tax collected via the PAYE code for the following tax year. HMRC will normally only collect the estimated tax in this way if the income is not more than £10,000.

6.9.2 Collection of debts

Where the taxpayer is an employee or receives a pension and has outstanding debts owed to HMRC from earlier years, the debts may be collected via the PAYE code. The maximum amount of underpaid tax (and some other debts such as some tax credits) that can be collected in this way depends on the taxpayer's level of PAYE income, with an overall maximum amount of £17,000 recoverable in this way in a tax year.

7 Income tax and capital gains tax – penalties and interest

Section overview

- Penalties are used to enforce the self assessment system, for example for late submission of tax returns and for late payment of tax.

- Interest is payable by the taxpayer on late paid tax and penalties. Interest is payable by HMRC on overpaid tax.

7.1 Penalties

The self assessment system is enforced through a system of penalties, some of which were considered earlier in this chapter, including those for late filing of returns.

7.2 Penalties for late payment of tax

The penalties for late payment of income tax or capital gains tax are:

- 5% of tax unpaid 30 days after the payment due date, known as the penalty date
- Further 5% penalty where tax remains unpaid six months after the payment due date
- Further 5% penalty where the tax remains unpaid 12 months after the payment due date

This gives a maximum penalty of 15% of the unpaid tax.

A penalty may be charged on late payment of:

- Balancing payments under self assessment
- Additional tax payment arising from amendments to a self assessment
- Tax payable under a discovery assessment (see later in this chapter)

Note that penalties do not apply to payments on account.

Late payment penalties can be suspended where the taxpayer agrees a time to pay arrangement, unless he abuses the arrangement.

Worked example: Penalty for late payment of tax

Arslan gives you the following information about his payments of tax relating to 2014/15:

First payment on account of £2,000 paid in full on 31 March 2015

Second payment on account of £2,000 paid in full on 31 July 2015

Balancing payment of £3,000 paid in full on 16 March 2016

Requirement

Calculate any penalties due.

Solution

First payment on account due 31 January 2015, paid 31 March 2015, but no penalties on payments on account.

Second payment on account paid on due date 31 July 2015.

Balancing payment due 31 January 2016, paid 16 March 2016. Initial penalty of 5% of tax due of £150 (5% × £3,000). No further penalty due as the tax was paid within six months of the payment due date.

Interactive question 2: Penalties

[Difficulty level: Exam standard]

State the maximum penalties for the following events.

Question	Fill in your answer
Notified HMRC of new source of income for 2015/16 on 5 December 2016, paid all £4,000 of tax due on 25 January 2017	
Tax return for 2015/16 issued May 2016, submitted return electronically on 30 March 2017	
Balancing payment of tax of £2,000 for 2015/16 paid 30 April 2017	
Destroyed supporting records for 2015/16 on 1 May 2017	
Tax return for 2015/16 issued June 2016, submitted electronically on 15 September 2017, tax liability £1,000	
Balancing payment of tax of £3,000 for 2015/16 paid 30 September 2017	

See **Answer** at the end of this chapter.

7.3 Late payment interest

A taxpayer is liable to interest on late payment of income tax, capital gains tax, national insurance and penalties.

Interest on payments on account, balancing payments and penalties runs from the due date of payment to the day the payment is made. However, HMRC interprets this to mean for the period between those two dates – ie HMRC does not count the actual due date or the date of payment.

Interest on additional tax payments due to amendments to a self assessment and tax payable under a discovery assessment runs from the **annual** submission date to the day before the payment is made.

Worked example: Interest on late paid tax

Arslan gives you the following information about his payments of tax relating to 2014/15:

First payment on account of £2,000 paid in full on 31 March 2015
Second payment on account of £2,000 paid in full on 31 July 2015
Balancing payment of £3,000 paid in full on 16 March 2016

Requirement

Calculate the interest due (interest rate on overdue tax is 3%), working to the nearest day and pound. Assume that any penalties are paid on time.

Solution

First payment on account due 31 January 2015, paid 31 March 2015, 58 days late (1.2.15 – 30.3.15). Interest = 58/365 × £2,000 × 3% = £10

Second payment on account paid on due date 31 July 2015, so no interest due.

Balancing payment due 31 January 2016, paid 16 March 2016, 44 days late (1.2.16 – 15.3.16). Interest 44/366 × £3,000 × 3% = £11

7.4 Repayment interest

Repayment interest is payable by HMRC on overpaid payments on account, balancing payments and penalties. Repayment interest runs from the later of the date that the tax was paid to HMRC and the due date for payment of the tax, to the day before the repayment is made. Repayment interest is exempt from income tax.

8 Corporation tax – returns

Section overview

- If a company has taxable total profits it must notify HMRC of its chargeability to corporation tax.

- HMRC will issue a company with a tax return shortly after the end of its period of account.

- The tax return includes a tax computation and the company must also submit accounts and supporting calculations.

8.1 Issue of tax return

Companies have an obligation to notify HMRC when their first accounting period begins. The company must give written notice to HMRC within three months of the start of the first accounting period. The notice must state when the first accounting period began.

If a company fails to notify HMRC, a penalty may be payable (see Section 9.1).

Most companies prepare their accounts to the same date each year. HMRC normally issues a notice requiring a company to submit a corporation tax return within a few weeks of the end of each period of account.

Where a notice and/or return is not issued, a company is required to notify HMRC where it has taxable total profits for an accounting period. Notification of chargeability must be made within twelve months of the end of the accounting period. If notification is not given, a penalty may be payable (see Section 2).

8.2 Full tax return

A full corporation tax return (CT600) consists of an eight-page summary form and tax calculation, together with a number of supplementary forms.

The company is required to complete the summary form and tax calculation and such supplementary forms as are relevant. Note that there is **no** option for HMRC to calculate the tax liability of the company.

The company must also submit accounts for the period covered by the return and computations showing how entries on the return have been calculated from the figures in the accounts.

The tax return and supporting information must normally be submitted within twelve months of the end of the period of account.

8.3 Short tax return

The short corporation tax return (CT600 Short) is a four-page form. Most companies which do not have to make payments on account and which have straightforward tax affairs can use the short return, provided the form has boxes for all the entries it needs to make.

Use of the short return does not affect the filing deadline or the requirement for the company to calculate its own tax liability.

8.4 Online filing

All companies must submit their tax returns online and pay their tax liabilities electronically.

Additionally, tax computations and the accounts that form part of the Company Tax Return, must be submitted in Inline eXtensible Business Reporting Language (iXBRL) format. iXBRL is an IT standard designed specifically for business financial reporting.

8.5 Right to amend tax returns

HMRC has the right to amend a company's tax return so as to correct obvious errors or omissions in the return such as errors of principle and arithmetic errors. HMRC's powers to correct a return extend to correct 'anything else in the return that the officer has reason to believe is incorrect in the light of information available to the officer'.

HMRC corrections must be made within nine months of the date the return is actually filed.

The company has the right to amend its tax return for any reason within twelve months of the normal due submission date (not the actual submission date).

In addition, the company may make a claim for 'overpayment' relief for errors in the tax return where tax would be overcharged as a result. Such a claim must be made within four years of the end of the accounting period.

9 Corporation tax – penalties and interest

Section overview

- Penalties are payable, for example on late submission of tax returns and late payment of tax.

- Interest is payable by a company on late paid tax and penalties.

- Interest is payable by HMRC on overpaid tax.

9.1 Penalties

A fixed penalty is charged where a company fails to notify commencement of the first accounting period. Failure to notify commencement within three months can lead to a maximum penalty of £300. Failure to notify when no return is issued (see Section 8.1) also gives rise to penalties (see Section 2 above).

Penalties are also charged if a company submits a late return. Tax-geared penalties may also apply to returns submitted late. These penalties have been considered earlier in this chapter.

9.2 Penalties for late payment of tax

Details of the payment dates of corporation tax were given in Chapter 10 and you may want to revisit that section now.

The penalties for late payment of corporation tax are as follows:

- 5% of tax unpaid at the filing date
- Further 5% penalty where tax remains unpaid three months after the filing date
- Further 5% penalty where the tax remains unpaid nine months after the filing date

Remember that only this penalty regime is examinable even where the rules have not yet been implemented in practice.

Worked example: Penalties

K plc makes up accounts to 30 June each year.

For the year to 30 June 2015, K plc submits its tax return and pays its corporation tax on 1 February 2017.

The corporation tax liability of K plc for the year to 30 June 2015 is £50,000. K plc does not pay corporation tax by instalments and has made no payments of corporation tax in respect of this year.

Requirement

What is the maximum penalty payable by K plc?

Solution

Tax return should have been submitted by 30 June 2016. The return was therefore seven months late.

Maximum penalty for late filing of the return is:

£100 plus £900 (£10 per day × 90 days) plus (5% × £50,000)	**£3,500**

The tax liability was due to be paid on 1 April 2016. The tax was paid 10 months late.

Maximum penalty for late payment of tax is:

(10% × £50,000)	**£5,000**

There is a 5% penalty at the filing date and a further 5% penalty three months after the filing date. The tax had been paid by nine months after the filling date.

Interactive question 3: Penalties

[Difficulty level: Exam standard]

State the maximum penalties for the following events, briefly stating the reason for your answer.

Question	Fill in your answer
Notified HMRC on 10 January 2017 of chargeability for accounting period ended 30 November 2015. This is not the company's first accounting period. Corporation tax liability £7,500 paid on same date	
Tax return for accounting period ended 31 July 2015 submitted 30 September 2016	
Destroyed records on 10 August 2019 for accounting period ended 31 December 2015	
Tax return for accounting period ended 31 October 2015 submitted 30 November 2017, corporation tax due of £10,000 paid 30 September 2017	

See **Answer** at the end of this chapter.

9.3 Interest on late paid corporation tax

Interest is payable on late paid corporation tax. Interest runs from the date the tax should have been paid to the day the tax is actually paid. However, HMRC interprets this to mean for the period between those two dates – ie HMRC does not count the actual due date or the date of payment.

Worked example: Interest on late paid tax

H Ltd does not pay corporation tax by instalments and makes up accounts to 30 September each year.

For the year to 30 September 2014, H Ltd had a corporation tax liability of £50,000. It paid this on 14 September 2015.

Requirement

What is the interest payable by H Ltd? Assume an interest rate of 3% on late paid corporation tax.

Solution

Corporation tax due 1 July 2015, paid 14 September 2015, so 74 days late.

Interest 74/365 × £50,000 × 3%   £304

Interest charged on late paid corporation tax is an allowable non-trading loan relationships expense.

9.4 Interest on overpaid corporation tax (repayment interest)

Repayment interest is payable by HMRC on overpaid corporation tax. Repayment interest runs from the later of the date the tax was originally paid and the date the tax was due to be paid.

Repayment interest is taxable as a non-trading loan relationships profit.

10 Value added tax – penalties and interest

Section overview

- There are penalties for late registration; late returns and late payments of VAT; and incorrect returns.

- Interest may be payable on late paid VAT and overpayments of VAT.

10.1 Late registration penalty

A taxable person who fails to register for VAT by the appropriate date may be liable to a late registration penalty (see Section 2 of this chapter).

10.2 Penalty for late filing of VAT returns

The penalty regime for the late filing of returns (see Section 4 of this chapter) also applies to VAT but as returns are typically filed at intervals of less than one year, a separate set of rules apply.

The rules apply to a 'penalty period'. Once a penalty period has started, each subsequent late return in that period causes the penalty period to be extended to the twelve months from the due filing date for that late return.

Penalties for further late returns within a penalty period gradually increase as the number of late returns increases.

Although the late-filing penalty regime is being implemented over a number of years, only the new late filing penalties explained here are examinable. This is the case even where the rules have not yet been implemented in practice.

The penalties are as follows:

	Monthly returns	Quarterly returns
Initial penalty	£100	£100
Further late returns within penalty period (expires 12 months after the most recent late return)	1st to 5th late return: £100 6th and subsequent late return: £200	1st late return: £200 2nd late return: £300 3rd or subsequent late return: £400

If a return is still outstanding after six months a further penalty applies of 5% of the tax due.

If a return is still outstanding after 12 months a further penalty applies:

- 100% of tax due where withholding of information is deliberate and concealed
- 70% of tax due where withholding of information is deliberate but not concealed
- 5% of tax due in other cases

The tax-geared penalties are all subject to a minimum of £300. They can be reduced for disclosure, with higher reductions if the disclosure is unprompted (see earlier in this chapter).

Worked example: Late filing of VAT returns

Gate Ltd has submitted its recent VAT returns as follows:

VAT quarter end	Date submitted
30.4.15	10.6.15
31.7.15	29.8.15
31.10.15	30.11.15
31.1.16	16.3.16

The company is not currently in a penalty period.

Requirement

What penalties will be payable by Gate Ltd for the late filing of its VAT returns?

Solution

The VAT return for the quarter ended 30 April 2015 was due by 7 June 2015. This is the first failure so will start a penalty period for the company for twelve months until 7 June 2016. It will also result in a fixed penalty of £100.

The VAT return for the quarters ended 31 July 2015 and 31 October 2015 were submitted on time so there is no penalty and no change to the penalty period.

The VAT return for the quarter ended 31 January 2016 was due on 7 March 2016 and was therefore submitted late. A penalty of £200 will be charged and the penalty period will be extended to 7 March 2017.

If the taxpayer can satisfy HMRC that there is 'reasonable excuse' for the late filing of the return, no penalty is payable nor does the failure count for the purpose of starting a penalty period to run.

10.3 Penalty for late payment of VAT

The new penalty regime for the late payment of tax also applies to VAT. However as liabilities are more frequent, because the return period is usually less than six months, a system based on penalty periods applies in a similar way to the penalties for late returns (above).

The first late payment of VAT does not attract a penalty but it starts a twelve month 'penalty period' that runs from the payment due date.

If a further late payment of VAT occurs within the penalty period, a penalty is charged, based on the amount of tax paid late. The penalty period is also extended for a further twelve months.

The penalties are as follows:

	Monthly returns	Quarterly returns
Penalty for default within penalty period	1st, 2nd or 3rd default: 1% 4th, 5th or 6th default: 2% 7th, 8th or 9th default: 3% 10th or subsequent default: 4%	1st default: 2% 2nd default: 3% 3rd or subsequent default: 4%
After 6 months	Further penalty of 5% of tax still unpaid	
After 12 months	Further penalty of 5% of tax still unpaid	

Late payment penalties can be suspended where the taxpayer agrees a time to pay arrangement, unless he abuses the arrangement.

Although the late-payment penalty regime is being implemented over a number of years, only the new late filing penalties explained here are examinable. This is the case even where the rules have not yet been implemented in practice.

Worked example: Late payment of VAT

Gate Ltd has paid the VAT due from its recent quarterly returns as follows:

VAT quarter end	VAT due £	Date VAT paid
30.4.15	30,000	14.6.15
31.7.15	26,000	29.8.15
31.10.15	28,500	21.12.15
31.1.16	31,200	21.9.16

The company is not currently in a penalty period.

Requirement

What penalties will be payable by Gate Ltd for the late payment of VAT?

Solution

The VAT payment for the quarter ended 30 April 2015 was due by 7 June 2015. This is the first default and will initiate a penalty period for the company for twelve months until 7 June 2016. There is no penalty charged for the first default.

The VAT for the quarter ended 31 July 2015 was paid on time so there is no penalty and no change to the penalty period.

The VAT due for the quarter ended 31 October 2015 was due on 7 December 2015 and was therefore paid late. As this is the first default within the penalty period the penalty charged is 2% of the tax due of £28,500, which is £570. The penalty period is extended to 7 December 2016.

The VAT due for the quarter ended 31 January 2016 was due on 7 March 2016. The VAT was paid late. The penalty for a second default within a penalty period is 3% of the tax due of £31,200. There will be a penalty of £936 and an extension to the penalty period to 7 March 2017. In addition as the VAT due is not paid until 21 September 2016 it is over six months late. A further penalty will be payable as this is a prolonged failure. The penalty will be 5% of the VAT due, which is £1,560.

10.4 VAT errors

The common penalty regime for making errors in tax returns discussed in Section 1 of this chapter also applies to value added tax.

An error made on a VAT return can be corrected on the next return provided it was not deliberate and does not exceed the greater of:

- £10,000 (net under-declaration minus over-declaration); or
- 1% × net VAT turnover for return period (maximum £50,000)

Alternatively, a small careless (not deliberate) error may be corrected on form VAT652. A tax payer may choose to both correct a small careless error on the VAT return and also submit form VAT652.

'Large' errors or deliberate small errors should be notified to HMRC on form VAT652.

In both cases a penalty for error may be imposed. Correction of an error on a later return is not, of, itself an unprompted disclosure of the error and fuller disclosure is required for the penalty to be reduced.

However if the inaccuracy in the return was neither careless nor deliberate when the return was made and the net value of the inaccuracy was below the de minimis limit and the error was corrected in a later VAT return HMRC will deem reasonable steps to have been taken to inform it of the inaccuracy and no penalty will be due.

In addition, as discussed in Section 2 of this chapter, a penalty may not be due if the trader can show there is reasonable excuse for the failure.

10.5 Interest on unpaid VAT

A taxable person may be charged interest where:

- HMRC raises an assessment for output VAT under declared or input VAT over claimed; or
- The taxpayer voluntarily discloses an error and the net value of errors exceeds the 'error reporting threshold' (see above).

Interest runs from the date the VAT should have been paid until the date of payment.

10.6 Interest on overpaid VAT

A taxable person may receive repayment interest only where there has been an error by HMRC leading to overpayment of output VAT or an under claim of input VAT.

Interest runs from the later of the date of payment to HMRC and the due date for payment, to the date of repayment.

11 Compliance checks and appeals

Section overview

- HMRC may conduct a compliance check into a tax return and can make determinations or discovery assessments.
- Appeals may be made by the taxpayer, for example against discovery assessments. HMRC may raise an assessment of VAT where a return is not submitted, or is incomplete or incorrect.

11.1 Compliance checks and enquiries

HMRC has the power to conduct a compliance check or enquire into an individual's or company's tax return.

Some taxpayers are selected at random, others for a particular reason, for example, if HMRC believes that there has been an underpayment of tax due to the taxpayer's failure to comply with tax legislation.

There are two main types of checks:

- Pre-return compliance checks, some of which are carried out by telephone, and
- Formal enquiries into returns, claims or elections which have already been submitted.

Examples of when a pre-return compliance check may be carried out in practice include:

- To assist with clearances or ruling requests

- Where a previous check has identified poor record-keeping
- To check that computer systems will produce the information needed to support a return
- To find out about planning or avoidance schemes
- Where fraud is suspected
- Where a person regularly discloses an error after the submission of a VAT return.

Notice must be given by HMRC of the intention to enquire into a submitted return by:

- The first anniversary of the actual submission date; or

- If the return is filed after the due submission date, the quarter day following the first anniversary of the actual submission date. The quarter days are 31 January, 30 April, 31 July and 31 October.

HMRC has only one opportunity to open a formal enquiry and a tax return cannot be subject to a formal enquiry more than once.

In addition, HMRC may conduct a check after a return has become final (or where no return has been submitted) where it believes that an assessment or determination may need to be issued under the discovery provisions (see further below).

11.2 HMRC determinations

If a return is not received by the filing date, HMRC may make a determination (to the best of its information and belief) of the tax due. This may include a determination of any amounts added or deducted in the computation of the tax payable, or any amount from which those figures are derived. The determination must be made within three years of the statutory filing date.

The determination is treated as if it were a self assessment. This enables HMRC to enforce payment of tax demanded, to charge interest and to levy tax geared penalties. A determination may be displaced by a self-assessment.

11.3 Discovery assessments

A determination may only be raised if no return has been submitted, and, once a return has been filed, there are strict deadlines for opening a compliance check into a return. Although this normally gives the taxpayer certainty that its tax liabilities are agreed, HMRC has the power via a discovery assessment to collect extra tax where it discovers a loss of tax.

HMRC can make a discovery assessment after the usual time for a compliance check if it is discovered that full disclosure has not been made by the taxpayer.

If the reason for the discovery assessment is that the taxpayer has made an incomplete disclosure resulting in a loss of tax the time limits for a discovery assessment are:

Reason for loss of tax	Time limits
Not due to careless or deliberate behaviour	4 years
Due to 'careless' behaviour	6 years
Due to 'deliberate' behaviour	20 years

The time limits run from the end of the accounting period (corporation tax), tax year (income tax and CGT) or prescribed accounting period (VAT).

11.4 Appeals

A taxpayer may make an appeal against:

- A request by HMRC to submit documents, supporting records etc in the course of a compliance check
- Amendments made to a self assessment as the result of a compliance check
- HMRC's right to raise a discovery assessment
- A discovery assessment
- A VAT assessment
- Imposition of a penalty

The appeal must be made in writing within 30 days of the relevant event and must specify the grounds for the appeal.

The taxpayer may also apply to postpone payment of all or part of the tax whilst waiting for the appeal decision. This only applies in the case of appeal against a discovery assessment or tax payable as a result of a compliance check.

Most appeals are settled by agreement between the taxpayer and HMRC. The first step, offered by HMRC or requested by the taxpayer, may be an internal review by an officer of HMRC not connected with the case. The taxpayer can appeal the outcome of the review within 30 days. Appeals which are not settled are heard by the Tax Chamber of the First-tier Tribunal. Appeals can be made in writing within 56 days to the Upper Tribunal on a point of law, with the First-tier or Upper Tribunals' permission.

As VAT is a European Union tax, these cases may be referred by the UK courts to the European Court of Justice for a ruling on a point of law.

12 HMRC powers

Section overview

- HMRC may use its statutory powers to request information and documents from taxpayers and even third parties via a written information notice.

- HMRC can issue an inspection notice and enter the premises of a taxpayer whose liability is being checked.

- HMRC may issue a conduct notice if it has evidence of the dishonest conduct of a tax agent.

- HMRC can obtain access to the working papers of the tax agent in order to establish the extent of the dishonesty.

- HMRC can impose a penalty of between £5,000 and £50,000 for dishonest conduct.

12.1 Information and inspection powers

HMRC has one set of information and inspection powers covering income tax, capital gains tax, corporation tax, VAT and PAYE, to ensure taxpayers comply with their obligations, claim the correct reliefs and allowances and pay the right amount of tax at the right time.

These powers allow HMRC to make compliance checks by:

- Asking taxpayers and third parties for information and documents
- Visiting business premises to inspect the premises, assets and records

12.2 Information powers

12.2.1 General provisions

HMRC may make informal requests for information from taxpayers in connection with their tax affairs. If, however, a taxpayer does not co-operate fully, HMRC can use its statutory powers to request information and documents from taxpayers and even third parties via a written 'information notice'.

12.2.2 Taxpayer notices

HMRC can only issue an information notice to a taxpayer if the information and documents requested are 'reasonably required' for the purpose of checking the taxpayer's tax position.

A taxpayer notice may be issued either with or without the approval of the First-tier Tribunal. An authorised HMRC officer must agree before the request is referred to the First-tier Tribunal.

HMRC can request both statutory records and supplementary information, such as appointment diaries, notes of board meetings, correspondence and contracts.

12.2.3 Third party notices

An information notice issued to a third party must be issued with the agreement of the taxpayer or the approval of the First-tier Tribunal, unless the information relates only to the taxpayer's statutory VAT records.

The taxpayer to whom the notice relates must receive a summary of the reasons for the third party notice unless the Tribunal believes it would prejudice the assessment or collection of tax.

Tax advisers and auditors cannot be asked to provide information connected with their functions. For example, a tax adviser does not have to provide access to his working papers used in the preparation of the taxpayer's return.

In addition, HMRC cannot ask a tax adviser to provide communications between himself and either the taxpayer or his other advisers.

12.2.4 Unknown-identity notices

In addition to the above HMRC also has the power, to require any person to provide information or documents which are required to check the tax position of a person(s) for whom HMRC does not hold full identity details where HMRC believes there is a serious loss of tax.

This power extends to require any person to provide basic identity information ie name, last known address and date of birth without HMRC having to have grounds to suspect there is a serious loss of tax.

12.2.5 Data-holder notices

HMRC may issue a data-holder notice to certain data-holders (for example, employers and banks) requiring them to provide 'relevant data', which may be general data or data relating to particular persons or matters. It may include personal data such as names and addresses of individuals.

HMRC may use this power for general effective risk assessment and also to target non-compliant taxpayers. Where this power overlaps with the general information powers detailed above, those general powers take priority.

12.2.6 Right of appeal

The recipient of an information notice has a right of appeal against that notice, unless:

- The First-tier Tribunal has approved the issue of the notice, or
- The information or documents relate to the taxpayer's statutory records.

12.3 Inspection powers

An authorised HMRC officer can enter the business premises of a taxpayer whose liability is being checked and inspect the premises, and the business assets and business documents that are on the premises. The power does not extend to any part of the premises used solely as a dwelling. If an information notice has been issued, the documents required in that notice can be inspected at the same time. The inspection must be reasonably required for the purposes of checking the taxpayer's tax position.

HMRC will usually agree a time for the inspection with the taxpayer. However, an inspection can be carried out at 'any reasonable time' if either:

(a) The taxpayer receives at least seven days' written notice, or
(b) The inspection is carried out by, or with the approval of, an authorised HMRC officer.

There is no right of appeal against an inspection notice.

12.4 Dishonest conduct by tax agents

12.4.1 Introduction

HMRC has a number of powers that it can use when it has evidence that a tax agent (ie an individual who, in the course of business, assists clients with their tax affairs) has done something dishonest that leads to a loss of tax.

12.4.2 HMRC powers

HMRC can:

(a) Issue a conduct notice if it has determined that the agent has engaged in dishonest conduct.

(b) Issue a file access notice to obtain the working papers of a tax agent found to have engaged in dishonest conduct (subject to prior approval by the First-tier Tribunal).

(c) Publish information about the tax agent, including his name and address, if a penalty for dishonest conduct (see below) exceeds £5,000.

In addition, HMRC can disclose details of the dishonest conduct to the tax agent's professional body if he is a member of one.

12.4.3 Penalties

HMRC can issue a **civil penalty for dishonest conduct**. The minimum penalty is £5,000 (although this can be reduced in 'special circumstances') and can be as high as £50,000, depending on the tax agent's behaviour.

It can also impose a penalty of £300 for failure to comply with a file access notice, with additional daily penalties of up to £60.

Interest is payable on late paid penalties.

12.4.4 Right of appeal

The tax agent may appeal, in writing within 30 days, against both a conduct notice and any penalty imposed.

He may not, however, appeal against a file access notice, although if HMRC has issued the notice to a third party (eg the taxpayer) because the working papers are no longer in the agent's possession, that third party can appeal.

13 Business Payment Support Service

HMRC's Business Payment Support Service (BPSS) is in place to assist businesses and individuals unable to pay the amount owed to HMRC by the relevant deadline.

Provided the BPSS is contacted before any tax is overdue, HMRC will review the circumstances of the taxpayer and may offer the option of payment by instalments. Late payment penalties will not be charged on payments included in the arrangement, provided the taxpayer makes payments in line with the arrangement. However interest will run from the normal due date until payment is made.

14 Budget payment plans

A budget payment plan can be set up to make regular payments in advance. Under a budget payment plan, a taxpayer makes regular Direct Debit payments towards future self-assessment liabilities.

A taxpayer wishing to set up a budget payment plan must be up to date with previous tax payments. The taxpayer can choose the amount of the regular weekly or monthly payments. The taxpayer can also suspend collection for a period of up to six months.

If the total paid in advance of the usual payment date does not cover the tax payable, the taxpayer must pay the difference by the usual payment deadline.

Summary

```
                    ┌─────────────────────┐      ┌─────────────────────┐
                    │  Common penalty     │─────▶│  Information and     │
                    │  regime             │      │  inspection powers   │
                    └─────────────────────┘      └─────────────────────┘
        ┌────────────────┬──────────────┬──────────────────┬──────────────────┐
  ┌───────────────┐ ┌───────────────┐ ┌───────────────┐ ┌───────────────┐
  │ Inaccurate    │ │ Failure to    │ │ Late filing   │ │ Record        │
  │ returns       │ │ notify        │ │ of returns    │ │ keeping       │
  └───────────────┘ └───────────────┘ └───────────────┘ └───────────────┘
          │                                                      │
  ┌──────────────────┐                                  ┌──────────────┐
  │ Percentage of    │                                  │ £3,000 pa    │
  │ PLR –            │                                  └──────────────┘
  │ reduction for    │
  │ disclosure       │
  └──────────────────┘
```

```
┌──────────────────┐      ┌──────────────────┐                  ┌──────────────┐
│ Self assessment  │      │ Self-assessment  │                  │ VAT          │
│ for individuals  │      │ for companies    │                  └──────────────┘
│ and partnerships │      └──────────────────┘                         │
└──────────────────┘                                          ┌──────────────┐
                                                              │ Penalties    │
                                                              └──────────────┘
```

Notification of liability by 5 October

Tax return: submit electronically by later of 31 January or three months after issue or on paper later of 31 October or three months after issue:
– full
– short (paper return only)
– partnership

Notification of liability: by 3 months after start of first chargeable accounting period by 12 months after end of continuing chargeable accounting periods

Penalties:
Late notification
Late returns
Failure to keep records

Late submission of return or payment of VAT

Late payment of tax

Assessments: if no return or incorrect return
Appeals: to First-tier tribunal

Compliance checks and discovery assessment Appeals

Penalties for late submission of return, failure to retain records

Payment of tax: Payments on account of income tax and Class 4 NICs, balancing payment of income tax, Class 4 NICs, all of Class 2 NIC and all of CGT

Tax return submitted by 12 months after end of accounting period

Compliance checks and discovery assessment Appeals

Penalties for late payment of tax

Interest on: late paid tax overpaid tax

Payment of tax: Large companies by 4 equal instalments Other companies 9 months and 1 day after end of chargeable accounting period

Interest: On late paid tax On overpaid tax

Self-test

Answer the following questions.

1   Jane submitted her 2015/16 tax return electronically on 13 January 2017. The return had been issued to her in May 2016.

   By what date must HMRC give notice if it wishes to check Jane's entitlement to the reliefs claimed in the return?

   A   13 January 2018
   B   31 January 2018
   C   30 April 2018
   D   13 February 2018

2   Zeta is a sole trader. She submitted a paper tax return for 2015/16 on 15 August 2016.

   What is the latest date by which HMRC can correct an obvious error in her return?

   A   31 January 2017
   B   15 May 2017
   C   31 August 2017
   D   31 January 2018

3   James has never received a tax return. He started a business on 5 May 2015.

   By what date must he give notice to HMRC that he has chargeable income?

   A   5 October 2015
   B   5 April 2016
   C   5 October 2016
   D   5 April 2017

4   Todd was issued with a tax return for 2014/15 on 20 October 2015. He filed it online on 15 March 2016 and paid the tax due of £1,700 on the same date.

   What is the maximum penalty for late submission of the tax return that could be imposed?

   A   £0
   B   £100
   C   £900
   D   £1,000

5   Susan's only source of income is savings income. She submits her tax return for 2015/16 on 1 October 2016.

   Until which date must she retain the records used to complete her return?

   A   31 January 2017
   B   30 September 2017
   C   31 January 2018
   D   31 January 2022

6   Y Ltd makes up a 12-month set of accounts to 31 May 2015.

   By what date must Y Ltd submit its tax return?

   A   1 March 2016
   B   31 May 2016
   C   31 January 2017
   D   31 May 2017

7   P Ltd makes up a 12-month set of accounts to 31 March 2016.

   Until which date must P Ltd retain its records relating to this accounting period?

   A   31 March 2017
   B   31 March 2018
   C   31 March 2021
   D   31 March 2022

8   U Ltd prepares accounts to 30 September each year. U Ltd has never paid tax by instalments. It has paid tax and filed returns as set out below:

y/e	CT due	Tax return submitted	CT paid
30.09.15	£70,000	14.05.17	21.06.17

What is the maximum penalty payable by U Ltd for the year ended 30 September 2015 for the late filing of its return?

A   £100
B   £1,000
C   £4,500

What is the maximum penalty payable by U Ltd for the year ended 30 September 2015 for the late payment of its tax?

D   £3,500
E   £7,000
F   £10,500

9   John files his tax return for 2015/16 on 31 January 2017. This shows property income of £54,000. John has purposely overstated the property expenses by £7,000 by creating false invoices for the additional expenses. HMRC initiates an investigation into John's return and in reply John then makes a disclosure of the error.

The minimum penalty that could be charged by HMRC for his error is

A   £2,800
B   £1,960
C   £1,400
D   £980

10 Amelia has submitted an inaccurate return to HMRC. The error is deliberate and concealed.

What is the maximum penalty HMRC could levy on Amelia?

A   100% of potential lost revenue
B   70% of potential lost revenue
C   30% of potential lost revenue

Amelia makes an unprompted disclosure of the error to HMRC.

What is the minimum penalty HMRC could levy on Amelia?

D   20% of potential lost revenue
E   30% of potential lost revenue
F   50% of potential lost revenue

11 Employers are required to pay their PAYE and Class 1 national insurance contributions electronically if they have

A   At least 250 employees
B   At least 100 employees
C   At least 50 employees
D   Any number of employees

Now, go back to the Learning objectives in the Introduction. If you are satisfied you have achieved these objectives, please tick them off.

Technical reference

Legislation

Penalties for incorrect returns	Sch 24 FA 2007
HMRC's powers	Sch 36 FA 2008
Records	Sch 37 FA 2008
Penalties for failure to notify	Sch 41 FA 2008
Duties of senior accounting officers	Sch 46 FA 2009
Penalties for late filing or late payment	Schs 55 & 56 FA 2009

Income tax and Capital gains tax – References relating to Taxes Management Act 1970 (*TMA 1970*) unless otherwise stated

Notification of liability to income tax and CGT	s.7
Personal return	s.8
Partnership return	s.12AA
HMRC corrections	s.9ZB
Taxpayer amendments	s.9ZA
Notice of enquiry	s.9A
Discovery assessments	s.29
Appeals	ss.48-54
Payments on account	s.59A
Balancing payment	s.59B
Penalty for failure to make return	s.93
Interest on overdue tax	s.86
Overpayment relief claim	Sch 1AB

Corporation tax – References relate to Finance Act 1998 (*FA 1998*) Schedule 18 unless otherwise stated

Notification of liability within three months of the start of the first accounting period	FA 2004 s.55
Tax return	para 3
HMRC corrections	para 16
Company amendments	para 15
Overpayment relief claim	paras 51-51G
Notice of enquiry	para 24
Discovery assessments	para 41
Payment of tax	FA 1998 s.30
Interest on late paid tax	FA 1998 s.33
Interest on overpaid tax	FA 1998 s.34

VAT – References relate to Value Added Tax Act 1994 (*VATA 1994*) unless otherwise stated

Assessments	s.73
Appeals	SI 1986/590
Late registration penalty	s.67
Interest on late paid tax	s.74
Repayment interest	s.79

HMRC manuals

Income Tax Self Assessment: The Legal Framework (Found at
http://www.hmrc.gov.uk/manuals/salfmanual/Index.htm)

Payment of Tax: Payments on Account	SALF303
Payment of Tax: Balancing Payments	SALF304
Payment of Tax: Automatic Interest and Late Payment Penalties: Interest Charged on Late Payments of Tax	SALF305
Payment of Tax: Automatic Interest and Late Payment Penalties: Late Payment Penalties on Unpaid Income Tax and Capital Gains Tax	SALF308A
Enquiring into Tax Returns: Introduction	SALF402

For corporation tax there is the company taxation manual. This can be found at
http://www.hmrc.gov.uk/manuals/ctmanual/index.htm

To find out more practical information about VAT, access the relevant section of the gov.uk website
through the page https://www.gov.uk/government/organisations/hm-revenue-customs .

Information is available online at https://www.gov.uk/business-tax/vat

Information about the range of special schemes and options to simplify VAT for small businesses is
available is available under the heading 'Accounting for VAT'

There is also a VAT telephone helpline: 0300 200 3700

> This technical reference section is designed to assist you. It should help you to know where to look for
> further information on the topics covered in this chapter. **You will not be examined on the contents
> of this section in your examination.**

Answers to Interactive questions

Answer to Interactive question 1

Question	Fill in your answer
Normal due date for tax return for 2015/16 issued 20 November 2016, taxpayer to submit an electronic return online	Later of 31 January 2017 and 20 February 2017, ie 20 February 2017
Notify HMRC of need to issue tax return for 2015/16	5 October 2016
Overpayment relief claim relating to 2015/16	5 April 2020
Keep business records for 2015/16	31 January 2022
Normal due date for tax return for 2015/16 issued 31 May 2016, HMRC to calculate tax and paper return to be submitted	Later of 31 October 2016 and 31 July 2016, ie 31 October 2016
Keep personal records for 2015/16	31 January 2018
Amend tax return for 2015/16 submitted 30 November 2016	31 January 2018

Answer to Interactive question 2

Question	Fill in your answer
Notified HMRC of new source of income for 2015/16 on 5 December 2016, paid all £4,000 of tax due on 25 January 2017	Maximum £1,200 penalty (for failure to notify – 30% × potential lost revenue). This may be reduced to nil for unprompted disclosure and payment in full within 12 months.
Tax return for 2015/16 issued May 2016, submitted return electronically 30 March 2017	Due date was 31 January 2017, less than three months late. Penalty of £100.
Balancing payment of tax of £2,000 for 2015/16 paid 30 April 2017	£2,000 × 5% = £100 – due date was 31 January 2017 so penalty due after 30 days (2 March 2017), no further penalty as paid within six months of payment due date.
Destroyed supporting records for 2015/16 on 1 May 2017	£3,000
Tax return for 2015/16 issued June 2016, submitted electronically on 15 September 2017, tax due £1,000	Due date was 31 January 2017, over 6 months late. Initial penalty of £100, daily penalty of £10 for 90 days (£900), 5% of tax due but subject to minimum of £300 once six months late.
Balancing payment of tax of £3,000 for 2015/16 paid 30 September 2017	£3,000 × 10% = £300 – due date was 31 January 2017, 5% penalty after 30 days (2 March 2017) and further 5% after six months (2 August 2017).

Answer to Interactive question 3

Question	Fill in your answer
Notified HMRC on 10 January 2017 of chargeability for accounting period ended 30 November 2015. This is not the company's first accounting period. Corporation tax liability £7,500 paid on same date	Maximum penalty 30% × potential lost revenue (£2,250). If disclosure is unprompted then may be reduced to nil. Notification should be by 30 November 2016, therefore less than 12 months late
Tax return for accounting period ended 31 July 2015 submitted 30 September 2016	£100 – return due 31 July 2016, ie less than three months late
Destroyed records on 10 August 2019 for accounting period ended 31 December 2015	£3,000 – should have kept records until 31 December 2021
Tax return for accounting period ended 31 October 2015 submitted 30 November 2017, corporation tax due of £10,000 paid 30 September 2017	£2,000 – for return filed late. The return was due 31 October 2016, ie over 12 months late so £100 plus £900 plus £500 (5% of tax due subject to minimum of £300) plus further £500 once 12 months late (unless deemed to be as a result of the deliberate withholding of information in which case penalty could be up to 100% of the tax due)

£1,500 – for tax paid late. 5% penalty at filing date and at three and nine months after filing date

Total penalty for late filing and late payment is £2,000 + £1,500 = £3,500 |

Answers to Self-test

1   A – 13 January 2018

The return was due on 31 January 2018 and was submitted on time. HMRC has until the first anniversary of the actual submission of the return to give notice of a formal check of the submitted return.

2   B – 15 May 2017

HMRC has nine months from the actual submission date to make corrections to a self assessment.

3   C – 5 October 2016

The business began in 2015/16 (5 May 2015) and James must notify HMRC by 5 October following the end of that tax year.

4   B – £100

The tax return was due on 31 January 2016 and so is less than three months late.

5   C – 31 January 2018

Personal tax records must be retained for one year after 31 January following the end of the tax year (for 2015/16, 31 January 2018).

6   B – by 31 May 2016

7   D – 31 March 2022

Records must be kept for a minimum period of six years after the end of the accounting period.

8   C – £4,500

Tax return submitted between six and twelve months late. There is an initial £100 penalty, £900 from a daily penalty of £10 per day for 90 days and 5% of tax due (£3,500).

E – £7,000

Tax due on 1 July 2016. Penalty of 5% of tax unpaid on filing date and a further 5% of tax unpaid three months after the filing date (31 December 2016). Tax has been paid by nine months after the filing date so no further penalty.

9   C – £1,400

The PLR as a result of John's error is £7,000 × 40%   £2,800

John's error is deliberate and concealed (active steps to conceal the error by the creation of false invoices) but he has made a prompted disclosure so the minimum penalty is 50% of £2,800 which is £1,400.

10 A – 100% of potential lost revenue.

E – 30% of potential lost revenue.

11 A – Only employers with at least 250 employees are required to make payments electronically.

PRINCIPLES OF TAXATION

Tax Tables Finance Acts 2015

The tax tables reproduced on the following pages are identical to the tax tables you will be given in the exam. Familiarise yourself with the content so that you know what you need to learn and what you can access in the exam from the tax tables.

In the actual exam, for ease of use on screen, your tax tables are divided into sections in accordance with the five key syllabus areas. You will find that for each question in the actual exam you will only be able to access the part of the tax tables relevant to that part of the syllabus. This is to minimise the amount of time you will need to spend scrolling through the tax tables.

Questions on each syllabus area will therefore only be able to access the pages of the tax tables as follows:

ICAEW – CERTIFICATE LEVEL

TAX TABLES FINANCE ACTS 2015

SYLLABUS AREA: ADMINISTRATION

SUBMISSION DATES

Submission dates for 2015/16 personal self-assessment tax returns

Return filed online	Later of: • 31 January 2017 • 3 months from the date of issue of return
Paper returns: [1]	Later of: • 31 October 2016 • 3 months from the date of issue of return

(1)   If HMRC is to calculate tax due on a paper return, the filing date is the later of 31 October 2016 and two months from the date the notice to make a return was issued.

Submission dates for corporation tax returns

Must be filed by 12 months from the end of the period of account

Submission dates for PAYE information: Real Time Information

Information	Filing date
Full Payment Submission (FPS)	On or before the day the employee is paid
P60 (to employees)	31 May following the tax year end
P9D and P11D	6 July following the tax year end

PAYMENT DATES

Payment dates for income tax

Payment	Filing date
First interim payment [1]	31 January in the tax year
Second interim payment [1]	31 July following the tax year end
Balancing payment	31 January following the tax year end

(1)   Interim payments are not required if the tax paid by assessment for the previous year was less than:
- £1,000; or
- 20% of the total tax liability (income tax and Class 4)

Payment dates for capital gains tax

Capital gains tax is payable by 31 January following the tax year end

Payment dates for corporation tax

Corporation tax	Nine months and one day after the end of an accounting period
Corporation tax by instalments	The 14th day of months 7, 10, 13 and 16 counted from the start of a 12-month accounting period

Payment dates for VAT

	Due date
Electronic payment	7 calendar days after the last day of the month following the end of the return period
Direct debit payment	Collected automatically 3 working days after electronic payment due date

ICAEW – CERTIFICATE LEVEL

TAX TABLES FINANCE ACTS 2015

SYLLABUS AREA: ADMINISTRATION

MAIN PENALTY PROVISIONS

Individuals: penalties

Offence	Maximum penalty
Failure to notify chargeability by 5 October following tax year end	See below: penalties for failure to notify
Late return	See below: penalties for late filing of returns
Late payment of income tax or capital gains tax: [1] • Unpaid 30 days after payment due date • Unpaid 6 months after payment due date • Unpaid 12 months after payment due date	 5% of tax unpaid Further 5% of tax unpaid Further 5% of tax unpaid
Failure to keep and retain tax records	See below: record keeping penalties

(1)   Late payment penalties do not apply to payments on account

Companies: penalties

Offence	Maximum penalty
Failure to notify commencement of the first accounting period within 3 months of start	Fixed rate penalty not exceeding £300
Failure to notify chargeability within 12 months of end of accounting period	See below: penalties for failure to notify
Late return	See below: penalties for late filing of returns
Late payment of corporation tax: • Unpaid at filing date • Unpaid 3 months after due filing date • Unpaid 9 months after due filing date	 5% of tax unpaid Further 5% of tax unpaid Further 5% of tax unpaid
Failure to keep and retain records	See below: record keeping penalties

PAYE: penalties for late returns/ submissions

Number of employees	Monthly penalty
1 to 9	£100
10 to 49	£200
50 to 249	£300
250 or more	£400

If the form is more than three months late, an additional penalty is due of 5% of the tax and NIC that should have been reported.

Additionally, there is a £300 penalty per late P9D or P11D return, with an extra £60 per day charged if the delay continues.

PAYE: penalties for late payment

Penalties for late payment of in-year PAYE depend on the number of defaults in the tax year	No of late payments	% of tax unpaid[1]
	1st	nil
	2nd, 3rd & 4th	1%
	5th, 6th & 7th	2%
	8th, 9th & 10th	3%
	11th or more	4%
Where a penalty has been imposed and the tax remains unpaid at 6 months		5%[2]
Where a penalty has been imposed and the tax remains unpaid at 12 months		5%[2]

(1)   The percentage penalty is applied to the total amount that is late in the relevant tax month. However, no default is charged in respect of the first late payment in the year.

(2)   The 6 month and the possible further 12 month penalties are in addition to the initial penalty for late payment.

ICAEW – CERTIFICATE LEVEL

TAX TABLES FINANCE ACTS 2015

SYLLABUS AREA: ADMINISTRATION

VAT: penalties

Offence	Maximum penalty
Failure to notify liability for registration or change in nature of supplies by person exempted from registration	See below: penalties for failure to notify
Failure to keep and retain tax records	See below: record keeping penalties

VAT: penalty for late filing of VAT returns

	Monthly returns	Quarterly returns
Initial penalty	£100	£100
Further late returns within penalty period (expires 12 months after the most recent late return)	1st to 5th late return: £100 6th and subsequent late return: £200	1st late return: £200 2nd late return: £300 3rd or subsequent late return: £400
Further penalty if return still unfiled after 6 months	Further penalty of 5% of the tax due (minimum £300)	
Further penalty if return still unfiled after 12 months	Further tax geared penalties apply (minimum £300): • 100% of tax due if deliberate and concealed • 70% of tax due if deliberate but not concealed • 5% of tax due in all other cases	

VAT: penalty for late payment of VAT

Amounts in respect of	Monthly returns	Quarterly returns
Penalty for default within penalty period	1st, 2nd or 3rd default: 1% 4th, 5th or 6th default: 2% 7th, 8th or 9th default: 3% 10th or subsequent default: 4%	1st default: 2% 2nd default: 3% 3rd or subsequent default: 4%
After 6 months	Further penalty of 5% of tax still unpaid	
After 12 months	Further penalty of 5% of tax still unpaid	

VAT errors

An error made on a VAT return can be corrected on the next return provided it was not deliberate and does not exceed the greater of:

• £10,000 (net under-declaration minus over-declaration); or
• 1% x net VAT turnover for return period (maximum £50,000)

Alternatively, a 'small' error which is not deliberate may be corrected via the submission of form VAT652. Errors which are not 'small' or errors which are deliberate should be notified to HMRC on form VAT652.

RECORD KEEPING PENALTY

Offence	Maximum penalty
Failure to keep and retain tax records	£3,000 per tax year/ accounting period

SYLLABUS AREA: ADMINISTRATION

PENALTIES FOR INCORRECT RETURNS

The penalties are a percentage of the potential lost revenue

Reason for penalty	Maximum penalty	Minimum penalty with unprompted disclosure	Minimum penalty with prompted disclosure
Careless action	30%	Nil	15%
Deliberate but not concealed action	70%	20%	35%
Deliberate and concealed action	100%	30%	50%

PENALTIES FOR FAILURE TO NOTIFY

Failures to notify chargeability to tax, or liability to register for tax that leads to a loss of tax will result in a penalty. The penalties are a percentage of the potential lost revenue.

Reason for penalty	Maximum penalty	Minimum penalty with unprompted disclosure		Minimum penalty with prompted disclosure	
Deliberate and concealed action	100%	30%		50%	
Deliberate but not concealed action	70%	20%		35%	
		>12m	<12m	>12m	<12m
Any other case	30%	10%	Nil	20%	10%

PENALTIES FOR LATE FILING OF RETURNS

The penalties for late filing of a return are as follows:

Offence	Maximum penalty
Late return	Immediate £100 fixed penalty
Return more than 3 months late	Daily fixed penalties of up to £10 per day for maximum 90 days
Return more than 6 months but less than 12 months late	Further tax geared penalty of 5% of tax due (minimum £300)
Return 12 months late	Further tax geared penalties apply (minimum £300): <ul><li>100% if deliberate and concealed[1]</li><li>70% if deliberate but not concealed[1]</li><li>5% in all other cases</li></ul>

(1)   These tax geared penalties are reduced for disclosure as per penalties for incorrect returns.

INCOME TAX RATES

	2015/16
Starting rate for savings income only	0%
Basic rate for non-savings and savings income only	20%
Basic rate for dividends	10%
Higher rate for non-savings and savings income only	40%
Higher rate for dividends	32.5%
Additional rate for non-savings and savings income only	45%
Additional rate for dividends	37.5%

Basic rate band	£1 – £31,785
Higher rate band	£31,786 – £150,000
Starting rate band for savings income only	£1 – £5,000

ICAEW – CERTIFICATE LEVEL

TAX TABLES FINANCE ACTS 2015

SYLLABUS AREA: ADMINISTRATION

INCOME TAX RELIEFS	**2015/16**
Personal allowance for individuals born after 5 April 1938	£10,600
Personal allowance for individuals born before 6 April 1938	£10,660

CGT RATES	**2015/16**
Gains falling within the remaining basic rate band	18%
Gains exceeding the basic rate band	28%

CORPORATION TAX RATES	**FY 2015**
Tax rate	20%
Augmented profits limit for corporation tax payment dates	£1,500,000

NATIONAL INSURANCE CONTRIBUTIONS

NIC CLASS 1 CONTRIBUTIONS	2015/16		
	Annual	**Monthly**	**Weekly**
Lower earnings limit (LEL)	£5,824	£486	£112
Primary threshold (PT)	£8,060	£672	£155
Secondary threshold (ST)	£8,112	£676	£156
Upper earnings limit (UEL)	£42,385	£3,532	£815
Upper secondary threshold (UST) for under 21s	£42,385	£3,532	£815

Employment allowance (per year, per employer)	£2,000
Class 1 Primary contributions on earnings between PT & UEL	12%
Class 1 Primary contributions on earnings above UEL	2%
Class 1 Secondary contributions on earnings above ST where employee aged 21 or over	13.8%
Class 1 Secondary contributions on earnings between ST & UST for employees under the age of 21	0%
Class 1 Secondary contributions on earnings above UST for employees under the age of 21	13.8%
Class 1A contributions	13.8%

NIC CLASS 2 CONTRIBUTIONS	**2015/16**
Normal rate	£2.80 pw
Small profits threshold	£5,965 pa

NIC CLASS 4 CONTRIBUTIONS	
Annual lower profits limit (LPL)	£8,060
Annual upper profits limit (UPL)	£42,385
Percentage rate between LPL & UPL	9%
Percentage rate above UPL	2%

VAT	
Standard rate of VAT	20%
Reduced rate of VAT	5%

ICAEW – CERTIFICATE LEVEL

TAX TABLES FINANCE ACTS 2015

SYLLABUS AREA: INCOME TAX & NIC

INCOME TAX RATES	2015/16
Starting rate for savings income only	0%
Basic rate for non-savings and savings income only	20%
Basic rate for dividends	10%
Higher rate for non-savings and savings income only	40%
Higher rate for dividends	32.5%
Additional rate for non-savings and savings income only	45%
Additional rate for dividends	37.5%

Basic rate band	£1 – £31,785
Higher rate band	£31,786 – £150,000
Starting rate band for savings income only	£1 – £5,000

INCOME TAX RELIEFS	2015/16
Personal allowance for individuals born after 5 April 1938[1]	£10,600
Personal allowance for individuals born before 6 April 1938[1]	£10,660
Marriage allowance where both born after 5 April 1935[2]	
– Marriage allowance	£1,060
Married couple's allowance (relief is given at 10%)	
– At least one spouse/partner born before 6 April 1935	£8,355
– Maximum income before abatement of relief[3]	£27,700
– Minimum allowance	£3,220

(1) The personal allowance of any individual with adjusted net income above £100,000 is reduced by £1 for every £2 of adjusted net income above the £100,000 limit.

(2) A spouse or civil partner with an income of less than the personal allowance is allowed to transfer £1,060 (ie 10%) of their personal allowance to their spouse/civil partner provided the recipient spouse is a basic rate taxpayer.

(3) This is the income limit for abatement of the higher personal allowances and then the married couple's allowance by £1 for every £2 over the limit.

COMPANY CARS, VANS AND FUEL

Company cars

Cash equivalent 5% of list price for cars emitting 0 – 50g/km
9% of list price for cars emitting 51 – 75g/km
13% of list price for cars emitting 76 – 94g/km
14% of list price for cars emitting 95 – 99g/km
Increased by 1% per 5g/km over the 95g/km relevant threshold
Capped at 37% of list price
3% supplement on all diesel cars (subject to 37% cap)

Private fuel provided for company car

£22,100 x company car %

Van scale charge

£3,150 if van has CO_2 emissions and £630 if it has zero CO_2 emissions

Additional £594 if private fuel provided for the van

Neither charge applies if there is insignificant private usage

SYLLABUS AREA: INCOME TAX & NIC

CAPITAL ALLOWANCES

First year allowances available

100% on new and unused zero emissions goods vehicles
100% on new energy saving plant or machinery
100% on new and unused low emission cars ie electrically propelled or with CO_2 emissions of not more than 75g/km (95g/km before 1 April 2015)

Annual investment allowance

£500,000 pa of expenditure incurred by any business on certain plant and machinery between 6 April 2014 and 31 December 2015.

Writing down allowances

18% pa in the main pool

NATIONAL INSURANCE CONTRIBUTIONS

		2015/16	
NIC CLASS 1 CONTRIBUTIONS	Annual	Monthly	Weekly
Lower earnings limit (LEL)	£5,824	£486	£112
Primary threshold (PT)	£8,060	£672	£155
Secondary threshold (ST)	£8,112	£676	£156
Upper earnings limit (UEL)	£42,385	£3,532	£815
Upper secondary threshold (UST) for under 21s	£42,385	£3,532	£815

Employment allowance (per year, per employer)	£2,000
Class 1 Primary contributions on earnings between PT & UEL	12%
Class 1 Primary contributions on earnings above UEL	2%
Class 1 Secondary contributions on earnings above ST where employee aged 21 or over	13.8%
Class 1 Secondary contributions on earnings between ST & UST for employees under the age of 21	0%
Class 1 Secondary contributions on earnings above UST for employees under the age of 21	13.8%
Class 1A contributions	13.8%

NIC CLASS 2 CONTRIBUTIONS	2015/16
Normal rate	£2.80 pw
Small profits threshold	£5,965 pa

NIC CLASS 4 CONTRIBUTIONS	
Annual lower profits limit (LPL)	£8,060
Annual upper profits limit (UPL)	£42,385
Percentage rate between LPL & UPL	9%
Percentage rate above UPL	2%

PAYE CODES

L   tax code with basic personal allowance

M   tax code with basic personal allowance plus claiming marriage allowance

N   tax code with basic personal allowance less surrendered marriage allowance

Y   tax code with full personal allowance for those born before 6 April 1938

K   total allowances are less than total deductions

SYLLABUS AREA: CAPITAL GAINS

	2015/16
Annual exempt amount	£11,100
Gains falling within the remaining basic rate band	18%
Gains exceeding the basic rate band	28%
Basic rate band	£1 – £31,785

SYLLABUS AREA: CORPORATION TAX

	FY 2015
Financial year	
Tax rate	20%
Augmented profits limit for corporation tax payment dates	£1,500,000

CAPITAL ALLOWANCES

First year allowances available

100% on new and unused zero emissions goods vehicles
100% on new energy saving plant or machinery
100% on new and unused low emission cars ie electrically propelled or with CO_2 emissions of not more than 75g/km (95g/km before 1 April 2015)

Annual investment allowance

£500,000 pa of expenditure incurred by any company on certain plant and machinery between 1 April 2014 and 31 December 2015.

Writing down allowances

18% pa in the main pool

SYLLABUS AREA: VALUE ADDED TAX

Standard rate		20%
Reduced rate		5%
Annual registration limit	From 1 April 2015	£82,000
De-registration limit	From 1 April 2015	£80,000
VAT fraction (standard rated)		1/6

Cash accounting	**£**
Turnover threshold to join scheme	1,350,000
Turnover threshold to leave scheme	1,600,000

Annual accounting	
Turnover threshold to join scheme	1,350,000
Turnover threshold to leave scheme	1,600,000

Flat rate scheme	
Annual taxable turnover limit (excluding VAT) to join scheme	150,000
Annual total income (including VAT) to leave scheme	230,000

Glossary of terms

Accounting period	Period for which a company's taxable total profits are charged to corporation tax.
Actual basis	For income tax purposes, the basis of assessment in the first tax year that a business operates is the actual basis. This means that the taxable trading profits for the first tax year are the taxable trading profits of the business from the date of commencement to the following 5 April.
Additional State Pension	An extra amount of money payable with the basic State Pension. The actual amount is based on the taxpayer's National Insurance contributions. It was previously known as the State Second Pension or S2P.
Adjustment to profits	The process whereby an accounting profit or loss is adjusted to accord with tax law.
Advocacy threat	May occur when a professional accountant promotes a position or opinion to the point that objectivity may be compromised.
Allowable expenditure	Expenditure incurred wholly and exclusively for the purposes of the trade which is not specifically disallowed by legislation.
Annual accounting scheme for VAT	A scheme available to small businesses which allows them to make payments on account of VAT during the year based on the previous year's VAT liability. A single VAT return for the year is then filed within two months of the year end together with any balancing payment of VAT due.
Annual exempt amount (AEA)	The amount of gains on which no CGT is payable.
Annual investment allowance (AIA)	A type of capital allowance, which offers tax relief at 100% on qualifying expenditure in the year of purchase. The maximum deductible from taxable profits is currently £500,000.
Appropriations of profit	Withdrawals from a business (such as the payment of a 'salary' to a sole trader or partner, or dividends paid by a company to shareholders) after tax ie they are not allowable for tax purposes.
Augmented profits	Taxable total profits plus franked investment income.
Badges of trade	As there is no statutory definition of 'trading' the Courts have developed a number of tests to determine whether an entity is trading. Collectively these tests are known as the 'badges of trade'.
Balancing allowance	If too few capital allowances have been given on an asset over its lifetime, a balancing allowance may arise. This might happen if an asset is sold for an amount less than its tax written down value.
	A balancing allowance can only arise on the main pool if the business comes to an end. Balancing allowances can arise on single asset pools when the asset is sold, even when the business has not ended.
Balancing charge	If too many capital allowances have been given on an asset over its lifetime, a balancing charge arises. This might happen if an asset is sold for an amount in excess of its tax written down value.
	A balancing charge can occur on the main pool and on single asset pools at any time.
Budget cycle	The process by which UK statutory tax law is developed. UK tax law is amended each year by the Finance Act. This is based on proposals from the Chancellor of the Exchequer. Some of these are outlined in the Autumn Statement, a pre-budget report. Further proposals are then put forward in the Budget (Financial Statement) in March or April each year. A new Finance Bill is presented to Parliament each year to enact the proposals made by the Chancellor and bring them into law. This process is complete once the Finance Bill receives Royal Assent, becoming an Act.

Business Payment Support Service (BPSS)	Assists businesses which are unable, or anticipate they will be unable, to meet income tax, national insurance, corporation tax, VAT or other payments owed to HMRC.
	The service reviews the circumstances of the business and may arrange temporary options such as for payments to be made over a longer period. Additional late payment penalties will not be charged on payments included in the arrangement, provided the tax payer makes payments in line with the arrangement. However interest will continue to be payable as applicable.
Capital allowances	Tax allowances for certain types of capital expenditure. Depreciation on assets is not allowable for tax purposes. Instead, capital allowances give tax relief by allowing part of the cost of capital assets each year.
Capital gains tax (CGT)	Paid by individuals on their taxable gains.
Careless inaccuracy	The taxpayer has not taken reasonable care in completing the return.
Cash accounting scheme for VAT	Allows small businesses to account for VAT on the basis of cash paid and received, rather than on invoices received and issued.
Cash basis	Certain small unincorporated businesses may elect to use the cash basis rather than accrual accounting for the purposes of calculating their taxable trading income. Under the cash basis, a business is taxed on its cash receipts less any cash payments of allowable expenses.
Chattels	An item of tangible moveable property. Specifically excludes goodwill, shares and leases.
Common penalty regime	Relates to situations where a taxpayer has made an error/inaccuracy in a tax return. The regime covers income tax, national insurance contributions, corporation tax and value added tax. Penalties are based on the Potential Lost Revenue (PLR) and range from 30% to 100% of the PLR. Penalties may be reduced or suspended.
Company	A company is a legal person formed by incorporation under the Companies Acts. It is legally separate from its owners (shareholders) and its managers (directors).
Compliance checks	HMRC may conduct two main types of compliance checks into taxpayer returns:
	• Pre-return checks and • Enquiries into returns, claims or elections which have already been submitted.
	In addition, HMRC may conduct a check after a return has become final (or where no return has been submitted) where it believes that an assessment or determination may need to be issued under the discovery provisions.
Confidentiality	Professional accountants are required to respect the confidentiality of information acquired as a result of professional and business relationships and, therefore, not disclose such information without proper and specific authority unless there is a legal or professional right or duty to disclose, nor use the information for their personal advantage or the advantage of third parties.
Corporation tax	Paid by companies on their taxable total profits for an accounting period.

Criminal property	Includes (but is by no means limited to)
	• The proceeds of tax evasion, other tax-related offences or any other crime
	• A benefit obtained through bribery and corruption (including both the receipt of a bribe and the income received from a contract obtained through bribery or the promise of a bribe)
	• Benefits obtained, or income received, through the operation of a criminal cartel
	• Benefits (in the form of saved costs) arising from a failure to comply with a regulatory requirement, where that failure is a criminal offence
Current year basis (CYB)	For income tax purposes, the CYB is the basis on which trading profits are taxed. Under the CYB, the basis period for the tax year is the taxable trading profits for the 12-month period of account ending in that tax year.
Deliberate and concealed inaccuracy	The taxpayer has deliberately made an inaccurate return and has positively done something to conceal the inaccuracy such as produced false invoices or bank statements.
Deliberate but not concealed inaccuracy	The taxpayer has deliberately made an inaccurate return but has not positively done anything to conceal the inaccuracy
Determinations	If a return is not received by the filing date HMRC may make a determination (to the best of its information and belief) of the tax due. This may include a determination of any amounts added or deducted in the computation of the tax payable, or any amount from which those figures are derived. The determination must be made within three years of the statutory filing date. The determination is treated as if it were a self assessment.
Direct taxes	Paid by those who generate the funds to pay the tax eg income tax.
Discovery assessments	HMRC has the power via a discovery assessment to collect extra tax where it discovers a loss of tax even if the normal time period in which it could open an enquiry has passed.

HMRC can make a discovery assessment after the usual time for a compliance check if it is discovered that full disclosure has not been made by the taxpayer. |
Dividend income	Distributions paid to shareholders by companies.
Dormant company	One which is not carrying on a trade or business.
Employment income	Includes income arising from an employment and the income of an office holder such as a director. There are two types of employment income:
	• General earnings
	• Specific employment income (not in your syllabus).
European Union	The overall aim of the European Union (EU) is the creation of a single European market with no internal trade barriers between member states and common policies relating to trade outside the EU.
Excluded employment	Employees in excluded employment are sometimes called 'P9D' employees. This is because their employers are required to submit form P9D to HMRC under the PAYE system giving details of their taxable benefits. This applies particularly to employees earning less than £8,500 pa.
Exempt supplies	One on which output VAT cannot be charged. In general, input VAT cannot be recovered by a trader making exempt supplies.

Familiarity threat	May occur when, because of a close relationship, a professional accountant becomes too sympathetic to the interests of others.
Finance Act	Each year the Chancellor of the Exchequer presents the Budget, which contains all the tax measures for the year ahead. Traditionally the Budget has been in March, prior to the start of the tax year on 6 April. The statutory provisions to effect these tax measures are set out in a single Bill: the annual Finance Bill which once enacted becomes the Finance Act.
Financial year	Runs from 1 April in one calendar year to 31 March in the next calendar year. The financial year running from 1 April 2015 to 31 March 2016 is called Financial Year (FY) 2015.
First year allowance	A type of capital allowance, which offers tax relief at 100% on qualifying expenditure in the year of purchase. There is no limit on the qualifying amount although the qualifying assets are very restricted.
Flat rate scheme for VAT	Allows small businesses to calculate net VAT due by applying a flat rate percentage to their VAT inclusive turnover rather than accounting for VAT on individual sales and purchases.
Franked investment income (FII)	Exempt dividends and tax credits received from UK and overseas companies, other than those received from companies which are 51% subsidiaries of the receiving company. The net dividend received needs to be grossed up by 100/90 to arrive at FII.
Future prospects test for VAT	A person must register for VAT if, at any time, there are reasonable grounds for believing that the taxable turnover in the next 30 days alone will exceed the threshold.
	If a person is liable to register under the future prospects test, he must notify HMRC by the end of the 30-day period in which the threshold is expected to be exceeded. This 30-day period includes the date the trader becomes aware that the threshold is likely to be exceeded.
	Registration takes effect from the beginning of the 30-day period.
General earnings	A category of employment income including any salary, wages or fee, any gratuity or other profit or incidental benefit of any kind obtained by an employee consisting of money or money's worth, and anything else constituting an emolument of the employment, together with anything treated under any statutory provision as earnings (eg benefits).
Gift Aid	Gives tax relief for cash donations made by individuals to charities.
Gross income	Income before any form of deduction has been made.
Historic test for VAT	A person must register for VAT if, at the end of any month, the taxable turnover in the prior period exceeds the threshold. The prior period is the previous 12 months or the period from the commencement of the business, whichever is the shorter.
	If a person is liable to register under the historic test, he must notify HMRC within thirty days of the end of the month in which the threshold was exceeded (the relevant month).
Her Majesty's Revenue & Customs	HMRC was established in 2005 as the UK's tax and customs authority, responsible for making sure that money is available to fund the UK's public services and for helping families and individuals with targeted financial support. Through its customs service it facilitates legitimate trade and protects the UK's economic, social and physical security.
Income tax	Paid by individuals (employees, investors, partners and self-employed) on their taxable income.

Income tax payable or repayable	The amount of income tax payable by a taxpayer (or repayable by HMRC) under self assessment after taking into account tax deducted at source.
Indirect taxes	Relate to consumption. It is up to individuals whether they spend money on such goods eg value added tax
Input VAT	Each VAT registered business receives credit for any VAT that it has suffered on its purchases. This credit is deducted from its output VAT to reduce how much it owes to HMRC.
Integrity	Professional accountants are required to be straightforward and honest in all professional and business relationships.
Intimidation threat	May occur when a professional accountant may be deterred from acting objectively by actual or perceived pressures, including attempts to exercise undue influence over the professional accountant.
Job related accommodation	Accommodation is job related if:

(a)   The accommodation is necessary for the proper performance of the employee's duties (eg caretaker); or

(b)   The accommodation is provided for the better performance of the employee's duties and the employment is of a kind in which it is customary for accommodation to be provided (eg police officers); or

(c)   The accommodation is provided as part of arrangements in force because of a special threat to the employee's security (eg members of the government).

A director can only claim one of the first two exemptions if he owns 5% or less of the shares in the employer company and either he is a full-time working director or the company is non-profit making or is a charity.

Loan relationship	A company has a loan relationship if it loans money as a creditor or is loaned money as a debtor. A loan relationship includes bank and building society accounts, bank overdrafts, government gilt-edged securities and loans to and from other companies which are often in the form of debentures. It does not include trade debts.
Marriage allowance	A spouse or civil partner may elect to transfer £1,060 of their personal allowance to their spouse/civil partner provided the transferor spouse either has no income tax liability or would be a basic rate taxpayer after the transfer, and the recipient spouse is a basic rate taxpayer.
Married couple's allowance (MCA)	Additional allowance available for older married couples and registered civil partners. The married couple's allowance (MCA) is not deducted from net income to arrive at taxable income like the personal allowance. Instead the MCA reduces an individual's income tax liability and is called a **tax reducer**. The MCA tax reducer is calculated at a fixed rate of 10% of the relevant MCA amount.
Modified VAT invoice	A 'less detailed', or modified, invoice can be issued for retail supplies over £250.
Money laundering	The term used for a number of offences involving the proceeds of crime or terrorist funds. It includes possessing, or in any way dealing with, or concealing, the proceeds of any crime.
Money laundering reporting officer (MLRO)	All firms who are subject to the anti-money laundering (AML) rules must appoint a MLRO. The MLRO is responsible for oversight of the firm's compliance with its AML obligations and should act as a focal point for the firm's AML activity.

National Insurance Contributions (NIC)	Paid by self-employed individuals, employees and employers. The contributions are used to bear part of the liability of the government to pay state benefits such as jobseekers allowance and state pensions.
National Crime Agency (NCA)	The NCA became operational in 2013 and replaced the Serious Organised Crime Agency (SOCA).
	NCA tackles serious and organised crime, strengthens UK borders, fights fraud and cyber-crime, and protects children and young people from sexual abuse and exploitation.
	As the UK's financial intelligence unit it receives suspicious activity reports about money laundering and terrorist financing.
Net income	For income tax purposes, it is the total chargeable income before deducting the personal allowance.
Non-savings income	Employment income, Trading profits, Property income, Miscellaneous income. Income that is not categorised as from a specific source is taxed as miscellaneous income.
Non-wasting chattel	One with a predictable life at the date of disposal of more than 50 years. Examples include antiques, jewellery and works of art.
Objectivity	Professional accountants are required to not allow bias, conflict of interest or the undue influence of others to override professional or business judgements.
OECD	The Organisation for Economic Cooperation and Development: the OECD's model tax treaty forms the basis of many of the UK's international tax treaties.
Output VAT	As the goods or services go through the production and distribution process, each VAT registered business charges VAT on the value of the goods or services it supplies. This VAT is collected on behalf of HMRC.
Overlap profits	For income tax purposes, choosing a period of account which ends on a date other than 5 April will result in double counting of trading profits. Such profits are taxed more than once.
Partnership	A partnership is a group of persons carrying on a business together with a view to making a profit.
Pay As You Earn (PAYE)	Pay As You Earn (PAYE) is HMRC's system for collecting income tax and national insurance contributions from employees. The employer deducts tax and national insurance contributions directly from employment income or occupational pensions on behalf of HMRC.
Period of account	The period for which a company has prepared its accounts.
Personal age allowance (PAA)	A higher personal allowance available to older taxpayers, instead of the basic personal allowance. The amount of the allowance is dependent on the level of the taxpayer's net income.
Personal allowance	The amount of income on which no income tax is charged.
Potential lost revenue (PLR)	The amount of tax outstanding at the end of the tax year (income tax and CGT) or accounting period (corporation tax). For VAT purposes it is the amount outstanding as a result of the failure.
Proceeds of Crime Act 2002 (POCA)	POCA criminalises all forms of money laundering and creates other offences such as failing to report a suspicion of money laundering and 'tipping off'.
Professional accountant	A member of the ICAEW.

Professional behaviour	Professional accountants are required to comply with relevant laws and regulations and avoid any action that discredits the profession.
Professional competence and due care	Professional accountants are required to maintain professional knowledge and skill at the level required to ensure that clients or employers receive competent professional service based on current developments in practice, legislation and techniques and act diligently in accordance with applicable technical and professional standards when providing professional services.
Profit sharing ratio	The taxable trading profits of a partnership are allocated between the partners according to the profit-sharing ratio agreed for the period of account.
Progressive taxes	Rise as a proportion of income as that income rises. For example, the lowest rate of income tax is 0% on the first few thousand pounds of certain taxable income, whereas the rate of income tax on income of over £42,385 is 40% and that on taxable income of over £150,000 is 45%.
Qualifying donations	The amount paid by a company to a charity in the accounting period.
Real Time Information (RTI)	Employers are required to inform HMRC about tax, NICs and other deductions every time a payment is made to an employee, rather than after the end of each tax year.
Regressive taxes	Rise as a proportion of income as income falls. The amount of duty paid on a packet of cigarettes is the same, regardless of the income of the purchaser. That amount will be a greater proportion of the income of a person with a low income than a person with a higher income.
Related 51% group company	Companies A and B are related 51% group companies if A is a 51% subsidiary of B, or B is a 51% subsidiary of A, or both A and B are 51% subsidiaries of the same company. B is a 51% subsidiary of A if more than 50% of B's ordinary share capital is owned directly or indirectly by A.
Safeguards	Safeguards are measures that may eliminate threats or reduce them to an acceptable level.
Savings income	Interest from investments.
Self-interest threat	May occur as a result of the financial or other interests of a professional accountant or of an immediate or close family member.
Self-review threat	May occur when a previous judgment needs to be re-evaluated by the professional accountant responsible for that judgment.
Senior accounting officer (SAO)	Is the director who, in the company's reasonable opinion, has overall responsibility for the company's financial accounting. The SAO must take reasonable steps to establish and maintain accounting systems within their companies that are adequate for the purposes of accurate tax reporting.
Simplified VAT invoice	A 'less detailed', or simplified, invoice can be issued for supplies under £250.
Small pool limit	If the balance on the main pool is less than the small pool limit of £1,000 at the end of the accounting period, a WDA can be claimed up to the value of the small pool limit. This means that the main pool may be written down to nil, rather than a small balance being carried forward on which allowances have to be claimed each year.
Small profits threshold	Class 2 NICs are not payable where an individual's financial accounts net profit figure is below the small profits threshold (previously known as the small earnings exception).
State pension age	The age at which an individual is entitled to receive the basic state pension and cease paying NICs.

Supplies outside the scope of VAT	A supply which has no effect for VAT purposes eg the payment of wages or dividends.
Suspicious activity report (SAR)	A report made to the National Crime Agency about suspicions of money laundering or terrorist financing. This is commonly known as a 'SAR'.
Taxable income	For income tax purposes, this is the net income after deduction of the personal allowance.
Taxable person for VAT	A person making taxable supplies who is, or who is required to be, registered for VAT. Person includes a sole trader, a partnership (not the individual partners) and a company.
Taxable supply for VAT	Any supply of goods or services made in the UK other than an exempt supply or a supply outside the scope of VAT.
Taxable total profits (TTP)	The sum of a company's income and gains less its qualifying donations paid for an accounting period.
Taxation at source	Some income is received by the taxpayer net of tax, which means that tax is already deducted at the source of the income. This simplifies the collection of tax for HMRC.
Tax avoidance	Any legal method of reducing a taxpayer's liability. The fact that avoidance is legal does not mean that it will always be acceptable.
Tax evasion	An illegal method of seeking to pay less tax than is due by deliberately misleading HMRC. This may be attempted by either:
	suppressing information to which HMRC is entitled, for example by
	– Failing to notify HMRC of a liability to tax, or
	– Understating income or gains
	or providing HMRC with false information, for example by
	– Deducting expenses that have not been incurred, or
	– Claiming capital allowances on plant that has not been purchased.
Tax liability	The total amount of tax due from a taxpayer.
Tax point for VAT	VAT becomes due on a supply of goods or services at the time of supply. Normally VAT must be accounted for on the VAT return for the period in which the tax point occurs.
	The basic tax point is the date on which goods are removed or made available to the customer or the date on which services are completed.
	However, the actual tax point may occur before or after the basic tax point.
Tax year	Runs from 6 April in one calendar year to 5 April in the next calendar year. The tax year running from 6 April 2015 to 5 April 2016 is called the 2015/16 tax year.
Tax written down value (TWDV)	Once the writing down allowance has been deducted from the pool balance, the remainder of the value of the pool is then carried forward to the start of the next period of account. This amount is called the TWDV. It continues to be written down on a reducing balance basis.
Unit taxes	Calculated as a flat rate per item, regardless of value.
Value Added Tax (VAT)	A tax payable on the consumption of goods and services by the final consumer.

VAT fraction   VAT charged on taxable supplies is based on the VAT exclusive value of the supply. For standard rated items, the rate of VAT is 20%. If the VAT inclusive price is given, the VAT component of the consideration is:

$$\frac{20}{120} \text{ or } \frac{1}{6}$$

Value taxes   Based on a percentage of the value of the item, such as value added tax.

Wasting chattel   One with a predictable life at the date of disposal not exceeding 50 years. Examples include caravans, boats, and computers and animals. Plant and machinery are always treated as having a useful life of less than 50 years.

Writing down allowance (WDA)   For each period of account a business may claim a capital allowance known as a WDA on a proportion of the value of its capital assets.

Index

Notes

ICAEW

REVIEW FORM – PRINCIPLES OF TAXATION STUDY MANUAL

Your ratings, comments and suggestions would be appreciated on the following areas of this Study Manual.

	Very useful	Useful	Not useful
Chapter Introductions	☐	☐	☐
Examination context	☐	☐	☐
Worked examples	☐	☐	☐
Interactive questions	☐	☐	☐
Quality of explanations	☐	☐	☐
Technical references (where relevant)	☐	☐	☐
Self-test questions	☐	☐	☐
Self-test answers	☐	☐	☐
Index	☐	☐	☐

	Excellent	Good	Adequate	Poor
Overall opinion of this Study Manual	☐	☐	☐	☐

Please add further comments below:

Please return completed form to:

The Learning Team
Learning and Professional Department
ICAEW
Metropolitan House
321 Avebury Boulevard
Milton Keynes
MK9 2FZ
E learning@icaew.com